Exploring Children's Literature

Second edition

Nikki Gamble and Sally Yates

SAGE Publications

Los Angeles • London • New Delhi • Singapore

First published 2008

SAGE Publications Ltd
1 Oliver's Yard
55 City Road
London EC1Y 1SP

SAGE Publications Inc.
2455 Teller Road
Thousand Oaks, California 91320

SAGE Publications India Pvt Ltd
B 1/I 1 Mohan Cooperative Industrial Area
Mathura Road
New Delhi 110 044

SAGE Publications Asia-Pacific Pte Ltd
33 Pekin Street #02-01
Far East Square
Singapore 048763

Library of Congress Control Number: 2007928381

British Library Cataloguing in Publication Data

A catalogue record for this book is available from the British Library

ISBN 978-1-4129-3012-3
ISBN 978-1-4129-3013-0 (pbk)

Typeset by Dorwyn, Wells, Somerset
Printed in India by Replika Press
Printed on paper from sustainable resources

Contents

Contents

Chapter 1

Developing Personal Knowledge About Books

This chapter covers your personal knowledge about literature for children.
  In this chapter we shall:

- consider your personal reading history;
- discuss social and cultural influences on reading;
- review the scope of your own knowledge about literature for children;
- consider ways of recording your reading and setting targets for further reading.

Effective teaching and learning in language and literature depends upon strong subject knowledge, of both a range of texts and of approaches to studying them. As Eve Bearne puts it in an article where she shares the reflective work of some 'enlightening' teachers,

> Not only must children be able to read their own and others' representations of the world sharply and analytically, but so must teachers. Not only must children's implicit knowledge of a range of texts and contexts be brought out into the open, but, crucially, teachers' own understandings need to be made explicit in order to help forge clear views of how best to tackle the classroom demands involved in helping children to energize their experience of an increasingly complex range of texts. (1996: 318)

This chapter, then, focuses on how you can review and analyse your personal knowledge about literature for children and how you can determine your own targets for broadening and extending your knowledge.

Social and cultural influences on reading

A good starting point is your own childhood reading history. We have produced short examples of our own histories as a starting point.

Childhood reading history 1

Books have been part of my life for as long as I can remember. The first book I owned was Beatrix Potter's *The Tale of Mrs Tittlemouse*. It was read to me many times until I knew it by heart and could read aloud to myself. My copy was in the original Frederick Warne small format that Beatrix Potter herself had insisted upon (made for little hands). I used to scrutinize the endpapers, which depicted characters from other Potter tales, checking to see which of the books I already knew and which were still to be discovered. Then came *Where the Wild Things Are*. I was about 3 years old at the time it was published. I remember my Dad, a graphic artist, getting really excited about it; his enthusiasm was infectious. Dad started reading aloud to me when I was very young. Frequently he would choose poetry. A.A. Milne's *When We Were Very Young* and *Now We Are Six* came first and then we progressed to Walter de la Mare's *Peacock Pie*, *A Book of Nonsense* and Louis Untermeyer's *Golden Treasury of Poetry*. I developed a

▶

1

repertoire of favourites that I would ask for every night and I knew many poems by heart. From *Struwelpeter* I could recite 'Shockheaded Peter', 'Harriet and the Matches', and 'Little Johnny Head in Air'. The untimely deaths of the disobedient children were not in the least off-putting, and neither did I believe that I would meet a similar end if I sucked my thumb or refused to eat my soup. But there was one poem in the collection that unsettled me, 'The Story of the Inky Boys'. I would even turn the pages quickly so that I wouldn't have to see the illustrations. Fiction was also on the storytime menu. Oscar Wilde's collection, *The Happy Prince and Other Stories*, was well thumbed. His stories made me cry; they were so painful but I thought they were beautiful as well. When I was about seven, Dad read John Masefield's *The Midnight Folk*; scary but thrilling. This was followed by Tolkien's *The Hobbit* and then *The Lord of the Rings*. It was always a bittersweet experience when we got to the final chapter of a good book and I often re-read them independently afterwards. Books were usually given as birthday and Christmas presents from friends and relatives.

Each year I had a copy of the *Rupert Annual* and was disappointed one Christmas when I discovered that Rupert had been given to my younger brother and I had to make do with the *Mandy Annual*. A cousin, who was a teacher, always bought prize-winning books: Elizabeth Goudge's *The Little White Horse* and Alan Garner's *Elidor* became personal favourites. I have been told that I was reading before I started school and perhaps this is the reason that I don't recall any early reading books but I do have clear memories of storytime. In the infants we were treated to Ursula Moray Williams's *Adventures of the Little Wooden Horse*, then Mary Norton's *The Borrowers*. Storytime ceased in the junior school. We were supposed to select something to read from a shelf of tatty books at the back of the classroom. I recall that the books were mainly non-fiction with titles such as *My Life as a Roman Centurion* covered in inkblots with dog-eared pages. I spent more time changing books than reading them. Once I started junior school I was allowed to go to the library on Saturday morning while mum and dad did the weekly grocery shopping. I worked my way through Andrew Lang's colour fairy books and Roger Lancelyn Green's retellings of Greek myths and Arthurian legend. And on Sunday mornings I cycled to the newsagent to collect a *Bunty* comic. At around the age of 11 I abandoned *Bunty* for *Jackie* – everyone I knew read *Jackie* – the problem page was read aloud on the way to school. But secretly I preferred my brother's *Marvel* comics. At home the radio was another rich source of stories. *The Hobbit* was dramatized for the radio on Sunday afternoon and children's books were serialized at teatime. Later when we acquired our first black-and-white television set (I was about 10 years old) I would rush home to watch Jackanory. I also enjoyed serialized drama: Frances Hodgson Burnett's *A Little Princess* and Nina Bawden's *The Witch's Daughter* were particularly memorable.

Childhood reading history 2

My earliest memories of reading are of some Ladybird books, stories told in rhyme about anthropomorphized animals. One was called *Downy Duckling*, and the other was about 'Bunnies'. These books fascinated me as I learnt the story through the rhyme and can still remember the cadences of this. I was rather threatened by some of the illustrations though, which I found macabre. I much preferred the pictures in the Noddy books by Enid Blyton which I read avidly, and still remember the thrill of seeing Noddy move on a neighbour's television (something exotic we had yet to acquire), albeit in black and white. I know I could read before I went to school and found the *Janet and John* books with their broad pastel stripe at the bottom of the page rather tedious. Until, that is, I was allowed to progress through them to the coveted *Once Upon a Time* which included the story of Chicken Licken. That was followed by *The Five and a Half Club*, which was a real adventure.

At home I had my comic delivered weekly – *Playhour* first, and later *Bunty* – although there may have been something in between. I shared with my sisters an enthusiasm for the adventure stories produced by Enid Blyton and Malcolm Saville, and our awareness of my Dad's disapproval of these did not deter our addiction. I was never attracted to Blyton's school stories, as I moved on from the Secret Seven and Famous Five to the stories of Noel Streatfeild, Malcolm Saville and Edith Nesbit. *The Treasure Seekers* and *Five Children and It* were magical and much discussed. We went regularly to the public library on our way to and from the shops and I have fond memories of a circular padded bench on which I used to sit, but I loved owning books most of all. I still have a coveted copy of *Milly Molly Mandy* which I won for attendance at Sunday school, and numerous versions of Bible stories with colour plates from the same source.

At Christmas we would receive *Golden Wonder* Books, anthologies containing Greek myths, traditional tales, poetry, short stories and extracts from longer books. I first met 'Augustus who would not eat his soup', and 'the great long red-legged scissor man' from these collections. We would also receive annuals relative to our current comic from an Auntie who worked in a paper shop. The advent of the paperback meant that Puffins were in the Christmas stocking too: Noel Streatfeild's *Ballet Shoes* and *The Painted Garden*, based on *The Secret Garden,* and the Worzel Gummidge books by Barbara Euphan Todd were favourites, and I think the latter had been broadcast on the wireless.

I had Eleanor Farjeon's *Book of Stories, Verse and Plays* with illustrations by Edward Ardizzone, and the *Book of a Thousand Poems*. We had also, most treasured, some books of my Mum's: *Black Beauty*, *Little Women*, *Heidi* and *What Katy Did* and their sequels, all in hardback and all still treasured. Very feminine choices, but absolutely adored by my sisters and I who read and reread them. *Heidi* I seem to recall being on television when we at last acquired a set, but it was always the book which was the magical version for me.

What I remember, too, is loving the whole business of books: the organizing, shelving, bookmarks and bookplates, and collecting of series and authors. Although my mother encouraged us to read, in the wider family, sitting reading when there were better things to do was not encouraged and I was viewed as a bit of a book worm.

Commentary

We found it interesting to compare and contrast our experiences. We were both avid readers from early childhood and were encouraged to both own and borrow books from the public library. We varied in the amount we were read to at home and that affected the range of texts to which we were introduced. However, sharing books with others in the family, including siblings, was an encouragement and allowed book talk to be engaged in and enjoyed. We both benefited from the development of the paperback book market and the genesis of the Puffin, which brought new writers' work to the fore to complement the classics our parents knew. Although we were both good readers, the range of texts read included, for both of us, easier books, series and books we re-read, and demanding reads which challenged us. Having a sibling of the opposite gender close in age and a father who read to her meant that Nikki had access to a wider range of genres than I did: I shared books with two sisters as my brother was much younger, and my mother was the main reader. We had a very gendered collection of texts, in contrast to Nikki's more varied diet. The attitude to reading as a pastime in our families was also different. Thus our social and cultural contexts for reading have shaped us in different ways.

ACTIVITY

Personal childhood reading history

Record your own personal childhood reading history. Points you might consider in completing this:

- What are your earliest memories of reading?
- Do you recall being read to by others at home and/or at school?

▶

- Do you have favourite books from different stages of childhood?
- Do your memories include particular times and places where you read?
- Did you read comics and other material?
- What was the source of your books (e.g. library, gifts, buying, borrowing)?
- Did you read with siblings and friends, or share their books?
- What was the attitude of the adults around you to your reading? Did they encourage you? Did they approve of your reading?
- Were there particular genres of books, authors or series you liked?
- How did you find out about which books to read?
- Was reading a pleasurable experience for you?
- Were there differences between reading at home and at school?
- Were there some books that you re-read?
- Which of the books you read would you consider to be 'good literature' and which 'popular fiction'?
- What is your pattern of reading now, as an adult?
- When you have completed your history, share it with others and consider what factors have contributed to your current attitude to reading. What social and cultural influences and attitudes do you bring to texts?

  Issues arising from this activity can also be related to the reading habits of the children with whom you will be working.

Commentary

A number of studies have focused on factors affecting children's range of reading experience. Margaret Clark in 1976 studied the behaviours at home and at school of children who were 'young fluent readers'. There was no one common methodology being used in the children's schools but, despite coming from varied backgrounds, with parents of varying levels of education, there were some common factors in their home experiences. The children:

- had parents who valued education and were interested in their progress;
- were initially interested in print generally, in the environment and television, rather than books;
- were very likely to belong to the public library and to read a wide range of books;
- commonly had an interested adult willing to read with and to them, and with whom they could discuss books.

Shirley Brice Heath's (1983) ethnographic study of three contrasting communities revealed differences in the perceptions of the place of reading and literature for children. Roadville and Trackton were two communities in the USA where the mill is the centre of the economy. Roadville was a white working-class community, stable in having several generations who had worked at the mill. Trackton was a black working-class community where traditional farm workers had moved in to work in the mill. In both communities literacy events were embedded in social and cultural practices. In Trackton literacy was functional, related to getting on with life or to the church and religion. No special texts were produced for children, but they were encouraged to read the print in the environment around them and given tasks to do such as shopping which required them to develop their reading skills. Reading for adults was a public, social event where newspapers or letters would be read aloud to a group and comment invited and expected. In church, the written words of the prayers and readings were interpreted and embellished by reader and congregation according to commonly agreed patterns: beyond the written text, the spoken word had a status and richness uniquely created and understood by the community. Children learnt about language and literacy by being apprenticed into these adult literacy events.

In Roadville, reading was valued and it was believed that children 'should' read. Adults acquired reading material – newspapers, magazines, brochures – but did not spend much time reading themselves. Children were provided with books for enjoyment and learning, and these were read to them, particularly at bedtime and for soothing. Early books were labelled pictures, alphabets and nursery rhymes, and typical adult behaviour when reading to the children was to ask questions and invite 'labelling' of the text and pictures. Environmental print was valued and children encouraged to read whatever they could. Television-related books were also bought as part of the range read by children as they grew older. There was a belief that 'behind the written word is an authority' and texts chosen and read were those which reflected and confirmed the values and rules of the community. Texts open to interpretation with meanings beyond those which were commonly understood as realities and meanings within the community sat uneasily here as reading was for learning how to become a member of that society.

These two communities were contrasted with the townspeople, both black and white; the 'mainstreamers'. The townspeople used literacy and language in every part of their lives and were very 'school oriented'.

As the children of the townspeople learn the distinction between contextualized first-hand experiences and decontextualized representations of experience, they come to act like literates before they can read (Heath, 1983: 262).

Not only were these communities in contrast to each other, they also contrasted with the demands and expectations of school cultures of literacy. School demands very specific literacy behaviours, and dissonance between experience at home and at school can make tremendous demands on the child. The concept of 'story' was different in each community and the teachers' expectations of the children in creating fantasies in school posed challenges for the children in conceptualizing the parameters of the activity. Shirley Brice Heath worked with teachers to consider ways of exploring, understanding and working with the literacies practised and valued by the communities. Her aim was to enable teachers and pupils to bridge language and culture differences and 'to recognize and use language as power' (1983: 266). Understanding the concepts of literacy in the communities with which you work can make this bridge building more effective.

In her work with young bilingual learners, Helen Bromley (1996) provides examples of such bridging behaviour. She describes the behaviour of Momahl, a young girl fluent in Urdu sharing books within the reception class. Initially, Momahl was inducted into sharing picture books by a more confident and experienced reader. Momahl demonstrated her awareness of nursery rhymes through her responses to the Ahlbergs' *Each Peach Pear Plum*, singing the rhymes related to characters as they appeared. Although not yet speaking English fluently, she had learnt the songs with her family and recognized the characters. In this behaviour she in turn supported Katy, a child who had clearly no such familiarity with the rhymes and who learnt them from Momahl. Each child in Helen's class was recognized as bringing different previous experience and cultural expectations into school, and she saw her role as not merely inducting them into the culture of school, but as drawing on what she learnt about them to create shared and valid experience and opportunities for learning. In considering which books you might consider to be 'good literature', or worthy texts, as opposed to 'popular fiction' or texts perhaps considered to be less worthy reading material, consider what factors guided your decision.

Keeping a reading journal

- Set up a reading journal to record your reflections on reading, and your responses to the activities suggested in this book.
- Your personal reading history might be a useful first entry.
- The journal will enable you to track your growing knowledge and understanding of children's literature and literary theory, and should provide a good source of ideas and inspiration for your work in schools with young people.
- At various points in this book further suggestions will be made about entries you might make in your journal to support you in your critical reflection.

Patterns of children's reading

In 1994 Christine Hall and Martin Coles conducted a survey into children's reading habits. Their research repeated a study conducted in the 1970s by Frank Whitehead and allowed them to see whether children's habits had changed over time. Over 2500 children at ages 10, 12 and 14 were surveyed and the data analysed in a number of different ways. They extended Whitehead's original survey as they wanted to investigate current concerns about the relationship between reading and the use of computers, about book and magazine purchasing patterns, about the influence of family reading habits of children (Hall and Coles, 1999).

This included gathering data on children for whom English was an additional language and on gender, class and ethnicity. The data collected through questionnaires and interviews included investigating children's:

- magazine and comic reading;
- amount and type of book reading;
- favourite authors and series;
- places and times for reading;
- book ownership;
- library membership;
- patterns of re-reading;
- rejection of books before completion;
- computer use;
- linguistic and family background.

The close analysis of the data has provided many insights into children's reading habits. Girls were found to read more than boys, and there were some gender differences in the genres of books read. The girls read more horror and ghost stories, romance and school-related books, and tended to share series books, while boys read more science fiction/fantasy books, comedy and sports-related books.

Ethnicity did not affect the amount of reading children engaged in but class did, and also affected the genres read. Children from lower socio-economic groups read fewer books generally and fewer horror and romance books than those in higher social classes. Children from higher socio-economic groups were more likely to use the library, thus extending the range of books available to them.

The main, reassuring, finding was that, despite computers and other media absorbing children's interest, children had not abandoned book reading, with a slight increase in the reading of 10- and 12-year olds. Children read a wide range of books, adventure stories being particularly popular, and the interest in school stories, humour, animal and sports stories decreased after the age of 10. Children read lots of series books and television tie-ins, with Roald Dahl and Enid Blyton the most read authors. There was a minority interest in science fiction, horror and ghost stories, and stories featuring the war. Children were mostly reading books marketed for children although some read both adults' and children's books, and 10 per cent read only adults' books. Children were on the whole positive about reading (Hall and Coles, 1999).

A more recent study by Hopper (2005) has corroborated Hall and Coles's data and found similar percentages of secondary pupils reading books. However, a high proportion of the young people involved were reading significantly more non-book material including use of the Internet. The most popular fiction read in Hopper's study was the *Harry Potte*r and *The Lord of the Rings* books, texts that had been recently released in film versions. Girls were also reading the work of Jacqueline Wilson, and Hopper notes that 'issues-based books appear increasingly to dominate the teenage book market' (2005: 116). The appearance of a book was 'significant in choice' and Hopper refers to the phenomenon of having a number of titles now published 'in two simultaneous versions for the teenage and adult markets' as impacting on these adolescents' choices of text. There were some differences in the genres cited as popular in this study, but 'fantasy, magic, horror/scary, magic and sorcery, school, romance and true story' were specifically mentioned (2005: 118).

A survey conducted by The National Literacy Trust of 8000 primary and secondary pupils in England (December 2005) explored the reasons that some pupils chose to read while others did not. Key findings indicated that half of the sample claimed to enjoy reading and that generally positive attitudes towards reading were held. A diverse range of material was read outside the classroom with about half expressing enjoyment of reading fiction, especially in the genres of adventure, comedy, horror and ghost stories. The activities that were most likely to promote reading were involvement in design of websites and magazines, and meeting authors. The full report is available at http://www.literacytrust.org.uk/Research/readsurvey.html.

Knowing the children with whom you work will enable you to understand the impact of their homes and communities on their learning in school, and to help you plan appropriately to 'build bridges'.

ACTIVITY

Exploring the patterns of children's reading

Conduct a small-scale survey of your own with children with whom you work, to explore the range of their reading both within and beyond school. You could do this through interviews or reading conferences, or through the use of simple question-naires. Hopper's study was conducted with PGCE students and her report on this provides a good model to follow. This small study should enable you to gain a picture of each individual's experience as a reader at home and school. Aim to address the areas covered by Hall and Coles's study, and perhaps also explore the points you covered when writing your own histories. Your skill in relaxing each child and opening up possibilities of what counts as reading will affect how much you find out, particu-larly if you are working with children you do not know well. Children schooled to believe that the only reading that 'counts' is the 'reading book' from the classroom collection may say they do not read much at home if they think the school book is your main focus. They may also initially be reticent to admit to reading texts of which they feel you may not approve, so encourage them to talk about reading-related activities and behaviours. It is likely that your investigation will also reveal the range of popular reading current among the age group you surveyed.

Consider your findings in relation to the studies mentioned in this chapter on ethnography and reading choices.

Commentary

Recent developments in publishing, not least the 'Harry Potter' phenomenon, may make your findings, like Hopper's, differ from the 1994 study, but look too for constants. Of course, the small scale of your investigation will make compari-son invalid statistically, but understanding changing trends in children's reading will support you in understanding children's needs and interests. One teacher who found that a cult of reading 'Goosebumps' and other horror series was preoccupy-ing her class created a display of ghost, mystery and horror stories from a range of writers, reading some of them aloud. This enabled her to tune in to but extend the children's current enthusiasm. Having, for example, Penelope Lively's *Fanny and the Monsters, Astercote* and *The Ghost of Thomas Kempe*, Bel Mooney's *The Stove Haunting* and some of Catherine Sefton's ghost stories available motivated the chil-dren to read not just their 'scary' stories, but to then indulge in the series readers' behaviour of gathering together other books by the same author, thus broadening their interest. This role in recommending books to children is vital. Hall and Coles's study found that children did not rate highly parents' recommendations of books to read, finding them boring, and Hopper's study found that teacher rec-ommendation rated low for adolescents. Examples of books recommended, such as *Treasure Island*, indicate that some parents may have relied on their own mem-ories of reading and were not tuned in to the needs of a new generation of read-ers. However, the age of the children may affect this. Children under 10 may be more open to adult suggestion, and the 'enabling adult' in school may exert a dif-ferent influence.

Aidan Chambers (1991) discusses the role of the 'enabling adult' who influences book selection, makes time for reading and encourages responses (Figure 1.1). With an informed and enthusiastic adult as guide, children may be motivated to take risks with what they read.

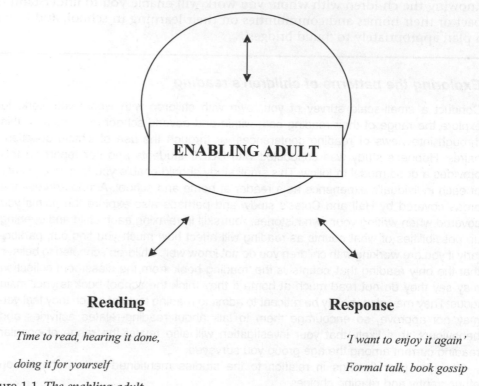

Selection

Bookstock, availability, accessibility, presentation

ENABLING ADULT

Reading

Time to read, hearing it done,

doing it for yourself

Response

'I want to enjoy it again'

Formal talk, book gossip

Figure 1.1 *The enabling adult*

A fascinating example of this is provided by Gabrielle Cliff Hodges (1996) in an article entitled 'Encountering the Different'. She describes introducing Jill Paton Walsh's *Gaffer Samson's Luck* to some children who at first had a less than enthusiastic response. The children kept journals and through analysis of these we can see that Brian, for example, moves from,

> It sounds boring because there are no secret alien bases, no tripods striding across the skyline and no UFOs zapping people's brains …

to

> Quite good …

to

> Brilliant. Miles better than what I expected. I am really into the book now and I love it. (Styles et al., 1996: 265)

The comments reveal how engaged Brian became with the text once he had been persuaded to read it. His teacher's sound knowledge about books ensured that she chose a text with the potential to draw him in. Children with access to a knowledgeable and enthusiastic adult to introduce books and read them aloud, will build up trust and be tolerant of the introduction of a broad range of texts. They will take risks with their reading, rather than staying with what they know is 'safe'.

Auditing your personal knowledge about books: range

Use the chapters on specific genres and the list of suggestions for a book collection in Chapter 10 to audit your own knowledge. Use the grids in Appendix 1.1 to record books you have read within each genre. A blank copy is available for you to ensure you can expand as required. You can draw on the sources of information outlined in Chapter 11 to guide you. Aim to enter six books for each genre in your reading log, three easier and three more demanding texts. Myths, Legends, Folktales, Fairy Tales, 'Issues', Fantasy, Science Fiction, Classics, Ghost Stories, Horror, Historical, Adventure, Animal Story, Biography, Autobiography, Narrative Non-fiction, Poetry Anthology, Thematic Poetry Collection, Single Poet Collection, Picture Books for Older Readers, Short Story Collections.

Commentary

From the completed grid you will be able to see where you need to prioritize your reading. Many of us can think of examples to fill the boxes under genres that we like to read but may struggle with others. However, to be an enabling adult, you need to know just the right book to suggest to, for example, a reluctant reader in your class aged 9 who loves reading anything about aliens. So guard against just indulging your own passions and neglecting genres with which you are less familiar. Courses of teacher training often require students to read at least 50 books during their first year to provide a broad base, and it would be beneficial to set yourself a target of reading at least a book a week to expand your repertoire of known texts.

Auditing your personal knowledge about books: authors and illustrators

Besides ensuring familiarity with a range of genres, you need to be familiar with the work of different authors and illustrators. Use the list below as a starting point for reviewing your knowledge about particular authors, but expand from this, drawing on the sources listed in Chapter 11. Providing any sort of list of recommended authors will inevitably lead to criticism of what has been included and those omitted. This list, therefore, is not intended to be definitive, but a reasonable reflection of some significant authors writing for children today. In any case, the critical discussion engendered by a list is a good opportunity to 'talk books' and discover other people's recommendations:

Janet and Allan Ahlberg	Melvin Burgess	Ime Dros
Joan Aiken	Frances Hodgson Burnett	Helen Dunmore
David Almond	John Burningham	Sara Fanelli
Rachel Anderson	Lauren Child	Anne Fine
Bernard Ashley	Eoin Colfer	Michael Foreman
Steve Barlow and Steve	Helen Cooper	Fiona French
Skidmore	Susan Cooper	Cornelia Funke
Nina Bawden	Sharon Creech	Neil Gaiman
James Berry	Gary Crew	Sally Gardner
Stephen Biesty	Gillian Cross	Leon Garfield
Malorie Blackman	Kevin Crossley-Holland	Jamila Gavin
Quentin Blake	Roald Dahl	Adele Geras
Frank Cottrell Boyce	Nicola Davies	Morris Gleitzman
Theresa Breslin	Alexis Deacon	Julia Golding
Raymond Briggs	Terry Deary	Emily Gravatt
Kevin Brooks	Narinda Dhami	Mini Grey
Ruth Brown	Peter Dickinson	Grace Hallsworth
Anthony Browne	Berlie Doherty	Frances Hardinge

▶

Sonya Hartnett	Margaret Mahy	Philip Ridley
Lian Hearn	Jan Mark	Michael Rosen
Russell Hoban	Bel Mooney	Meg Rosoff
Mary Hoffman	Michael Morpurgo	Tony Ross
Janni Howker	Jill Murphy	J.K. Rowling
Shirley Hughes	Beverley Naidoo	Jon Scieszka
Ted Hughes	Edith Nesbit	Marcus Sedgwick
Pat Hutchins	Linda Newbery	Maurice Sendak
Simon James	Garth Nix	Ivan Southall
Oliver Jeffers	Mary Norton	Jerry Spinelli
Pete Johnson	Robert C. O'Brien	Catherine Storr
Reinhardt Jung	Hiawyn Oram	Rosemary Sutcliff
Charles Keeping	Helen Oxenbury	Robert Swindells
Dick King-Smith	Siobhan Parkinson	Shaun Tan
Satoshi Kitamura	Brian Patten	Colin Thompson
Elizabeth Laird	Philippa Pearce	Kate Thompson
Ursula Le Guin	Mal Peet	Ann Turnbull
C.S. Lewis	Daniel Pennac	Jean Ure
Penelope Lively	Richard Platt	Chris van Allsburg
Arnold Lobel	Terry Pratchett	Max Velthuijs
Lois Lowry	Susan Price	Cynthia Voigt
Geraldine McCaughrean	Philip Pullman	Martin Waddell
Roger McGough	John Quinn	Jill Paton Walsh
David McKee	Bali Rai	Robert Westall
Patricia MacLachlan	Celia Rees	Jacqueline Wilson
Michelle Magorian	Philip Reeve	Benjamin Zephaniah

Commentary

You will also be able to review over time the pattern of your reading and consider whether you have met your targets for expanding your experience to meet children's needs. I had in the past a tendency to buy myself yet another historically focused story and had to force myself to choose science fiction. However, reading what I felt I ought to read instead of what I most waned to has provided me with some of my most pleasurable reading surprises. Lesley Howarth's books, such as *Maphead*, for example, have been worth taking the risk of dipping into a less favoured genre and I have enjoyed science fiction and works on futuristic dystopias by Philip Reeve (*Mortal Engines*), Susan Price (*The Sterkarm Handshake*) and Jan Mark (*Riding Tycho, Useless Idiots*). I first read Jan Mark's *Thunders and Lightnings* because I judged from the cover, which had two boys and a range of warplanes on it, that it might be good to motivate some reluctant young male readers I was teaching. What I discovered was a book rich in humour, pathos, moral issues, wonderfully drawn characters and relationships, and a central focus on planes: a book which, when read aloud to a class, motivated those who loved the planes and the airfield, but did not detract from the enjoyment of those who, like me, would not initially have been drawn to the book by the cover.

ACTIVITY

Reflecting on your reading

In your journal, make notes on the texts you read. A short reflection on your response to the text can enable you to track your own growth as a reader, and make connections between texts. As you read the remaining chapters of this book, you will learn different ways of looking at texts and your response should be more informed. For some books you may wish only to make a short record, but for others you may want to engage in deeper analysis and reflection. If you are re-reading texts you have read before, particularly if you read them as a child, make notes on your recollections of previous reading. It will be interesting to note whether your later reading reinforces impressions gained in earlier readings or challenges them.

Commentary

The reflections in your reading journal will be particularly revealing when you read beyond your 'comfort zone', and also when you re-read books. Re-reading helps you to look more closely at the text and pay attention to the 'constructed-ness' of the text and the devices the author has used to create the narrative.

ACTIVITY

Keeping track of your books

It is a good idea to set up a database or card index of children's books as you read them, cross-referencing them to other related books or themes to help you identify books quickly when you need them. Note the details of each book including the source (e.g. own collection, public library/university library, borrowed) so that you will know how to track it down should you wish to read it again, and note the date when you read it.

Commentary

My first log was a card index of genres and themes, such as moving house (*Thunders and Lightnings*), death (*Badger's Parting Gifts, Walk Two Moons*). I entered each book I read under as many headings as was relevant. It would certainly be beneficial to include headings related to the literary devices you will want to address with children, for example. Searching for a book with dramatic irony, or flashbacks or a particular narrative perspective is made easier in this way. A computer database will allow you to make sophisticated searches and keep track of your book repertoire more easily. Students at the University of Sunderland on teacher education programmes set up databases to support their reading which ensures they can readily identify suitable texts for supporting children's learning in their placements in school, and also support their choices of books to read aloud for pleasure and for recommending to individuals.

In addition to keeping records of your own reading, tracking children's individual reading allows you to understand their previous experiences, preferences for reading, to monitor and review their choices and to engage in dialogue with individual children to support their continued reading.

In this chapter we have:

- considered your own personal reading histories and how you can draw on the histories and experience of children to meet their needs;
- audited your own knowledge of children's books and set targets to extend your reading;
- considered some studies relating to the patterns of children's reading and the social and cultural influences on this;
- introduced some approaches, including a reading journal to keeping track of your own reading experience.

Further reading

Chambers, A. (1991) *The Reading Environment*. Stroud: Thimble Press.

Chambers, A. (1993) *Tell Me: Children, Reading and Talk*. Stroud: Thimble Press.

Coles, M. and Hall, C. (2002) 'Gendered readings: learning from children's reading choices', *Journal of Research in Reading*, 25 (1), 96–108.

Hall, C. and Coles, M. (1999) *Children's Reading Choices*. London: Routledge.

Hopper, R. (2005) 'What are teenagers reading? Adolescent reading habits and reading choices', *Literacy*, 39 (3), 113–20.

Ivey, G. and Broaddus, K. (2001) '"Just plain reading": a survey of what makes students want to read in middle school classrooms', *Reading Research Quarterly*, 36, 350–77.

Millard, E. and Marsh, J. (2001) 'Sending Minnie the Minx home: comics and reading choices', *Cambridge Journal of Education*, 31, 25–38.

Wilkinson, K. (2003) 'Children's favourite books', *Journal of Early Childhood Literacy*, 3 (3), 275–301.

Appendix 1.1: Setting targets for personal reading

Aim to enter six books for each genre, three easier and three more demanding texts.

Fantasy	Science fiction	Classics	Adventure	Contemporary realism	Fairy-tale versions

Horror	Adventure	Traditional tales	Books about 'issues'	Historical	Animal stories

Setting targets for personal reading

Chapter 2

Reading and Responding

In this chapter we shall:

- consider the nature of literature;
- consider how children respond to texts;
- be introduced to critical theory on reader response;
- explore factors affecting children's comprehension of texts;
- consider how teachers can best support children's understanding of how to read literature.

The nature of literature

It may be helpful to begin by defining our terms. A broad definition of literature encompasses all written and spoken material: prose (fiction and non-fiction), drama or poetry. The term is sometimes used to describe spoken genres from the oral tradition such as epic, legend, myth, ballad and folktale. This broad view of literature includes essays and speeches, such as Martin Luther King's 'I Have a Dream …' and Winston Churchill's 'Fight them on the beaches …' speeches. However, other definitions focus on the special qualities of literature: its fictionality, special use of language, lack of pragmatic function and the facility to arouse different levels of interpretation:

Fictionality

It might be argued that what counts as literature is the product of a writer's imagination – a work of fiction (this can be applied equally to drama and poetry). However, it is not always possible to determine whether a text is indeed fact or fiction. Perception of a text as fictitious or factual is to some extent dependent on the reader's prior knowledge and attitude. For instance, if reading some passages from Roald Dahl's *Boy*, it might be difficult to determine what is autobiographical and what the product of Dahl's imagination. It would be possible to read entire chapters believing them to be fiction, only later to learn that they are autobiographical.

Special language use

Linguist Roman Jakobsen (1960) drew attention to the poetic function of literary texts. He argued that literature draws attention to the language it utilizes, making everyday words seem fresh and original. However, texts that might not be regarded as 'literature' may also employ language in special ways. Newspaper headlines, clever adverts, descriptions of food in menus might use figurative language, puns, rhyme or alliteration to create particular effects. So the claim that language use is a defining characteristic of literature is not uncontested.

Non-pragmatic

It is sometimes asserted that texts such as newspaper articles, gardening manuals, and recipe books have a pragmatic function, as the reason for their existence is to help us do something practical. On the other hand literary texts may not be intended to have any specific purpose; indeed the writer may not have had a particular audience in mind when writing. However, this assertion also needs to be qualified. How we read texts depends on the individual. Some people will read fictional texts because they are interested in their basis in fact. For example, they may read Beverley Naidoo's *Burn My Heart* because they want to understand something of the history of the Mau Mau. They may find that by reading novels they have an increased understanding of human motivation and behaviour that allows them to deal with day-to-day problems. Conversely I enjoy reading cookery writers like Nigel Slater and Nigella Lawson as much for their delicious descriptions of food and the stories behind their recipes as for the instructions on how to prepare a meal. So again the distinction between the literary and non-literary text is not as straightforward as it might appear.

Polysemic

A literary text might be considered one that is ambiguous or open to interpretation, in a way that a non-literary text is not. So while we expect a recipe to create exactly the result we are expecting no matter who is doing the cooking, a literary text might be interpreted in different ways by different readers.

It is evident that any description of what constitutes literature is problematic and not wholly satisfactory. Nevertheless, we can acknowledge that some texts offer more for readers to reflect upon: they say interesting things and say them in interesting ways. We argue that it is important that teachers choose with care texts to read with and to young readers, offering those that provide challenge in content, form and language. However, we do not take the elitist position that children should only read books that are considered by adults to be 'good for them'. Just as adults may choose a quick light read or relax by watching an intellectually undemanding reality programme on television so children will enjoy returning to favourite texts, reading books in series or reading an action-centred story. These books may well be the ones that get them 'hooked on reading' and they should not be discouraged from reading them. However, as teachers we will want to present other possibilities and introduce books that deal with powerful themes in ways that engage, provoke and stimulate the imagination.

ACTIVITY	In your journal make some notes about the concept of literature and its usefulness when thinking about children and their texts.

Reading and creativity

Reading involves processing the words on the page to create meanings. Assuming the child can decode the words, this chapter seeks to explore how children make sense of what has been written, creating meaningful narratives from the words on the page. It is generally acknowledged among educators that meaning is created when readers interact with texts. However, the relative importance played by the text and the reader in this active process is a matter of divergent opinion, even among those who acknowledge that the text is not the only place where the meaning resides. For example, Wolfgang Iser (1978) attributes equal importance to the reader and the text in his notion of two poles: 'the artistic', which is the author's text and 'the aesthetic', which is the response of an accomplished reader. For Iser, a work of literature lies between these two poles, being neither the actual printed text, nor the reader's subjective response. In contrast Stanley Fish argues that the reader is central. He writes, 'the reader's activities are at the center of attention, where they are regarded not as leading to meaning but as *having* meaning' (1980: 158). Fish argues that it is impossible to recover the author's intended meaning and any attempt to do so can only produce an interpretation. Reader response theories have been influential in the development of pedagogical approaches for teaching reading and literature and converge with the current focus on creativity in education.

There has been in recent years a renewed and growing interest in creativity in the curriculum. Following from the *All Our Futures* report (DFEE, 1999), QCA's creativity project defines creativity as:

- thinking or behaving imaginatively;
- purposeful activity;
- generating something original;
- an outcome which is of value.

This definition challenges a commonly held view that creativity is limited to physical outcomes, the arts and the domain of a few specially talented and creative individuals. Central to this definition of creativity is the notion that all humans have the capacity to be creative. Such a definition allows for thinking and reading to be classed as creative acts. Outcomes of creative reading include the dialogue between readers, the responses kept in reading journals, and the shifts in thinking that occur when the mind engages with a text that challenges preconceptions or confirms a provisionally held idea.

ACTIVITY

> Make notes, or discuss with a partner, the extent to which reading is a creative act. Exemplify with illustration from your own reading experience.

Commentary

Readers respond creatively to texts in many ways. They might for instance bring to mind their own images based on an author's description of character or setting. The individual nature of these responses may be highlighted when a film of known books is viewed. Perhaps you have had the experience of being dissatisfied with the way a character has been interpreted in film because they don't fit with the image that has been created in your mind. Some readers might 'rewrite' the text in their heads, selecting alternative endings or expressing a preference for a different ending to the one that the author has written. Graves and Hodge (1948) state that imaginative readers rewrite books to suit their own taste, omitting and mentally altering as they read. Beyond this readers create their own internal reality; their construction of the world is built partially on what is read. The imaginative landscape is furnished from the vicarious experience of bringing readers, through the pages of book, into contact with experiences they will never encounter in real life.

Filling the gaps

Stephens (1992) claims that the idea of the implied reader is an important concept for children's literature and he is critical of the text-oriented focus of much of the work on reader response in children's literature. He criticizes Chambers's work on discussions of text as assuming an ideal reader and paying too little attention to the 'socialization' aspect of text. The role of the enabling adult in this case might be to support the child in recognizing more of the clues and facilitating discussion of a range of interpretations, drawing on evidence from within the text and from prior knowledge external to the text to draw inferences and create meanings. There may be no consensus in such discussions, but there would, one would hope, be challenge and extension of understanding a range of perspectives. The author uses language and literary devices to create paths for the reader through the text so that the reader can understand the narrative. How tightly the author defines the paths is variable. Some authors use a narrative style and format the content so that there are few ambiguities and the narrator signifies clearly to the reader how the text is to be read. The role of the narrator is explored in more detail in Chapter 3.

Other authors, though, in exploring changing perspectives on the role of the reader, encourage different behaviours from the adult reading with the child. Children may already be familiar with spotting multiple levels of meaning in text from their experience of picture books. The classic picturebook *Rosie's Walk* by Pat Hutchins will open up the possibility that the story told by the words on the page at a literal level may not be the whole or only story. This is a book which children will commonly first encounter through having it read to them by an adult, so the adult reader takes on the voice of the narrator. Often the child 'reader' listening to the words enters into the game of predicting the events in the subtext of the pictures with the adult 'narrator/reader' as the unknowing reader having this pointed out to him or her by the knowing child. In *Titch* by Pat Hutchins, the simple declarative sentences with which the book starts, again tell only one aspect of the story: 'Titch was little. His sister Mary was a bit bigger. And his brother Pete was a lot bigger'. But looking at Titch's face on the second page, we can see that this is about something beyond the words narrated: the story is about how Titch feels about being the youngest and smallest.

ACTIVITY

Filling the gaps

Read these extracts from the opening pages of *Midnight Is a Place* by Joan Aiken. The central character of the book is introduced: Lucas Bell. Using the format in Appendix 2.1 record what you know so far about Lucas:

> The boy who sat curled up on a windowseat looking out at this dismal view had remained there for the past two hours only because he could think of nothing better to do. On a shelf to his right stood a row of schoolbooks. A partly written composition lay on an inkstained table. The composition's title was Why Industry is a Good Thing. Under this heading the boy had written, 'Industry is a good thing because it is better to work in a carpet factory than to be out in the rain with nothing to eat.' Having written these words he had stopped, wondering to himself, 'Is that true?' and had turned to look at the rainswept park …
>
> … He glanced over his shoulder at the meagre attempt at a fire smouldering under a black polished mantel. Across the dusky room he could hardly see it.
>
> Large fires were unknown in Midnight Court, as were bright lights or lively music, or laughter.
>
> The boy blew on the wide, rainstreaked windowpane and wrote the words, I'M LONELY, then added his name, and the date. Tomorrow would be his birthday. He wondered if anybody else had remembered the fact. The words LUCAS BELL, OCTOBER 30 1842 faded as the vapour from his breath dissolved … When some people arrived at the house he asked about them.
>
> … Business affairs of your guardian, the tutor, Mr Oakapple had said impatiently, no affair of yours. Nothing was ever explained to the boy; sometimes he felt like a ghost in the house …
>
> This was a bare, looted-looking apartment. Paler patches on the painted walls showed where pictures had been taken down. A hole in the ceiling was all that remained of a chandelier.

Commentary

Students and teachers completing this task have recorded the following about the central character, Lucas:

- He is bored.
- He is an orphan.
- It is his birthday.
- He has a guardian.
- He is rich.
- He might not have much money now.
- He lives in a town.
- No one tells him anything.

Some of these are facts about Lucas told to us by the author, for example, that he was lonely, that he had a tutor and a guardian and lived at Midnight Court. However, others have been inferred from clues provided by the writer, and you can record the clues which led you to your deduction:

- He is rich 'because he has a guardian and lives in a big house with gates'.
- He might not have so much money 'because there are gaps on the wall where there used to be pictures. Perhaps they have been sold'.

In this case, knowing that wealthy children, particularly those living in the past, might have had tutors at home rather than going to school helps to interpret the text. Children can glean this prior knowledge of cultural, social and literary contexts from media such as film and television as well as from previous book reading.

Traditional approaches to textual criticism make the assumption that the author creates the meaning in the text. Through choice of subject, narrative perspective, language and literary style, the author creates a text to communicate with the reader. Literary criticism and study of literature has often concentrated on the 'author's intentions' (Iser, 1978: 20), with the reader recreating the intended meaning. This assumes that the author writes with an 'implied reader' in mind who will pick up the clues in the text to recreate the intended meaning. Iser claims that this assumes a culturally shared understanding of the codes and signals in the text. The author, in writing, 'encodes' attitudes and norms within the text reflecting his or her cultural perspective within the belief system of the time. This is particularly apparent when reading texts written in previous centuries, which can prove difficult for the contemporary reader to understand. The further back in the past a text was written, the more likely it is that the reader will require some support such as footnotes or a glossary, to contextualize the behaviour and attitudes of the characters and to understand the language used. Shakespeare may be read more easily with a glossary and reading Chaucer, such a device is certainly necessary.

The notion of an implied reader, then, makes immense assumptions about the prior knowledge being brought to the text. In this critical perspective, the child reader without the prior knowledge necessary to recreate the author's implied meaning may require an enabling adult to help interpret the given meanings. It advantages those who share the social and cultural experience of the implied author and can be alienating for those who read the codes differently.

Students in discussions frequently share the 'deskilling' nature of some English teaching where they were made to 'feel stupid' when they did not share the same reading of the text as the teacher, having missed vital clues in interpreting the text. The role of the teacher in this case could be seen as inducting children into established modes of understanding to discover the 'true meaning' that lies within a text. Such behaviour is particularly apparent when reading works from the canon of established literature. An alternative perspective is to realize that besides the *implied* reader for whom the author might have been writing, there is the *real* child reader. The *real* reader reads the narrative, interpreting the text to create meanings. Thus the meaning resides not as a given in the text, but in the interaction between the reader and the text, mediated by the social and cultural experience of the reader. Each rereading of the text may create different understandings as the gaps in the text are filled by attention to and interpretation of the signifying clues within the text. This is particularly apparent, again, when looking at historical texts where we may interpret them very differently today.

Different meanings of the same text have emerged at different times, and, indeed, the same text read a second time will have a different effect from that of its first reading (Iser, 1978). Thus, the meaning of a text is not something static that lies within it: meaning is created by the real reader's engagement with the text and the bridges built to fill the gaps left by the author.

Understanding comprehension

Comprehension of a text, the creation of meaning from print, is more complex than the decoding of the words. The reader has to 'know the rules of the game the author is playing' (Meek, 1988: 18). Meek has demonstrated how the polysemic texts such as Burningham's *Mr Gumpy's Outing* invites children into reading them in complex ways. The book talk which accompanies readings is likely to be more challenging and analytical if the adult is aware of the complexities of the text. The level at which children can understand written text is much higher when the text is read aloud by a skilled adult reader than when read alone by the child. Reading aloud is a dramatic event: the adult reader's own interpretation and understanding allow him or her to emphasize the clues and signs required to fill in the gaps in the text using paralinguistic and prosodic cues in the reading performance and the listener can draw on these to help understand the narrative.

- **Prosodic features**
  How the words are spoken:
  Intonation, pitch, melody;
  Loudness;
  Stress;
  Tempo;
  Rhythm, pauses.

- **Paralinguistic features**
  The behaviour of the speaker beyond the words:
  Timbre, tone of voice, whisper, etc;
  Gesture;
  Accent;
  Facial expression;
  Body language.

Through use of intonation, gesture, dramatic pauses, reading aloud provides a 'soundtrack' which could be likened to the background music in a film. The reader may slow down and read quietly, anticipating some incipient action, and then speed up to indicate urgency, for example. The reader may pull dramatic faces and gesture to demonstrate a character's actions. The sharing itself allows for discussion, as it is a social activity whether engaged in at home or at school. When the child reader engages in independent reading of a text though, he has to become what Margaret Meek (1988: 10) calls the 'teller' (picking up the author's view and voice) and the 'told' (the recipient of the story, the interpreter).

ACTIVITY

Reading aloud

Choose a good book to read aloud to a child or group of children at a level slightly above their own independent reading levels, that is, at instructional level (see Chapter 10). Prepare for your reading noting any particular features of the book that may pose difficulties for children to comprehend. You will need to consider whether an introduction and discussion before you begin your reading might be necessary, to prepare the child(ren). Consider how your reading aloud will make the text more accessible, and annotate the text or write a plan to indicate how you will read. If possible, work with a partner and observe each other reading so you can gain some critical evaluation afterwards.

Commentary

Did your performance of the text support the child(ren)'s understanding of the narrative? If possible, try to share the book with a child who did not hear the reading aloud and see how the reader copes independently with reading the text. We know from Margaret Clark's work on young fluent readers that they often re-read. Children who have been read to regularly have some experience of the texts they read independently from having heard them read aloud, and this supports their solo reading. The child who has not such a broad repertoire of familiar texts read aloud will be clearly disadvantaged. Reading aloud continues to be important for children throughout their school years, providing a model for their future reading lives and setting up encounters with texts that they may not be ready to tackle alone.

According to Gray (in Melnik and Merritt, 1972), effective readers read at three levels. They should be able to:

- read the lines (literal level);
- read between the lines (inferential level);
- read beyond the lines (interpretative and evaluative level).

Barrett's taxonomy of comprehension takes this further, addressing the cognitive and affective dimensions of reading comprehension and creating further distinctions at each level of comprehension:

> 1.0 Literal comprehension
>   1.1 Recognition
>   of details;
>   of main ideas;
>   of a sequence;
>   of comparison;
>   of cause-and-effect relationships;
>   of character traits.
>   1.2 Recall
>   of details;
>   of main ideas;
>   of a sequence;
>   of comparison;
>   of cause-and-effect relationships;
>   of character traits.
> 2.0 Reorganization
>   classifying;
>   outlining;
>   summarizing;
>   synthesizing.
> 3.0 Inferential comprehension
>   inferring supporting details;
>   inferring main ideas;
>   inferring sequence;
>   inferring comparisons;
>   inferring cause-and-effect relationships;
>   inferring character traits;
>   predicting outcomes;
>   interpreting figurative language.
> 4.0 Evaluation
>   judgements of reality or fantasy;
>   judgements of fact or opinion;
>   judgements of adequacy and validity;
>   judgements of appropriateness;
>   judgements of worth, desirability and acceptability.

5.0 Appreciation
>   emotional response to the content;
>   identification with characters or incidents;
>   reactions to the author's use of language;
>   imagery.

Barrett does not imply that there is a linear progression through these dimensions, and children may be operating at different levels within the reading of a single text (in Melnik and Merritt, 1972). The child reader will benefit from the guided intervention of the 'enabling adult' (Chambers, 1991; 1993) for support in interpreting the text to create meanings at these levels, and the taxonomy can be used to help structure questions and discussion to foster comprehension.

Awareness of the multiplicity of comprehension can help guard against simplistic notions. However, taxonomies are problematic. For instance, Merritt's reservations regarding the use of taxonomies stress that they do not allow for the 'background which the reader brings to the comprehension task'.

Approaching a new book for the first time, the reader brings to the first reading prior knowledge that will help create sense of what is read. The prior knowledge drawn on to create meaning is of two kinds: (a) knowledge of story conventions and books; and (b) knowledge of the world, what Stephens (1992) calls 'experiential knowledge'. The prior knowledge the child reader brings to a text will be different from that of an adult reader, and the author of books for children makes varying concessions to this in creating the texts. The author's choice of language and literary devices creates paths through the text so that the reader can understand the narrative. As texts vary in the demands they make on readers, you will need to ensure that you are selecting texts that provide opportunities for developing complex levels of interpretation. Some books for children, while being good stories which motivate children to read, allow only for literal interpretation rather than for deeper interpretation. One of the criticisms of Enid Blyton's work has been her didactic, closed style which guides the reader so thoroughly through the plot. Her characters are unchanging and there is no character development for interpretation as the narrative progresses.

As we have suggested, challenging texts require readers to be more active in the creation of meaning. For example, in the following extract Henrietta Branford expects the reader to deduce who the main character may be:

> The wolves came down to the farm last night. They spoke to me of freedom.
>   I lay by the fire with my four feet turned towards the embers and the last of the heat warming my belly. I did not listen to the wolf talk. This is no time to think of freedom.
>   Tomorrow, in the morning, I will choose the place. Out in the byre, where the bedding is deep and the children cannot find me. My back aches from the pull of my belly. However long I lap from the cold cattle trough I am still thirsty. I think tomorrow is the day. I rest. The fire ticks. Grindecobbe grunts in her stall. Humble creeps in through the window and curls beside me, soft as smoke.
>   I can smell mouse on her. She has eaten, and come in to the fire for the warmth. (*Fire, Bed and Bone* by Henrietta Branford)

It is left to the reader to infer that this is not a person narrating: lapping from the cattle trough, referring to warming a belly, having four legs, understanding wolves, are all clues that this narrator may be a creature: it is in fact a dog. The setting is the country, and later, further clues will indicate that the story is set long ago. Barthes (1995) distinguishes between 'lisible' or 'readerly' texts, where the reader is passive, and led by the author through the text, and 'scriptable' or 'writerly' texts where the reader is active in creating meaning from the text. The writerly text allows room for interpretation: gaps are left in the texts by the author for the reader to fill. Bruner writes that 'texts which require readers to fill in gaps by forcing "meaning performance" upon the reader – will on the whole be better stories (that is higher quality visits to narrative worlds)' (pp. 4–5). According to Iser (1978) the reader draws on prior knowledge to 'build bridges' that help make sense of the text. Whenever the reader bridges the gaps, communication begins. Re-readings may allow the reader to notice more signs, make greater links and allow for further inferences to be drawn. Sometimes we are so good at filling the gaps that reading between and beyond the lines is an unconscious activity.

Reading between the lines: thought bubbles

On a large sheet of paper draw a thought bubble or print one using Word auto shapes. Underneath, copy the picture of Titch from the page which reads, 'His sister Mary was a bit bigger ...' and write what he might be thinking in the thought bubble. Alternatively, select another picturebook where the text does not state explicitly what the characters are thinking and feeling (e.g. Rosie the Hen in *Rosie's Walk*, Bernard in *Not Now, Bernard*). You can do this activity with children and discuss their responses with a colleague.

Commentary

Thought and speech bubbles are useful devices for considering what particular characters think or feel at key points in a narrative, and for allowing children to interpret what they have read.

Reading demands explanations beyond the information given about the surface features of language, important as that undoubtedly is (Meek, 1988). In *You'll Soon Grow into Them, Titch*, the written text tells the story of Titch receiving handed-down clothes and buying new ones. Meanwhile in the background pictures, we can see hints and clues about other events unspoken. Outside the window a bird builds a nest, lays eggs and eventually baby birds hatch out; Mum knits tiny clothes; plants in the house and garden grow and blossom; and, of course, Titch's mother shows unmistakable signs of pregnancy so that the denouement is a new baby to whom Titch can pass on his old clothes.

The traditional tale, too, offers scope for prediction, anticipation and interpretation for the reader. This story form is likely to be familiar to children so the prior knowledge they bring to the text will facilitate prediction and anticipation. The child reader is likely to know that, if a challenge is set, many difficulties will have to be endured before the hero succeeds. Transformations of beautiful to ugly, rich to poor, and back are common, although good and evil remain stable, with good triumphing over evil in most children's tales. The pattern of three is symbolic and it will often take three attempts to achieve something. This can make interpreting these tales much easier than other texts.

Genres are discussed in Chapters 5 to 9 but it is worth pausing here to explore the impact of form on comprehension in some children's books. The use of letters, diaries and journals for forming a narrative requires particular interpretation by the reader, who often has literally to fill in gaps to read the text. Some narrative forms, such as stories told in letters require the reader to work on the text and surmise what was said or written in between, rather like hearing one side of a telephone conversation. This is a good device for encouraging children to 'read between the lines'.

Beverley Cleary's *Dear Mr Henshaw* starts simply with a boy, Leigh, writing to his favourite author as an exercise set by his teacher. As the boy grows older, the letters to his favourite author become more complex and eventually the author with whom he is corresponding suggests that Leigh writes his letters as a diary for himself, and so it becomes an inner monologue with no respondent.

A more recent book, Sharon Creech's *Love That Dog*, is written in the form of a journal kept by Jack during poetry-writing sessions. The journal is addressed to his teacher, Miss Stretchberry, and again, the reader has to fill in the gaps in the dialogue between the two. On the opening page, it is not hard to work out what has gone before:

JACK
ROOM 105 – MISS STRETCHBERRY
SEPTEMBER 13
I don't want to
Because boys
Don't write poetry
Girls do.

And then, a few pages later,

DECEMBER 4
Why do you want
to type up what I wrote
about reading
the small poems?
It's not a poem.
Is it?
I guess you can
put it on the board
if you want to
but don't put
my name
on it
in case
other people
think
it's not a poem.

A changing relationship of mutual respect develops: Jack's confidence as a poet grows with his trust in his teacher. Other letters written in journal form include a number of Jacqueline Wilson's books including *The True Story of Tracy Beaker*. *Double Act* is a journal kept by identical twins, although the difference in style between the twins' inputs is an interesting device for exploring their growing awareness of their individuality.

Another book told as journal extracts written by different characters is *The Wanderer* by Sharon Creech. Sophie is sailing the Atlantic with two cousins and her uncles, and both she and her cousin, Cody, keep a log of the voyage. This allows us to have two narrative perspectives on the unfolding relationships of these family members cooped up on a small boat during the crossing. Malorie Blackman's verse novel, *Cloudbusting*, told in the form of a confessional journal, allows the reader to gradually piece together clues about the narrator and his relationship with the victim of class bullying.

Intertextuality

One of the signifying features the author uses to create meaning is intertextual reference. Narrative refers to other sources or contexts in creating layers of understanding and, if the reader can pick up the clues, then the references are shared. Yet again, the difference between the implied or ideal reader and the real reader will affect the interpretation of these intertextual signs. Janet and Allan Ahlberg's books are rich in intertextual references. In *Each Peach Pear Plum*, each opening contains objects signifying the next character or story which will appear. On the second page, Tom Thumb sits in the cupboard eating jam. His seat is a tin of dog food, and the child with prior knowledge of the rhyme 'Old Mother Hubbard, went to the cupboard, to get her poor dog a bone' will make a connection between the rhyme and the object. On the central page opening, Bo-peep sits on a well, and those who know the rhyme 'Jack and Jill', and who are aware of what a well looks like, will make the connection. The story still works as a viable narrative for those who do not make the connections and miss the intertextual references.

The Jolly Postman built on the success of *Each Peach Pear Plum*, taking such references further with inclusion of various cards and letters which children may recognize from their home experience. For older children, an earlier book, *Jeremiah in the Dark Woods*, plays with the reader's knowledge of other stories, although the reader can also understand it as a story without picking up the allusions:

> Jeremiah Obadiah Jackanory Jones lived with his grandma in the middle of the Dark Woods. Jeremiah's grandma's house was made of gingerbread and cakes, with window-panes of clear sugar and a roof of chocolate fudge.
> Jeremiah was very happy there. He was fond of his grandma and enjoyed eating the house.
> One morning Jeremiah's grandma said, 'Jeremiah, I am going to make some nice jam tarts for your auntie who lives beyond the hills and a great way off, and I want you to take them to her'. (*Jeremiah in the Dark Woods* by Janet and Allan Ahlberg)

Catherine Storr's *Clever Polly and the Stupid Wolf* also plays with the reader's knowledge of other books. In *The Journey of the Clever Man* by Ime Dros, a man in hiding from the Nazis in Holland recounts stories from the one text he has, to a listening child. The stories are from the *Odyssey*, although it is not immediately apparent and the connection could only be made by a reader with some familiarity with Homer. Encouraging children to make the connections between textual references opens up possibilities of what reading can be and will develop a skill to be extended with other texts later. The references need not be to actual texts, but to broader cultural referents. Biblical and classical allusions abound in literature and the knowing child may identify allegories of, for example, the Garden of Eden, in *The Secret Garden*. The genre, or story archetype, is another cultural referent.

The affective response

Benton describes the subject of the reader's response to text as 'the Loch Ness Monster of literary studies', with our attempts to define and describe what happens when we read as 'pictures of dubious authenticity' (in Hunt, 1999: 81). Analysing what happens when children read is a complex business. D.W. Harding described the reader as an 'onlooker', making analogies with someone looking on at events, and refers to a stage between being the actual witness of events and being the reader as the 'gossip', listening to a recount of events. He says that, first, the onlooker 'attends' and that, second, he evaluates. He evaluates, 'whether his attitude is one of faint liking or disliking, hardly above indifference, or strong, perhaps intensely emotional, and perhaps differentiated into pity, horror, contempt, respect, amusement, or any other of the shades and kinds of evaluation ... ' (in Meek, 1977: 59).

Harding claims that attention indicates interest and that leads to a response, which will be evaluative, welcoming or aversive. Psychological interpretations of children's responses as readers have been outlined by Tucker (1981) who criticizes the Freudian close analysis of the text for signifying features relating to, for example, Oedipal myth as 'hunting the symbol'. He criticizes the failure of many perspectives, particular Freudian interpretations, to take account of the social contexts in which children are reading. Harding, however, foreshadows the development of reader response theory in acknowledging that what the onlooker perceives is coloured by his or her own attitudes and social and cultural beliefs. Harding uses as an example the sight of two groups of people struggling: if we note that one group is the police, each onlooker might interpret the event differently depending on the set of assumptions about 'police' that are being brought to the situation. He claims that besides bringing values to the text, the texts themselves 'have, cumulatively, a deep and extensive influence on our systems and culture' (in Meek, 1977: 61).

In his study of readers, Appleyard (1990) describes five different roles that readers take when engaging with books, three of which relate to the child reader:

- *The Reader as Player* – In the pre-school years the child, not yet a reader but a listener to stories, becomes a confident player in a fantasy world that images realities, fears, and desires in forms that the child slowly learns to sort out and control.
- *The Reader as Hero and Heroine* – The school-age child is the central figure of a romance that is constantly being rewritten as the child's picture of the world and of how people behave in it is filled in and clarified. Stories here seem to be an alternative, more organized, and less ambiguous world than the world of pragmatic experience, one the reader easily escapes into and becomes involved with.
- *The Reader as Thinker* – The adolescent reader looks to stories to discover insights into the meaning of life, values and beliefs worthy of commitment, ideal images, and authentic role models for imitation. The truth of these ideas and ways of living is a severe criterion for judging them.

Appleyard also discusses how the reader searches for moral order through reading, but exploring in increasingly sophisticated ways. This reflects the Piagetian view of young children's reading, outlined by Tucker (1981), of the young child wanting consistency in social order, with reward and punishment for good and bad characters, and clearly worked out plots. Tucker calls reading a form of internalized play and suggests that the dilemmas and fear-inducing plots of children's books are an essential part of children's experience.

Although children initially want stability and predictability, with stories in which they can imagine themselves as the hero at the centre of the narrative, they also learn from 'cognitive dissonance'. Such dissonance in the books children read as they mature challenges the immature notions of right and wrong. Appleyard focuses on 'the transaction that occurs between reader and text', and particularly on 'changes in the reader that shape that transaction' (1990: 3). This change is also recognized by Tucker (1981: 182) who claims that there 'is a perpetual journey' in children's books. He claims that children see themselves in a naturally heroic way. He suggests that growing up is 'one long process of cutting down this heroic view and gradually coming to terms with what is' (1981: 185).

The values and beliefs the child brings to the text can be challenged, reinforced, refined or rejected through discussion and exploration. Tucker suggests that 'more gifted' writers take children on from their 'habitual ways of thinking by prodding them onwards, suggesting new avenues, new attitudes' (1981: 186). He discusses the child's concept of 'truth' being challenged by the introduction of 'shades of grey' in the moral certitudes of the texts read, and suggests that truth might be 'something you puzzle over and about which you are not too sure'. Appleyard (1990: 59) suggests that from the age of 6 childhood changes as the child moves 'beyond the family culture' with school and peer culture exerting pressures. Reading fiction provides information but so allows the child to focus on issues of identity, exploring 'an inner world'.

Danny the Champion of the World is an interesting text for exploring this. On the one hand, the book contains some of Dahl's stock good and bad characters, with 'baddie' Mr Hazell portrayed in a grotesquely unsympathetic way. However, Danny's relationship with his father is more delicately handled. A picture is painted of a close and trusting relationship between father and child, alone in the world and united through their shared loss of Danny's mother. The reader, like Danny, trusts in his father's strength and integrity. So when Danny wakes alone to find his father gone, there is a moment of high tension: he has been let down. When his father returns, trust is not restored initially, as Danny requires an explanation about why he had left. Then Danny has a second moral dilemma when he discovers that his father's absence was a result of his poaching. The reader has to wrestle, together with Danny, with the thorny question of whether poaching is stealing, and whether in this case it was justifiable, although Dahl rather ducks the issue by making Hazell so grotesque that young readers feel any action against him is acceptable. How the young reader grapples with such issues will depend on the attitudes and experience brought to bear on the text.

The tendency of authors to 'take upon themselves the task of trying to mould audience attitudes into "desirable" forms' (Stephens, 1992: 3) is addressed in

Chapters 3 and 10, but even the least zealous author's work will impact on the child's developing mind. Stephens refers to the 'emotional space' (Stephens, 1992: 14) which the reader can 'inhabit largely on his or her own terms' when responding to a literary text. This is the space where the child relates the text to his or her own experience, and so as to make it 'meaningful' the reader has to question 'who does the perceiving and who determines the meaningfulness' (Stephens, 1992: 15). So we are back to context, and the meaning created at the point of reading by the reader. Crago (1985), in a review of psychological perspectives on the impact of literature on the child, cites Nell's work on 'ludic reading' as demonstrating how the child can become 'lost' in a book. However, he also asserts that we have no way of knowing exactly how an individual experiences a book. Only in our discussions with children and in their written and spoken offerings following a reading can we glimpse their response, but the articulation, according to Crago, changes and shapes the response. He suggests, like Harding, that children's first responses to text are preferences – they either like or dislike the story. He develops this by claiming that aesthetic response reflects the preference and develops from it.

Stephens (1992), while acknowledging the impossibility of knowing what is actually in the child reader's mind, claims that we can look for 'determinable meaning' in a text. And so we return to the 'enabling adult' who can help provide opportunities for the reader to read and engage with the text in searching for meaning and pleasure.

ACTIVITY

Being an onlooker

Malorie Blackman's books are uncompromising in presenting realities of life and its dilemmas to children. Read *Pig Heart Boy* or *Hacker*. One deals with the first child to have a pig's heart transplanted into him, the other concerns computers and corruption. Either of these books would provide a good starting point for exploring children's responses to issues which are not clear-cut in moral and ethical terms.

Response journals

In Chapter 1 we introduced the idea of keeping a personal reading journal as a means of reflecting on your own reading experience. Journalling is also a useful tool for helping children develop reflective and critical reading as well as developing their understanding of what they read and can be used as a tool for supporting group discussion about books as well as one-to-one reading conferences with the teacher. Helpful prompts can be displayed in the classroom but should not be treated as checklists.

In the initial stages children will benefit from suggestions as to what and how they might record their responses. They might for example:

- record their likes and dislikes – Prompts: 'I dislike this story because ...', 'I really enjoyed reading this because ...';
- record their feelings – Prompts: 'I felt sad when ...', 'It made me angry when ...' 'I was surprised that ...';
- relate their reading to their own experience – Prompts: 'This reminds me of the time that ...', 'I can relate to ...';
- make connections between texts – Prompts: 'This reminds me of ...', 'I read another book that ...', 'This is similar to ...';
- make connections between their reading and knowledge of the world – Prompts: 'I heard about ... on the news', 'We have learnt about ... in science';
- reflect on characters;
- reflect on settings;
- make an evaluative comment: 'I thought this was an effective piece of writing because ...';

- make notes about confusions – Prompts: 'I don't understand why ...', 'A question I have is ...'.

ACTIVITY

Children's reading logs and journals

Set up reading journals with the children you teach and use them as the basis for discussion in reading conferences and literature circles/group reading on a regular basis. Small books are best for these, so that they can travel and be used wherever and whenever the child is reading. As with your own journal, the title and author/illustrator can be recorded and the source of the book. The date each book was started and finished enables you to see how long the child is spending on a book.

You might encourage the children to enter books they read at home. Many children, like many adult readers, keep several texts on the go, particularly if they have to have an approved 'school' book to read: they will often be reading a more popular text or series book outside school or for bedtime reading. Comic and magazine reading can be included, as well as non-fiction and functional reading.

You might want children to have separate sections for recording personal reading and the books that are being read as part of class/group reading activities. The written entries can be single reflections on a book on completion, or staged entries throughout the reading like the reflective journals.

Commentary

Having to write an evaluative comment on every book read could be tedious, but encouraging a swift evaluative response by a grading from 1 to 10 for the book can be useful. One teacher of reception children devised a record where she could complete the title of the book and record of who shared it with the child, but the child could contribute too by indicating a qualitative response by putting a smile or frown on a face (see Appendix 2.1). A colleague adapted this by adding a grid for colouring in a grade from 1 to 10 (see Appendix 2.2). These children were involved in recording and responding from an early stage, and although initially the teacher or assistant wrote the book details, the children insisted on copying the author's name and title for themselves after a while. Although initially the children awarded every book a high grade, eventually they would read a book that stood out and realize it was better than the others, and so they gradually started to make distinctions and discuss the reasons for their responses. Occasional reflective inputs can be required, particularly where children are taking books home to read prior to working on them in class. They should be discouraged from rewriting the story, and modelling a collective journal based on an ongoing shared book in class can help children to understand what form a reflective journal might take.

Many children enjoy making an evaluative comment and use their journals extensively. We would recommend always encouraging children to make an entry if they reject a book and leave it unfinished. This will allow you to discuss the text with the child who has genuinely made a mistaken choice or is finding it difficult to choose: such rejections can allow you to guide the child to books they might enjoy. It also tends to deter children who habitually flit and do not settle to read as, given the choice of reading a book or writing about why they do not want to read it, most will opt for the reading. Once started, they can easily be hooked in. Many teachers have read aloud a book to the whole class with the objective of winning over one reluctant or 'lost' reader, offering them the text for their own reading afterwards. Inevitably a book read aloud by the teacher becomes a hot favourite to read, so there will be a queue for the book and a cachet for the child who has read it first.

Extracts from one child's reading log

Read these extracts from Kareena's reading log and consider what you can discover about her reading behaviour and knowledge about books.

The Great Escape of Doreen Potts by Jo Nesbitt
This book was quite good. It was written by Jo Nesbitt … When I had finished my last book I wasn't going to choose this book but Lubina and Vanessa told me that it was good …

The Little Witch by Ottfried Preussler
When I had finished my last book I didn't know what book to choose. Thank god Emma came and told me to read this book … The witch isn't like any other witch horrible and nasty. She is very kind …

Hills End by Ivan Southall
This book that I have just finished reading was Absolutely Brilliant! I have never read a book so exciting as this before … When I had finished my last book I didn't have a chance to choose what I really wanted to read, instead I just picked up the book and sat at my desk and read … It took me a week to read this book. I would have finished before but it had 221 pages. Right in the middle of the book the most important part happened, the storm began. As I may have told you in some records I have mentioned that I read my books in the night. As I was reading this book I felt scared if they were going to die …

Pippi Longstocking by Astrid Lindgren
It took me about three days to read. I did like the first chapter because I liked the bit where they start to meet and introduce themselves. The best chapter I liked was when they find an old oak tree for a hiding place. At the end of the book I felt it was awkward to ask a question and not answer it. Although I think these stories are worth listening to.

No More School by Meg Harper and Oliver Jelfe
When I finished this book I sat down and thought of all the books I had read and the ones that were boring. All the time I have been reading all sorts of different books I think this one on no more school was boring and not exciting. As I read the blurb I thought this book was going to be good, but I was wrong. I think this book isn't my type to read …

Commentary

Kareena is a confident reader who is reading at home and at school. Most of the books she read came from school, although there was some swapping and borrowing of books owned by the children. She was an avid reader and had read many of the popular choices and was exploring beyond the commonly known authors.

It was interesting that she had persisted with a book she did not enjoy, and it is useful to discuss preferences and choices, and demonstrate that occasional rejection is acceptable. Reading books read by others in the class meant that she could engage in 'book talk' with other interested readers and benefit from peer recommendation. The sharing of questions or dilemmas arising from the reading, such as the 'awkward' question at the end of *Pippi Longstocking*, allows the teacher a chance to engage in discussion with the reader at reading conferences. However, it helps if you have read the books you are discussing, so get to know your classroom collection well. Teachers who keep records and know who has read what can also put children with shared experience in touch with each other for further sharing of experience. Kareena chose books on the recommendation of friends and by reading the blurb. She also liked reading books which had been read aloud in class. However, children are introduced to television, video and film at the same time or, even, earlier than they read books, and for many children their choice will be affected by this filmic 'publicity'.

Contexts for developing response

Guided reading

Guided reading involves the teacher working in depth with a group in order to develop reading strategies that will enable them to become independent readers. A lesson within a lesson, guided reading follows a teaching sequence that provides explicit instruction, opportunities for independent reading and for assessment (Figure 2.1). However, this teaching approach should not be regarded simply as a procedure: effective guided reading is contingent upon high-quality interactions between the teacher and pupil and this means knowing when to intervene and how to intervene in order to move children's reading forward. For children working at National Curriculum Level 3 and above the emphasis in guided reading will be the development of comprehension and thinking skills, though children will still need to develop more advanced skills for deciphering more complicated sentence structures and unfamiliar text types. Older children may well be reading at length between guided sessions so that most of the lesson is spent talking. A rationale for guided reading at KS2, examplar material, professional development sessions and recommended titles can be found in Hobsbaum et al.'s *Guiding Reading at KS2* (2006).

Introduction to text

Strategy check

Independent reading and related task

Return to the text

Developing the reposne

Review (reading target and next steps)

Evaluation

Figure 2.1 *Guided reading teaching sequence*

Group reading and literature circles

Group reading is distinct from guided reading in that the groups work independently, without the teacher. Through group reading children learn to become autonomous readers. Group reading provides an opportunity for developing shared understandings and creating a community of readers for whom enjoyment and purpose is paramount. They share the reading of a specific text over a series of lessons. Inexperienced groups will however need to have ways of working and expectations made clear and some modelling may be necessary to show groups how to organize themselves. Short tasks may be set and prompts given to aid discussion. You can read more about group reading or literature ciricles in Carol King and Jane Briggs's (2005) *Literature Circles: Better Talking, More Ideas* (2005).

Questions, statements, prompts

Questioning in guided and group reading involves not only the teacher structuring questions to lead discussion and exploration of the text, it also involves the children formulating their own questions for interrogating the text. This could be achieved through discussion, writing or drama activities. In *hot seating*, one child will be a character from the book and the other children have the chance to interrogate him or her about his role and motives. For example, for younger children, the wolf might be asked about his behaviour toward Little Red Riding Hood. For older children, Edmund could be questioned about his denial that he had been to Narnia in *The Lion, the Witch and the Wardrobe*; Gabriel in *A Little Lower Than the Angels* by Geraldine McCaughrean could be challenged about his motives in wanting to leave his master, the Mason. Another useful strategy is to have pairs of children working in role having telephone conversations. Either both or one of the children could be in role, so that the child could interrogate any character, or could set up dialogue between characters. For example, Baby Bear could ask Goldilocks why she had eaten his porridge, or Lucy could ask Edmund why he had denied that he had been to Narnia.

Where the teacher asks the questions, they should be carefully planned to encourage not just literal recall but deeper analysis of the text. Open questions, which invite wider responses, are preferable to closed questions for this. 'Did Edmund tell the truth about what happened when he went through the wardrobe?' invites a limited response. 'I wonder what would make Edmund deny he had been through the wardrobe?' invites an open and full response, and encourages speculation.

Some question types

- Literal questions: *What colour was Goldilocks's hair?*
- Inferential questions: *Will –stay or leave and what makes you think this?*
- Deductive questions: *What do you think will happen next? Why do you think that?*
- Justification questions: *Where does it imply that? What in the text makes you say that?*
- Evaluative questions: *Does the author successfully hook you into the story? Is this an effective piece of mystery writing?*
- Appreciation questions: *Do you like this story? Why? Why not?*
- Quality questions: *How many different ways can you imagine that .?.*
- Reorganization questions: *What would have happened if .?.How would the story have been different if .?.*
- Viewpoint questions: *If you were the King, what would you have thought of .?.*
- Involvement questions: *If you could travel to ..what would you expect to see?*
- Forced association questions: *In what ways are the stories of Sleeping Beauty and Cinderella alike? In what ways are Lord of the Rings and the film Star Wars alike?*

Questions, no matter how carefully planned, may not be the best way of stimulating discussion. Statements, challenges and prompts generate livelier debate. Using tag questions and other facilitating strategies can further the discussion, for example, 'go on …', 'Mmmm?', 'Can you say a little more about that?', or 'What is it in the book that makes you think that?'.

The 'tell me' approach developed by Aidan Chambers (1993) provides an excellent example of how discussion might be organized and guided. Chambers talks about the importance of accepting 'honourably reportable' contributions from children, where what they have to say is accepted and explored as valid, although the 'enabling adult' may challenge and extend such thinking through further 'book talk'.

ACTIVITY

Questioning the text
Choose one of the books from your personal collection and draw up a plan to explore the key themes, characters and events using questioning. Consider the questions you will ask and how you might facilitate wider discussion. Include questions that require literal, inferential and deductive reading. Include some role play to enable children to ask questions too.

Finally, devise an activity that requires children to generate their own questions in relation to a specific text.

Small group activities: directed activities related to texts

One of the most influential studies focused on improving children's responsive reading is the *Schools Council Project on The Effective Use of Reading*. The study focused on the different reading behaviours children need to cope with a range of reading tasks: skimming, scanning, receptive reading and reflective, or critical, reading (Lunzer and Gardner, 1979). It is the later two of these behaviours which we need to foster most in responding to fiction, although skimming and scanning can also be useful strategies when looking for evidence in narrative text to justify inferences. This major project produced suggestions for effective group reading activities which would support children's learning.

The focus on group reading was a move away from the 'reading round a group' which was seen as unproductive. Instead, children were to read and discuss texts in a much more active way within their groups. This approach has formed the basis for a number of more recent curriculum initiatives such as the guided reading in First Steps in Australia and the National Literacy Strategy in England. The strategies recommended for the group work were:

- prediction;
- questions;
- analysing text;
- sequencing;
- deletion/cloze;
- visual representations of text.

The strategies suggested are for working with both expository and narrative text. The first three can be achieved through structured discussion or through more tightly focused and directed activities.

Prediction

Pausing in the reading of a narrative to review events and to discuss character, plot, themes and setting allows children to presuppose what might happen next. This behaviour, which is modelled well and learnt in the early years in sharing and discussing picture books with readings and re-readings, can be continued throughout the school. Carole King's literature circles begin with children reviewing the outside of the book, looking at the covers, the illustrations, title, author's name, blurb and any other information provided. The children record in their journals their initial impressions and anticipate the beginning of the story. By the time they start to read, they have already brought their prior knowledge to bear on this initial scrutiny of the book and have made predictions about what to expect as they start to read in terms of genre, plot, characters and, even, style, particularly if the author's work is familiar.

There is some wonderful play on the functions and conventions of the book cover and the whole business of story-book production in the work of Jon Scieszka, as we have seen, and the recently published Lemony Snicket. In the Lemony Snicket stories, the covers provide endless clues as to the dreadful adventures contained within. The series title *A Series of Unfortunate Incidents*, and the first title in the series, *The Bad Beginning* both augur trouble to come. A doom-laden blurb confirms this:

> Dear Reader,
> I'm sorry to say that the book you are holding in your hands is extremely unpleasant. It tells an unhappy tale about three very unlucky children. Even though they are charming and clever, the Baudelaire siblings lead lives filled with misery and woe … (*The Bad Beginning* by Lemony Snicket)

The opening chapters of most narratives make significant demands on the reader, introducing the setting and characters and providing a framework for the later development of the story. Picking up on the clues necessary to predict, hypothesize and review needs support. Jon Scieszka plays with the concept of author by attributing *The True Story of the Three Little Pigs*:

> By A. Wolf
> As told to Jon Scieszka
> The wolf as narrator leads us into the story.
> Everybody knows the
> story of the Three Little Pigs.
> Or at least they think they do.
> But I'll let you in on a little secret.
> Nobody knows the real story,
> because nobody has ever heard
> *my* side of the story.
> I'm the wolf. Alexander T. Wolf.
> You can call me Al.
> I don't know how this whole Big Bad Wolf thing got started,
> but it's all wrong.

In discussion we can consider the devices the wolf is using to win us over even before he begins his story. We can discuss the intertextuality: we need to review the original story, the one 'everybody knows'. And we can begin already to consider whether this is the true story and whether we are going to believe the wolf. If we decide his claims are unreliable, then we predict that the story will have flaws in it, and as we turn the pages we shall be looking for evidence to back up this hypothesis.

ACTIVITY

Reading the clues to predict ahead

Read the following extract. Review what you know of the story so far and what information it provides about what the story might be about:

> There is no lake at Camp Green Lake. There was a very large lake here, the largest lake in Texas. That was over a hundred years ago. Now it is just a dry, flat, wasteland.
> There used to be a town of Green Lake as well. The town shrivelled and dried up along with the lake, and the people who lived there.
> During the summer the daytime temperature hovers around ninety-five degrees in the shade, if you can find any shade. There's not much shade in a big dry lake. The only trees are two old oaks on the eastern edge of the 'lake.' A hammock is stretched between the two trees, and a log cabin stands behind that.
>
> The campers are forbidden to lie in the hammock. It belongs to the Warden. The Warden owns the shade.
> Out on the lake, rattlesnakes and scorpions find shade under rocks and in the holes dug by the campers.
> Here's a good rule to remember about rattlesnakes and scorpions: If you don't bother them, they won't bother you.
> Usually.
> Being bitten by a scorpion or even a rattlesnake is not the worst thing that can happen to you. You won't die.
> Usually.
>
> The reader is probably asking: Why would anyone go to Camp Green Lake?
> Most campers weren't given a choice. Camp Green Lake is a camp for bad boys.
> If you take a bad boy and make him dig a hole every day in the hot sun, it will turn him into a good boy.
> That was what some people thought.
> Stanley Yelnats was given a choice. The judge said, 'You may go to jail, or you may go to Camp Green Lake.'
> Stanley was from a poor family. He had never been to camp before.
> (*Holes* by Louis Sachar)

Commentary

In describing the camp, Sachar paints a picture of desolation that demonstrates the contrast between the expectations produced by its name, and the harsh realities. He introduces the main character, Stanley, and exposes his naïvety. He also introduces the Warden as someone ruthless, selfish and uncaring. This is achieved in few words through a clever juxtaposition of statements. We can guess as we turn the page that Stanley will be cruelly disillusioned and that this will form the basis of the story. As we read through the text we can pause at different points to review our knowledge and make further predictions. Such anticipation of what might come next is predicated on textual scrutiny and gathering of evidence balanced with our own personal knowledge to support an argument: as such, it encourages further close reading. The teacher's choice of text can develop and expand children's use of predictive skills. Choosing to work on contrasting texts, for example will challenge preconceptions. The beginning of *The Lion, the Witch and the Wardrobe* is safe and comfortable, with no hint of what is to come. However, within three pages, Lucy has gone through the wardrobe into Narnia. The argument when she returns as the others disbelieve her account, fractures the closeness of the children's relationships and presages the changes in their lives to come.

Analysing text

As we have already seen, close textual analysis can focus children on language or structural aspects of the narrative. The possibilities are endless. Marking and annotating texts encourages close looking, and a good strategy is to copy extracts of no more than two pages into the centre of an A3 sheet. This allows space around the text for annotations, notes and queries. It is a good idea as you read children's books to note particular extracts at critical points in the story that might be good for such a focus. However, they should always be read within the context of reading the whole book, and not used as exercises divorced from the context.

ACTIVITY

Badger on the Barge
Copy this text onto the centre of a sheet of A3 paper. This format will provide space for you to annotate the text and record your initial response to the story. Who is it about? What is the setting and how has the author created the setting? What do you know about Helen? Are there any clues about the story and what it might be about? Has the author used any interesting language to describe the setting and characters so far?

October smelled of bonfires, even in Alfred Street. Down by the canal the yellow leaves of the big conker trees flickered and rustled like burning newspapers. In the still canal water black leaves floated on Helen's reflection.
'Come, ye thankful people, come,
Raise the song of harvest home.
All is safely gathered in
E're the winter storms begin . . .', she sang softly. Across the canal she could see King Alfred's Grammar School, high and holy on its hill above the empty cricket-field. Peter didn't go there any more.
At last Helen took the list out of her basket. All the names were crossed off except one. 'Miss Brady. The Barge. The Canal.' Underneath, Mrs Phillips, her teacher, had written: Boat moored on the canal just past the bridge. In her basket was the last box of fruit from their school harvest festival which she had to deliver to old age pensioners. So far Helen had not enjoyed knocking on the old people's doors, drinking cups of sweet tea and looking at photographs of smug grandchildren who never came to call.
Miss Brady would be the seventh, and the last.
She stood looking at the towers of the Grammar School for a few seconds more, then she turned and walked along the muddy towpath. Peter didn't go there any more. And, this morning, Dad had burnt his cricket bat on that terrible bonfire, while Mum had stood at the back door, silently watching. Mum had looked as worn and grey as a length of old string.
(*Badger on the Barge and Other Stories* by Janni Howker)

Commentary

When working with children you would probably proscribe the focus for the activity rather than looking at all the issues suggested here. You might have noted the mention of the barge as the address for Miss Brady, the old lady Helen has to visit as this relates to the title and so may be significant. You might track the references to the dying, falling leaves. This autumnal reference is significant, as autumn is a time of death and decay. October is linked to bonfires, and the leaves 'burn'. The bonfire is mentioned again later, referring to Helen's Dad's burning of Peter's cricket bat. The grammar school is mentioned twice, so seems significant 'high and holy on its hill'. Why does Peter not go there any more? You might surmise that Peter is Helen's brother, as he is mentioned in the family context. And you might have inferred that Peter not being there any more and not needing his cricket bat might be important clues to what the story might be about.

There is some interesting figurative language to be traced, and two styles of storytelling. There is the contemplative, slow beginning, referring to the bonfires, Peter and the school, and the central, more brisk style of the passage about the delivery of the basket, marked by 'At last Helen took ...'. Then a return to the contemplative style again, signifying perhaps, Helen's attention drifting away from the purpose of her visit to other preoccupations.

In *Dinner Ladies Don't Count* by Bernard Ashley, the character of Jason is quickly established as being the 'bad boy' of the class. An early analysis might be recorded on the character sheet in Appendix 2.3. However, later on, while all the other characters in the book continue to think of Jason as the class villain, we discover, through the narrator, information about Jason which leads us to amend our opinion of him, and we could go back and add more to the character portrait. It is important to understand though, that while the other characters still think badly of him and respond to him as such, we as readers now perceive this as unfair treatment: an example of dramatic irony. One way of exploring these multiple perspectives within a book and to make explicit with children what they may have perceived implicitly, is to use drama or writing to consider what is happening 'out of shot'. Possible activities might include working in pairs to role play conversations between characters, considering what they might be saying or thinking about Jason. In writing, large speech bubbles on A4 paper enable a similar exercise to be written as conversation or as thoughts.

Sequencing

With young children in particular, sequencing a text can help to consolidate their understanding of story structure. Cards with pictures or captions relating to the main events in a narrative can be used for this focus. The computer can also be used for this, to good effect. Older children can 'storyboard' main events in a more complex narrative, as if they were planning to film the story. The story can also be tracked or reviewed on a simple storyline. Tracking the plot on the framework provided can be helpful for examining story structure in simple tales and for understanding the structure of longer, more complex novels. There are a number of commercially produced story-tracking frameworks. Detailed frameworks support more in-depth analysis but will not work for all stories. A simple plot line like the one shown in Figure 4.1 (p. 81) can support analysis without being too intrusive.

ACTIVITY

> *Tracking the plot*
> Read or re-read a favourite traditional story. Use the plot line (Figure 4.1) to track the story. Try the same activity with a modern short story and a longer novel.

Commentary

It is useful to try this activity first with a traditional tale or a short story before considering how you might represent more complex stories. Consider whether individual episodic analyses, for example of one chapter, might supplement the analysis of the overall structure of a complex narrative. This analysis can also support children's understanding of narrative form in their own writing.

Visual representation of text

Children's understanding from a young age can be assessed and developed through their picturing of a story. They will often use such pictures as the basis for their own retellings, thus consolidating their knowledge and understanding. Older children, too, can benefit from diagrammatic or visual responses. Tracking the story in a storyboard in visual form can support understanding of story structures.

ACTIVITY

> Use these visual approaches to explore responses. Undertake them with children in school. Discuss the outcomes in groups or with a partner.
>
> - *Planning a film of the book:* Using the storyboard planner (Appendix 2.5), imagine you are planning to create a film version of 'Kate Crackernuts' or another traditional tale. Plot the opening sequence of images and annotate to provide additional detail.
> - *Designing a book jacket:* Choose a short story from your personal collection. Imagine you have been commissioned to make it into a short book. Design a jacket for the book, including cover pictures and blurb.
> - *Exploring setting:* Read *The Dark Is Rising* by Susan Cooper, *Plundering Paradise* by Geraldine McCaughrean or any other book with good descriptions of setting. By drawing or painting, try to recreate the picture created by the author in words, capturing the atmosphere of the written text.

Commentary

This is an effective way of encouraging close reading. It encourages literal and evaluative reading of the text, and may require children to consider how to represent the metaphorical images created by the author. Character can also be represented pictorially, and even some action, such as the life of Gollum outlined so evocatively in *The Hobbit*. Visual imaging can also be used to record children's responses to text beyond the literal level through their construction of mental images as they read, which can be articulated through discussion or pictorially. Just as some of the picture books mentioned earlier represent visually the affective domain, so children can represent their affective and interpretative readings of the text.

Cloze procedure

Cloze is a procedure, based on Gestalt psychology, where words are deleted from a text, and the reader is required to draw on cues from the context to fill the gaps and complete the text.

It can be used to:

- encourage readers to make full use of context cues (semantic and syntactic cues) when reading, particularly when they have been heavily dependent on grapho-phonic cues;
- encourage children to read for meaning when they are able to decode text, but do not fully comprehend what they read;

- focus on particular aspects of language, such as verbs or conjunctions, by deleting only that class of word in the text;
- assess reading attainment through using a text with a known level of difficulty;
- assess the level of difficulty of a text.

The usual level of deletions is approximately every seventh word, but easier passages may be prepared by deleting every tenth word, for example. Alternatively, you will prepare passages with carefully selected deletions in order to support your specific objectives (e.g. examples of figurative language, rhyme, speech verbs). The space left when words are deleted should be sufficiently large to allow the children to write in their substitution. The gap should not provide a clue as to the length of the deleted word, so all gaps should be the same length. In cloze procedure, the aim is not necessarily to have the children guess the original word, but to have them find an appropriate word which makes sense in the context. In some cases there can only be one possible word that fills the gap, for example 'a' or 'the' or a character's name. Sometimes there is a limited possibility and sometimes there is a wide range.

Variations include the deletion of phrases or sentences, such as a title or a key sentence in order to encourage discussion about key themes. Harrison (2004) also suggests a skeleton approach in which only the first and final lines of a paragraph are included. This can provide an interesting stimulus for discussing what a passage may be about and is a useful strategy for orienting pupils to the reading of a new text. The potential for learning using this procedure can be greatly enhanced through thoughtful organization. Having children complete them as individuals and then marking them right or wrong is very limiting. Two possible approaches which offer greater opportunities for collaborative learning are outlined here.

The children can complete a passage individually, then come together as a group to discuss what they have inserted. At each space, they should discuss the possibilities, articulating what has informed their choice of word. The group should reach agreement as to which word or words are acceptable in order to make sense of the text. The children tick their insertion if it is acceptable. Words which are not reasonable for the particular gap being filled should be circled and a better choice written in above. Thus the less confident child benefits from the discussion about why some words 'work' and others do not, and is helped to understand the clues within the text on which others are drawing. Intially these discussions may be teacher-led, but once the strategy has been modelled groups can review together and present their outcomes to the teacher. The teacher can review and analyse completed texts, rather like a miscue analysis, noting misconceptions and setting further targets.

Alternatively, the children can work in pairs and have one sheet only for them to complete together. In this approach, the discussion takes place prior to completion and consensus is required before choices are made. This can be further extended by moving from pairs to groups of four. Now each pair must explain and justify their word choices. A further consensus is achieved as the groups of four create their definitve set of word choices. These may be selected from their first attempts but the discussion may also prompt them to find words that had not emerged from the earlier discussion.

In both of these suggested ways of organizing group cloze activities, listening to the children discussing the possibilities provides an insight into their knowledge about language and literature and where they may need further support. Cloze procedure works very well on the interactive whiteboard and it is easy to complete in group contexts with everyone in the group looking at the screen. The texts used can vary in difficulty: differentiation can be through selection of text and/or number of words deleted. The children should be encouraged to read through the whole text before starting to complete the task.

A word of caution: the deleted words should not be provided, ready for insertion, as is often seen in published materials labelled as cloze procedure. Although there may be a place for matching given words to spaces, it is not cloze procedure and does not encourage the same close reading of the whole text when looking for clues. The pre-selected words limit the range of possibilities and there is less evidence of the child's thought processes in the completed text.

ACTIVITY

Cloze procedure
Complete the two passages below, inserting one word into each space. The deletions are not quite every seventh word, as I wanted to provide a particular range of challenges for you. If possible, compare your insertions with a colleague.

Once upon a .... in a hot sunny country, lived very .... bright .... beautiful parrot. He was red and .... and gold and blue, with a purple top to .... head. His real name was Lory. And he lived on .... There were .... of flowers growing among .... trees, so all he had to .... when he was hungry was to fly .... and lick the honey out of the flowers. As a matter of .... , he had a tongue that was specially .... for getting .... out of flowers. So he always had honey to eat, and managed very ....

With more than usual eagerness did Catherine .... to the Pumproom the next day, ... within herself of seeing Mr Tilney .... before the morning were over, and .... to meet him with a smile – .... no smile was demanded – Mr Tilney .... not appear. Every creature in Bath .... , himself, was to be seen in .... room at different periods of the .... hours; crowds of people were every .... passing in and out, up the .... and down; people whom nobody cared .... , and nobody wanted to see; and .... only was absent. 'What a delightful .... , Bath is,' said Mrs Allen, as .... sat down near the great clock .... parading the room till they were .... ; 'and how pleasant it would be if we had any acquaintance here.' (*Northanger Abbey* by Jane Austen)

When you have finished, decide which of the passages was the easier to complete. Analyse the factors that affected the ease with which you accomplished the task.

Commentary

You probably found the first passage least difficult. It is written in the form of a traditional tale, and you would have brought your prior knowledge of this genre and of story language to bear on the text. When choosing a colour to insert in line 2, you would have deleted from your possible choices the colours already mentioned and those which follow the space. You may have been initially challenged in line 3 to think what he could live on, but the clue comes later in the text – it is honey.

The second passage, from *Northanger Abbey* by Jane Austen, will probably have posed more challenges for you. As it was written a long time ago, the language constructions seem archaic in places, making familiar vocabulary suddenly very challenging to read. Although you will have managed to ascertain the gist of what was required, finding the right word to insert may not have been easy or straightforward. In line 1, did you insert 'go'? A more accurate choice might have been 'hie' or 'repair' if you were to choose language in a register appropriate to the 18th century when this was written. Towards the end of the text Mrs Allen and Catherine sit down at last, having paraded the room 'till they were'. One student completing this task suggested the word 'knackered' to complete this space, to much hilarity. It certainly works semantically, but is of course a register inappropriate to the context. Possible alternatives suggested which were more fitting included 'exhausted' and 'fatigued'.

Preparing cloze passages
Prepare some cloze passages from one of the books in your collection. Differentiate the passages you prepare through careful selection of the passage and rate of deletion. They can be prepared as electronic texts to be completed on screen, or as hard copy but remember to allow sufficient space for the child to write.

Subsequent studies on effective strategies for developing reading comprehension have reiterated the value of the strategies outlined earlier from Lunzer and Gardner's study. Wray (1995) refers to the work of Tregaskes and Daines (1984), for example, in using mind mapping and visual imaging for recording responses to a text, and to the value of summarizing, self-questioning, clarifying and predicting cited in the work of Miller et al. (in Wray, 1995). Pressley (2000) reviews the strategies that most effectively develop comprehension and the current focus in research into comprehension is on the role of metacognition in interpreting texts.

Effective plenary sessions

Following group reading activities a plenary will enable you to draw together the different strands of learning, make connections between different activities, help children articulate what they have learnt, help them make implicit learning explicit, discuss how they will apply what they have learnt in the future and outline next steps. During the plenary, you might

- ask a group to present their work to the rest of the class to generate feedback, discussion and clarification;
- challenge children to justify and refine their ideas and findings;
- provide feedback which aims to clarify, refine and extend the thinking of the children;
- identify the next steps with the class;
- set independent work to consolidate learning.

It is vital that plenaries are kept fresh and free from being overly routine and ritualized. Sometimes one group may be asked to lead the plenary, or each group might be asked to contribute one point.

In this chapter you have:

- considered various ways in which children respond to texts;
- explored the ways meaning is created by the interaction of the reader with the text;
- explored factors affecting children's comprehension of texts;
- considered a range of ways in which teachers can support children's understanding of how to read and understand literature.

Further reading

Applebee, A. (1978) *The Child's Concept of Story*. Chicago: University of Chicago Press.
Appleyard, J.A. (1990) *Becoming a Reader: The Experience of Fiction from Childhood to Adulthood*. Cambridge: Cambridge University Press.
Chambers, A. (1993) *Tell Me: Children, Reading and Talk*. Stroud: Thimble Press.
Harrison, C. (2004) *Understanding Reading Development*. London: Sage.
Iser, W. (1978) *The Art of Reading*. London: Routledge and Kegan Paul.
Lunzer, E. and Gardner, K. (eds) (1979) *The Effective Use of Reading*. London: Heinemann.
Stephens, J. (1992) *Language and Ideology in Children's Fiction*. Harlow: Longman.

Appendix 2.1: Book record 1

Book Record

Title ....

....

Author ....

Illustrator ....

I read this book with

My mum ▢   My teacher ▢

My dad ▢   My friend ▢

My brother ▢   ▢

My sister ▢

How I liked the book:

Story   Pictures

Appendix 2.1: Book record 1

Appendix 2.2: Book record 2

Book Record

Title   ....

        ....

Author ....

Illustrator ....

I read this book with

My mum   ☐   My teacher   ☐

My dad   ☐   My friend   ☐

My brother   ☐   ☐

My sister   ☐

How I liked the book:

Story

1	2	3	4	5	6	7	8	9	10	

Pictures

1	2	3	4	5	6	7	8	9	10	

Appendix 2.3

Record what you know about a character and add to it as the story progresses and you find out more about the character.

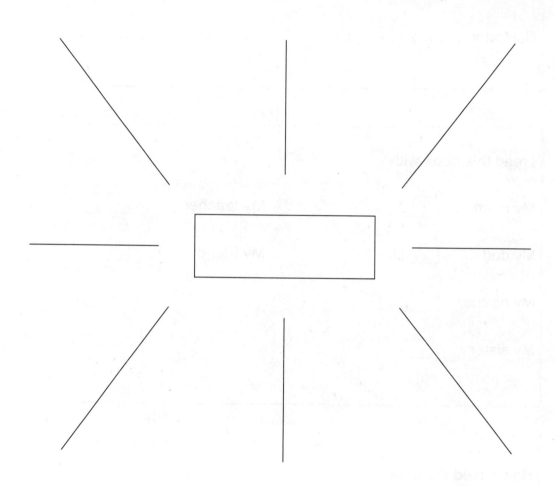

Appendix 2.4

How did you find out about the character? Sometimes the author tells us directly about a character and sometimes we have to work things out for ourselves.

In this table, record what you know about a character so far. Then show what evidence you have from the text for this. Can you see a difference between information the author has given you and information you have inferred by reading between the lines?

Character	Book:
What I know about	Evidence from the book

Appendix 2.5: Storyboard planner

Chapter 3

Narrative: Narration and Structure

This chapter introduces narrative, structure and narration. In this chapter we shall:

- define narrative;
- show that narrative is employed in fiction and non-fiction;
- demonstrate that a story can be told in different ways using third, second person or personal narration;
- see that the narrator presents a particular viewpoint and this may change in the course of the story;
- see that the point of view affects the reader's response to the story;
- see that different effects can be achieved by using the past or present tense;
- explain how narrative structure is the framework that holds the story together and gives it shape;
- see that there are common story shapes that recur;
- see how suspense is used to enable the reader to predict what will happen in the story and maintain interest;
- explain that fiction is temporal – time passes during the reading of the story and fictional time may or may not correspond to it;
- see how the narrative is held together through the use of cohesive devices.

What is narrative?

Commentary

A narrative text relates a sequence of events. In a seminal article, 'Narrative as a Primary Act of Mind', Barbara Hardy (1977) argues that narrative is not an aesthetic invention but the basic way in which we make sense of our experiences. She explains that we use 'inner' (in our heads) and 'outer' (to others) storytelling to shape our lives; for instance, recalling our dreams and talking about the things that happen to us as though they were stories. One of the first things families often do at the end of a working day is enquire of each other, 'How was your day?' By asking this question we are inviting each other to tell stories about the day's events and this is far more than listing a catalogue of events. We highlight exciting moments, build dramatic tension, pause for effect, turn funny incidents into jokes with punch lines. When we visit friends for dinner the conversation frequently develops into storytelling as we swap tales about nightmare holidays, embarrassing moments and reminiscences of childhood. A survey of television programming for one night included the serialization of a classic children's book, two episodes of The Simpsons, a situation comedy about an unconventional family, three soap operas, a courtroom drama, a documentary about the life of Arthur Lowe, Big Brother (the voice-over narration turning events into the house into a series of mini-stories), an American forensic science drama and, of course, the news bulletins covering 'the day's top stories'. In the commercial breaks there were yet more stories.

This evening I caught the latest installment in a series of adverts for a telephone company. The characters are a single mother, her two children and new partner. In each episode the family bonds have been developing though it has been uneasy at times. In the latest episode the family is viewing a new house but it looks rather pricey, perhaps they won't buy this house. However, the deal is clinched when they see the new phone system that has been installed. In the closing scene the estate agent shows them a room that would make 'an ideal nursery'. The couple exchanges a look that is pregnant with meaning, but open to different interpretations. The viewer is one step ahead predicting what will happen in the next installment. In less time than it takes to make a cup of tea the characters and setting have been introduced, a problem has arisen and been resolved. A cliff-hanger ending prepares us for the next episode in the story.

ACTIVITY

> ### Introductory
>
> Take a look at this list of words:
>
> apple
> alligator
> angry
> ambulance
> apologize
>
> - Can you read this list like a story?
> - Now try changing the order of the words. Does this alter the story?
> - Try to explain what happened when you made a story from the list of words. For example, did you try to imagine the characters, develop the plot, or imagine where the story took place?

Oral storytelling

As this brief introduction indicates, stories come in all sorts of forms: verbal, visual and textual. Oral stories have been around much longer than written ones. When the spoken word was the sole means of communication, people passed on their history, the law of the tribe, moral advice and warnings this way. To begin with, everyone would have been a storyteller but, over time, individuals came to be recognized for their storytelling prowess; the professional storyteller was born. The *seanachaidh* or bards (as they were known) would devote their lives to learning and perfecting their repertoires of stories. Today, we use written language to record history and pass it on to future generations. It is the means by which we preserve those stories that have official significance, such as cases of precedence in law. But family history and tales of personal experiences are still transmitted orally. Perhaps you have been aware of how transitory family history is as the oldest generation in your family dies out. You may have had an impulse to record those old family stories before they are forgotten forever. (See 'Traditional stories' in Chapter 5.)

ACTIVITY

> ### Investigation
>
> - Make a record of the different types of story that you hear (and see) in the course of one day.
> - Consider how you could use the information you have gathered to develop a unit of work that develops children's awareness of story.
> - Traditional stories lend themselves to oral retellings. Think of some ways in which you might develop children's oral storytelling of traditional stories. Theresa Grainger's *Traditional Storytelling in the Primary Classroom* has a wealth of practical suggestions.
> - See Chapter 5 for suggested traditional story collections.

Narrative non-fiction

In common parlance the terms 'narrative' and 'fiction' are sometimes used inter-changeably, but they are not the same thing. While it is true that fictional texts are usually written in narrative form, it is also true that factual texts can be written this way. Margaret Mallett (1992) has shown that very young children can detect that a narrative text is not necessarily a fictional one. To illustrate this let us have a look at some examples. The first extract from Janni Howker's *Walk With a Wolf*, which was written to challenge what she perceives to be the unfair stereotypical representation of the wolf in traditional stories and takes the reader on a journey with the wolves of the Yukon Territory in Canada. In her foreword she explains, 'Most wolves live in the far north of the world – in Alaska, Siberia and parts of the Yukon Territory where this story is set'. Notice that Howker explicitly uses the word 'story' to describe her study of the wolves' behaviour in their natural habitat. The second extract is taken from Meredith Hooper's *Ice Trap!*, an account of Sir Ernest Shackleton's amazing expedition to Antarctica. It is one of the greatest true-life adventure stories of all time

---

ACTIVITY

Read the following passages then make notes or discuss the following:

- What factual information is presented?
- What features of storytelling can you identify?
- Consider how Janni Howker's narrative technique affects your response to the wolf.
- In the extract from Meredith Hooper's *Ice Trap!*, what factual information is conveyed? To what extent is the passage subjective?

Walk with a wolf in the cold air before sunrise. She moves, quiet as mist, between spruce trees and birches. A silent grey shadow, she slides between boulders and trots over blue pebbles to the edge of the lake. She plunges through slush ice and laps the chill water, snaps at a feather that drifts down from a goose wing, then splashes to shore and shakes herself like a dog. There's deep snow on the mountains. Snow clouds bank in the east. Winter is coming, and the geese fly south. (*Walk With a Wolf* by Janni Howker)

'Stowaway! Stowaway!' The locker lid crashed back and Percy Blackborrow staggered out into the bitter air. For three days he'd crouched inside the dark locker under piles of clothes while the ship pitched through the ocean. Now he felt so seasick and hungry he didn't mind being discovered.

　　Sir Ernest Shackleton was standing above him roaring his anger. 'Do you know,' bellowed Shackleton, 'that on these expeditions we often get very hungry, and if there is a stowaway available he is the first to be eaten?' Percy looked up. Shackleton was a heavy, powerfully-built man. 'They'd get a lot more meat off you, sir!' he said. (*Ice Trap!* by Meredith Hooper)

Commentary

From the first passage we can gather the following information:

- wolves are active in the early morning;
- they live in forested areas;
- there are icy-cold lakes in the Yukon Territory;
- the wolf behaves in a similar manner to a dog;
- geese leave the Yukon Territory when winter comes.

To 'walk' with the wolf is to share a day in her life – a day that begins with a visit to the lake to drink water. The last sentence, 'Winter is coming, and the geese fly south', prepares the reader for the next stage in the story; at this point we might infer that the wolf does not travel south with the geese. We are being encouraged to anticipate as Howker builds suspense. What will the wolf do when winter comes? Howker's poetic prose elicits feelings of wonder and respect; the reader is invited to admire the wolf's agility and stealth, her ability to move 'quiet as mist'. It stimulates an emotional response. The wolf's behaviour mirrors that of a playful domestic animal as she 'snaps at a feather' in the way a pet might snap at a thrown ball. The image of her shaking water from her coat brings to view a pet dog that has plunged into a pond to chase a stick. The similarity is further emphasized by the direct comparison, 'like a dog'. So we can see that the information story presents facts in a way that encourages emotional involvement with the subject.

In the second passage Meredith Hooper employs narrative techniques that are commonly used in fiction. The attention-grabbing opener prompts us to immediately ask questions. How did the stowaway come to be there? What will happen to him now? The invention of dialogue is also a fiction. It can at best only be an approximation of what was actually said but it serves to draw the reader into the story and builds character. In this short extract we have the beginning of a sequence of events that will be extended as the story develops:

- Percy is discovered;
- Percy meets Shackleton.

It is evident that narrative allows greater freedom with the point of view. In the extract from *Walk With a Wolf*, the reader was positioned as a close companion of the wolf. *Ice Trap!* is written in the third person but we are seeing events through the eyes of Percy Blackborrow. We are privileged to know how he is feeling and our impression of Shackleton is filtered through his eyes. And it is not surprising that in a book written for children, Hooper has chosen the youngest crew member to focalize the beginning of the story. Hooper has also given us some key facts about this expedition:

- a young boy did stowaway on *Endurance*;
- Shackleton had a commanding personality.

For the young reader an information story can be a bridge from existing experiences to new ones. Margaret Mallett (1999: 38) writes, 'the security of a familiar narrative framework helps consolidate knowledge gained from experience while opening up new ideas and possibilities'. This is not, however, to suggest that the narrative format is only for immature readers unable to cope with 'real factual writing'.

ACTIVITY

Now read the following passage and consider:

- in what significant ways does this extract differ from *Walk With a Wolf* and *Ice Trap!*?
- what similarities does this passage have with the other passages?

I think I always wanted to farm. I would have had an idealized picture of the life, I suppose, but the wish had two strong roots: to continue to live in the country and to work with animals. It was all going to be so simple. The pets that I had always kept, the rabbits, the guinea-pigs, the fancy mice and rats, the ornamental pheasants, the budgerigars, would translate into cattle and pigs and poultry.

When I was eighteen, I determined to make a start, unconcerned that I was by nature unbusinesslike, that anything mechanical baffled me, and that my educational qualifications for the job were ten years of studying the classics. 'How blest beyond all blessings are farmers,' Virgil had said '… Far from the clash of arms.'
(*Chewing the Cud* by Dick King-Smith)

Commentary

This is the opening chapter of Dick King-Smith's autobiography, *Chewing the Cud*. The most obvious difference is that this extract is written in the first person: 'I think I always', 'I would'. Unlike the previous extracts, Dick King-Smith is telling his personal story from his own point of view. Autobiography is a special example of narrative non-fiction. While there are similarities with biography, and this is indicated by the simple addition of the prefix 'auto', autobiography also has much in common with fiction. Krause tells us that imagination is as important in autobiography as it is in fiction and that it can never function simply as a reflex mirror for the imitation of life. Other critics, such as Pascal, have highlighted the factual discrepancies that occur in a person's account of their life when compared with the actual events. So the interest in autobiography lies as much in the narration, how the writer constructs his or her life and the reflections on that life, as it does in factual recount. In this sense it can be said to be closer to fiction than non-fiction.

'In many (children's information) texts the author is hardly present at all, and the language so bland and impersonal that a computer might have written it'. Here Helen Arnold (1992:) is talking about the school information book, that special breed of text book that exists purely for schooling purposes. If we reflect on the pleasures that are to be had from reading non-fiction, the books that spring to mind are rarely information books of this kind. I have recently finished reading Andrew Smith's *Moondust*, a fascinating exploration of the lives of the 12 men who have walked on the moon following that momentous, life-changing experience. Equally interesting is Andrew Smith's engaging account of his connection with those men. Simply put, it is the narrator's voice that brings the book to life. Similarly, when I ask students about the non-fiction books they enjoy reading the will often cite books like Bill Bryson's *Notes from a Small Island*, and comment on the distinctive voice that makes the reading such a pleasurable experience. They will often mention 'hearing' the author talk directly to them. Alvarez explains,

> Real literature is about something else entirely and it's immune to speed-reading. That is, it's not about information, although you may gather information along the way. It's not even about storytelling, although sometimes that is one of its greatest pleasures. Imaginative literature is about listening to a voice. When you read a novel the voice is telling you a story; when you read a poem it's usually talking about what its owner is feeling; but neither the medium nor the message is the point. The point is that the voice is unlike any other voice you have ever heard and it is speaking directly to you, communing with you in private, right in your ear, and in its own distinctive way. (2005: 15)

Read the extracts in Appendix 3.1 and make notes about the narrative voice. Discuss with a partner or in group.

ACTIVITY

Have you read a narrative non-fiction book for children or adults that made you view the world differently? Why do you think this book had such a big impact on you? Was it wholly or partly narrative non-fiction?   Gather together a collection of books about a particular topic, include narrative non-fiction, information books and fiction. Make notes about the narrative voice used in each book. Which do you find engaging? How do these texts engage you? Alternatively, read the extracts in Appendix 3.2 and carry out the activity in the book.

ACTIVITY

Narration in fiction

In narrative texts we can distinguish between the story (what it is about) and narration (how the story is told). The same story can be told in various ways; events can be reordered, narrators can be changed, the viewpoint can be altered and the tone adopted might range from grave and portentous to wacky and humorous. Read the following passage from *The Secret Garden* by Frances Hodgson Burnett and then rewrite it with Mary telling the story.

ACTIVITY

▶

At first each day which passed by for Mary Lennox was exactly like the others. Every morning she awoke in her tapestried room and found Martha kneeling upon the hearth building her fire; every morning she ate her breakfast in the nursery which had nothing amusing in it; and after each breakfast she gazed out of the window across to the huge moor, which seemed to spread out on all sides and climb up to the sky, and after she had stared for a while she realized that if she did not go out she would have to stay in and do nothing – and so she went out. She did not know that this was the best thing she could have done, and she did not know that, when she began to walk quickly or even run along the paths and down the avenue, she was stirring her slow blood and making herself stronger by fighting with the wind which swept down from the moor. She ran only to make herself warm, and she hated the wind which rushed at her face and roared and held her back as if it were some giant she could not see. But the big breaths of rough fresh air blown over the heather filled her lungs with something which was good for her whole thin body and whipped some red colour into her cheeks and brightened her dull eyes when she did not know anything about it.

Now consider these questions and make notes in your journal:

- How easy or difficult did you find the task?
- Were some parts more difficult to write from Mary's point of view than others? Can you explain this?
- How has changing the point of view altered the story?

Commentary

Stories are narrated in different ways. The narrator (or narrators) is the imaginary person who provides the point of view and steers the reader's emotional and moral response.

Third-person narration

An omniscient narrator has complete access to the thoughts and feelings of all the characters. The term comes from Latin *omni* (all) + *scientia* (knowledge). But as we cannot have access to the innermost thoughts of others, full omniscience can push the boundaries of credibility. It is more usual for an author to opt for limited omniscience in which the third-person narration reveals the point of view of one or two characters. Usually the viewpoint of one character will be privileged above the others. This is the method of narration that Gillian Cross prefers: 'Except for *Chartbreak* all my novels are in the third person – but close to a character's point of view. I always imagine that I'm a particular person looking at the scene' (Gillian Cross, in Carter, 2001: 126). This is called focalization. Because children's literature is primarily concerned with the interests of children, authors intentionally writing for them will most usually focalize the narrative through the eyes of a child.

In *The Secret Garden*, Frances Hodgson Burnett employs a third-person narration, which is focalized largely through Mary's eyes. In the earlier extract, the first eight lines privilege Mary's point of view. When she wakes in her bedroom she sees the tapestry wall-hangings and Martha kneeling by the grate. It is Mary's perception that there is nothing to amuse her in the nursery and we are privy to her thoughts as she weighs up whether to stay indoors and do nothing, or go outside in the blustery weather. When you were transposing the text from the third person you probably found these lines easiest as they are already presenting Mary's viewpoint. At the end of line eight the viewpoint changes to a mature, knowledgeable perspective. An observer describes 'her thin body' and 'dull eyes' and comments on things that are beyond Mary's understanding; that the fresh air is good for her health. The perspective moves from an internal to an external awareness. The reader is able therefore to draw on different sources of information in the interpretation of Mary's character. Presented exclusively from an external point of view the reader would find it difficult to empathize with her; presented wholly from Mary's point of view the reader's understanding of how she appeared to others would be limited, and consequently the thematic focus of the novel would be diminished. It is likely that you found it difficult, if not impossible, to write these lines from a first-person perspective unless you adopted the retrospective stance of an older, wiser Mary looking back on her childhood. One of the advantages of third-person narration is the opportunity it provides for shifting perspectives. Philip Pullman sees a similarity with filming: 'I like the third person voice because I like swooping in and drawing back and giving a panoramic view – in the same way a film camera does. I like directing the story as one would direct a film' (in Carter, 2001: 12).

The Eye in the Sky

Notice in the following extract how Lesley Howarth's opening to *Weather Eye* positions the reader as though they were looking at the scene on a big screen moving from establishing shot to mid-shot and then into close-up.

> All night long the wind blew. Northern hemisphere isobars were going ape – and how – on every forecast map. The sinister-looking weather front had swirled in from mid-Atlantic. In the toe of south-west England, spit centre under the storm lay a moon flooded moor. On the moor stood a windfarm. On the windfarm, tucked among the wind turbines like a cat in mint, stood a stone-faced, six-eyed house. In the second-largest bedroom upstairs, behind blue and green curtains she'd agonized over when her room had been redecorated, stood Telly's bed. In the bed Telly and Race huddled, listening.

This technique has been termed the 'eye in the sky'. You might think that the invention of film has made it possible to visualize scenes in this way but, as Howarth (1996: 12) points out, Charles Dickens used the technique well before film had been invented:

> Right back in *Bleak House* you come in from the sky, zero down into part of London, then to a street in Chancery Lane, then to a man standing outside a particular shop, then into the shop – and you get to the scene. And that's what I did for the last scene in *Weather Eye*, coming in over the top of what's going on, and looking at different parts of it as if it were a painting.

Unintrusive and intrusive third-person narrative

In contemporary fiction the third-person narrator is usually unintrusive and does not intervene to make explicit comments or judgements on events or characters. But sometimes a narrator's voice does intrude into the story. For instance, in Rudyard Kipling's *Just So Stories* the narrator addresses the listener, 'O Best Beloved. ...'. This is called the transferred storyteller mode and when it is adopted we are most likely to be aware of the narrator's presence. Writing in this mode the author adopts the persona of a guide or companion through the story, addressing the reader directly and intimately.

One of the problems with authorial intrusion is that the narrator adopts a position of authority, and in children's literature this amplifies the existing unequal power relationship between adult narrator and child narratee.

The narrator as an authority is frequently in evidence in Enid Blyton's stories. Here is an example:

> Anne gazed out of her bedroom window over the moor. It looked so peaceful and serene under the April sun. No mystery about it now!
> 'All the same, it's a good name for you,' said Anne. 'You're full of mystery and adventure, and your last adventure waited for us to come and share it. I really think I'd call this adventure 'Five Go To Mystery Moor'.

> It's a good name, Anne. We'll call it that too! (*Five Go to Mystery Moor* by Enid Blyton)

Intrusion into the story is a way of exercising control; in this instance the narrator validates Anne's suggestion of a name for the moor. On other occasions Blyton's intrusions serve to comment on a character's behaviour, thus limiting the reader's opportunities for making independent moral judgments. Such heavily didactic narration was a product of its time and it is no longer fashionable. But in his recently published parody of Victorian children's fiction, *A Series of Unfortunate Events*, Lemony Snicket reduces the convention to absurdity:

> The three Baudelaire children lived with their parents in an enormous mansion at the heart of a dirty and busy city, and occasionally their parents gave them permission to take a rickety trolley – the word 'rickety,' you probably know, here means 'unsteady' or 'likely to collapse' – alone to the seashore, where they would spend the day as a sort of vacation as long as they were home for dinner. (*The Bad Beginning* by Lemony Snicket)

It is hardly necessary for the author to explain the word 'rickety'. Snicket is using the intrusive narrator to comic effect, commenting ironically on Victorian melodrama.

Personal narration

So far we have focused on third-person narration but another option is the use of personal narration, often referred to as the first person. Most frequently the personal narrator is one of the characters in the story. One of the first children's writers to experiment with first-person narration was E. Nesbit in her family adventure, *The Story of the Treasure Seekers*. It begins,

> There are some things that I must tell before I begin to tell about the treasure-seeking, because I have read books myself, and I know how beastly it is when a story begins, 'Alas!' said Hildegarde with a deep sigh, 'we must look our last on this ancestral home' – and then someone else says something – and you don't know for pages and pages where the home is, or who Hildegarde is, or anything about it. Our ancestral home is in the Lewisham Road. It is semi-detached and has a garden, not a large one. We are the Bastables … It is one of us that tells this story – but I shall not tell you which: only át the very end perhaps I will. While the story is going on you may be trying to guess, only I bet you don't.

The narration is rather inelegant in places ('It is one of us that tells this story') but, nevertheless, this was an early attempt to give the impression of a child telling his own story, avoiding the overbearing tone of adult narrator to child narratee. In spite of the challenge to identify narrator ('I bet you don't') the reader very quickly works out which of the Bastable children is telling the story. The narration clearly favours Oswald who is always presented in the best possible light; we are told he is the bravest and cleverest of all the children – he is not, however, very strong on modesty!

The diction of a first-person narrator may indicate class, culture and gender. For example Huck in *The Adventures of Huckleberry Finn* has a distinctive voice that locates him geographically and socially:

> By and by he rolled out and jumped up to his feet looking wild, and he see me and went for me. He chased me round and round the place with a clasp knife, calling me the Angel of death, and saying he would kill me, and then I couldn't come for him no more. I begged, and told him I was only Huck; but he laughed such a screechy laugh, an roared and cussed, and kept on chasing me up. (*The Adventures of Huckleberry Finn* by Mark Twain)

The colloquial diction is simple, informal and typical of a boy from the Southern states in that time period.

Personal narration may imply an autobiographical voice as it does in many of Michael Morpurgo's books including the *Wreck of the Zanzibar*. Morpurgo uses a variety of first-person narrative devices in this book including letters and the main method of narration – great-aunt Laura's diary. The story opens with the narrator describing a return to the Scilly Isles for the funeral of his Great-aunt Laura:

> My Great-aunt Laura died a few months ago. She was a hundred years old. She had her cocoa last thing at night, as she usually did, put the cat out, went to sleep and never woke up. There's no better way to die. I took the boat across to Scilly for the funeral, almost everyone in the family did. I met again cousins and aunts and uncles I hardly recognised, and who hardly recognised me. The little church on Bryher was packed, standing room only. Everyone on Bryher was there, and they came from all over the Scilly Isles, from St Mary's, St Martin's, St Agnes and Tresco.

After his aunt's funeral the narrator returns to her house and finds a letter addressed to him. Now it is elderly Great-aunt Laura's voice that takes over the storytelling. This letter cleverly provides a link in the narrative between the narrator's childhood and his aunt's:

> Dear Michael
>
> When you were little I told you lots and lots of stories about Bryher, about the Isles of Scilly. You know about the ghosts on Samson, about the bell that rings under the sea off St Martin's, about King Arthur still waiting in his cave under the Eastern Isles.

In *The Wreck of the Zanzibar*, it is the combination of first-person narrative techniques and the device of using his own first name that creates the illusion of authenticity that we associate with an autobiographical voice.

A more extended example of storytelling through letters is Berlie Doherty's *Dear Nobody*, in which a pregnant teenager writes to her unborn baby, the 'Dear Nobody' of the title. The epistolary novel (a story revealed through the exchange of letters) has a long tradition in English literature. It has the advantage of using a first-person narrative but allows different characters to present their stories, as Thomas Hardy wrote, 'The advantages of the letter system of telling a story are that, hearing what one side has to say, you are led constantly to the imagination of what the other side must be feeling, and at last are anxious to know if the other side does really feel what you imagine' (Abbs and Richardson, 1990: 138).

Jacqueline Wilson believes that first-person narration brings the writer closer to the main character: 'I find it much easier writing in the first person ... I think it's a more approachable, direct way of writing. You get to care about the main character more if they're narrating the story. The only disadvantage is that you can only see what happens through their eyes' (Jacqueline Wilson, in *Young Writer*, issue 15, p. 3).

But we should not leap to the assumption that a first-person narration provides a more 'intimate' experience for the reader. On occasions I have been convinced that a story has been written in the first person but, on returning to check, I find that this is not the case – the story is simply focalized through the eyes of the main character. Most of Morris Gleitzman's books achieve this effect.

One of the challenges facing a children's author using a first-person child narrator is that the relative inexperience of the narrator makes it difficult for them to reflect on the big themes and issues. It can test credibility if the child narrator is too wise or mature. In *The Tulip Touch*, Anne Fine tackles the subject of child abuse and the theme of moral responsibility. Her treatment is as committed as any author writing for an adult audience but her narrator, Natalie, is an 11-year-old girl.

Commentary

Read this extract and then consider how Anne Fine deals with the challenge of using an 11-year-old narrator. Do you find the passage convincing?

> What were we like then, the pair of us, Tulip and Natalie? I lift a photograph out of the box, and see us laughing. We look happy enough. But do old photos tell the truth? 'Smile!' someone orders you. 'I'm not wasting precious film on sour faces.' And so you smile. But what's behind? You take the one dad snapped by accident when Tulip came down the cellar steps just as he was fiddling in the dark with his camera. Suddenly the flash went off, and he caught her perfectly (if you don't count the rabbity pink eyes). She's a shadow in the arched entrance of that dark tunnel. And how does she look in that, the only one taken when no one was watching? Wary, would you say? Or something even stronger? One look at that pale apprehensive face, and you might even think haunted. But there's something else that springs to mind. I turn the photo in my hand, and try to push the word away. But it comes back at me, time and again. I can't get rid of it. If you didn't know her better, you'd have said she looked desolate. (*The Tulip Touch* by Anne Fine)

In this extract the retrospective narration presents two viewpoints. Fine makes us aware of the gap between Natalie's mature and inexperienced understandings of Tulip's circumstances. The smiling photo represents the younger Natalie's perspective but the ability to comment on the unposed photograph suggests an experienced understanding. Fine signals that this reflection is taking place after a considerable time with the opening sentence, 'What were we like then, the pair of us, Tulip and Natalie?' This is the sort of thing that adults say when reminiscing with old friends. The last two sentences emphasize the gap in the understanding of the mature Natalie and the inexperienced Natalie: 'If you didn't know her better you'd have said she looked desolate'. Retrospectively she can see Tulip's desolation but at the time she was just her lively, jokey friend. However, the implication is that the adults (Natalie's mother and father) should have recognized these signs. Fine's dual perspective raises issues about the moral responsibility of those closest to Tulip; she clearly supports the child and condemns the adults.

Objective viewpoint

An objective or dramatic viewpoint is one where the writer does not enter the minds of any of the characters. All is revealed through the action. The readers have to work out the meaning for themselves as no interpretation of events is provided. The objective viewpoint is present in texts for very young children, most notably in picture books, and responses show that they are able to interpret the story and make hypotheses about intentions. In the classic picture book, *Rosie's Walk* the text reads, 'Rosie the hen went for walk, across the yard, around the pond, over the haycock, past the mill, through the fence, under the beehives and got back in time for dinner'.

So how does the reader interpret this story? What is Rosie thinking or feeling? The text gives no clues. To understand the story the pictures need to be interpreted. Each stage of Rosie's journey is shown on two successive double-page spreads. Looking at the illustrations we are immediately aware that there is another participant in this story – a fox. Rosie is pictured apparently unaware that a fox is following her. A rake is placed dangerously in the path of the advancing fox. What is going to happen? We are not told, but the information we are shown in the pictures allows us to predict that the fox will step on the rake and Rosie will be free to continue her walk. Turning the page we find that our predictions are confirmed. This pattern is repeated throughout the book. We are never told, so must infer, what Rosie and the Fox are thinking. Does Rosie deliberately take a booby-trapped path through the farmyard? Or is she completely oblivious to the fox's presence? The reader must decide.

Consistent and multiple viewpoints

Texts that have a consistent point of view create an illusion of realism, but the disadvantage of a single viewpoint is that it places limits on interpretation. On the other hand a text that has multiple viewpoints opens up possibilities for exploring different perceptions but draws attention to the artifice of the narration.

An early example of dual narration is found in Robert Louis Stevenson's *Treasure Island*. An old sailor arrives at a West Country inn bearing a secret treasure map, said to mark the location of Captain Flint's buried treasure. When Jim Hawkins, the innkeeper's son discovers the map he takes it to Squire Trewlaney who commandeers a ship, *The Hispaniola*, and after employing a crew including the cook, Long John Silver, and with Jim as cabin boy, they set forth for Treasure Island. After a mutiny aboard two camps set up on the island, each determined to find the treasure. At the outset the story is narrated by Jim Hawkins. The diction is informal, though there are occasions where the persona of the narrator is less evident and the narration is closer to a third-person perspective (e.g. Silver's parley with Captain Smollett). A second narrator, Dr Livesey takes up the narration of Chapters 16–18, when Jim is separated from the rest of his companions. Livesey's narration is more formal and pays particular attention to the unhealthy conditions on the island. The point of view presented in Chapter 28 is also interesting as Stevenson invites the reader to view the mutineers from a different perspective to the way they are viewed from the position of Trelawney's camp, suggesting that the judgements made about behaviour are relative to the position of the person making those judgements.

Anthony Browne's *Voices in the Park*, as the title suggests, is a story told by different voices: Mrs Smythe, her son Charles, Mr Smith and his daughter Smudge. The adults are drawn as gorillas and the children as chimpanzees. The text is written in the first person. On the surface, each of the participants recalls a visit to a park. The distinctiveness of each is signalled by choice of font, sentence structure, vocabulary, illustrative techniques, association with objects and the natural world, and the way in which the illustrations are framed. Mrs Smythe is the first speaker: 'It was time to take Victoria, our pedigree Labrador, and Charles, our son, for a walk. When we arrived at the park, I let Victoria off her lead. Immediately some scruffy mongrel appeared and started bothering her. I shooed it off, but the horrible thing chased her all over the park'.

This text clearly presents Mrs Smythe's point of view. 'The scruffy mongrel' reflects her opinion not the reality that we see in the pictures. The first image places Mrs Smythe in front of a large white house with a neat picket fence. This contrasts with an image later in the book, which shows her returning home with Charles. The second image occurs in Charles's narrative and depicts a gloomy house surrounded by a moat. It is clear that to Charles home is a prison. By comparing the two illustrations we can deduce that the images of the house reveal a psychological rather than physical reality. The big white house with manicured lawns is Mrs Smythe's perception of the world she inhabits. From this we infer that she is house-proud and the phrase 'keeping up appearances' springs to mind. But the illustrations that accompany Mrs Smythe's story do not present a consistent point of view. In the fifth picture she is portrayed in an unflattering manner as she frantically calls her son to prevent him from playing with Smudge, who she regards as socially inferior. This picture is not like the first one; it is not Mrs Smythe's point of view but an authorial comment. The pictures provide a dialogic perspective in what is largely first-person narration.

Contemporary children's novels often employ dual or multiple narrations. Ann Turnbull's historical novels, *No Shame, No Fear* and sequel *Forged in the Fire* are set in 17-century England shortly after the civil war had erupted from the clashes in faith and culture. Seventeen-year-old William returns to his home in Hemsbury to begin an apprenticeship arranged by his wealthy father. Meanwhile, Susanna, a Quaker girl from the neighboring countryside, travels to Hemsbury to work as a servant. William and Susanna meet by chance and begin a secret courtship. The story is told in the alternating viewpoints of both William and Susanna providing access to the viewpoints of different sections of society during this period. Ann

Turnbull most usually employs a third-person narration but decided that these novels required a different approach. She explains,

> I had some difficulty settling on the viewpoint for the novel. I couldn't decide whether to write about Susanna or Will. Then I thought that perhaps I could have two main characters. I was worried that it wouldn't work, but they have very separate experiences at the beginning of the book, so the dual narration is the perfect solution. If I'd had one first person narration it wouldn't have worked, too much would have been related second hand.

> One thing I discovered from experimenting was that all my 'try outs' were in the first person, which was new to me. I did experiment with the third person but I was surprised that I had to use a lot more words. In effect the writing lost the vividness of the first person. I found that writing in the first person meant I could avoid tedious explanation. (from www. writeaway.org.uk)

Young readers are certainly capable of identifying shifting viewpoints in picture books. On one occasion when I was sharing *Zoom* by Istvan Banyai with a group of 8-year-olds, one boy told me that he had spotted a mistake in the book. We returned to have another look and he showed me a page. 'It's different here', he explained. He pointed to a picture of a man holding an airmail letter in his hand. Up to that page the pictures had zoomed out from an imaginary starting point: first a cockscomb, then the cockscomb on a cockerel's head, and then the cockerel in a farmyard, at which point our expectations are disrupted because the farmyard is a toy farm, and the toy farm is only on a poster. Eventually we discover that everything we have been shown is on a postage stamp on an airmail letter. This is the page that Nathan was showing me. And then the images start to zoom out from the postage stamp, no longer a tiny imaginary world but the real world, up into the sky, beyond the world's atmosphere until earth is just a tiny white speck on a black page. What that boy had noticed was a shift in viewpoint. A shift that is crucial to understanding the serious theme rather than enjoying it simply for visual play with images. The shifting viewpoint emphasizes the comparison of two worlds, real and imaginary. Having gasped incredulously, 'How can all of those things be on the postage stamp?', the final page leaves us to consider our own significance in a vast universe. And for one boy, spotting 'a mistake' opened a door to talking about points of view in books.

The unreliable narrator

A narrator is a guide through the story but the extent to which we can trust the narrator's take on events varies.

The True Story of the Three Little Pigs by Jon Scieszka and Lane Smith is a retelling of the traditional folk tale from the wolf's point of view:

> I'm the wolf. Alexander T. Wolf. You can call me Al. I don't know how this whole Big Bad Wolf thing got started, but it's all wrong. Maybe it's just because of our diet. Hey, it's not my fault wolves eat cute little animals like bunnies and sheep and pigs. That's just they way we are. If cheeseburgers were cute, folks would probably think you were Big and Bad too.

Does *The True Story of the Three Little Pigs* present a case for a genuine miscarriage of justice? Does it simply retell the story from an alternative point of view? Well, hardly, the narrative clues alert the reader that the wolf is not to be trusted – he is an unreliable narrator. From the very first page when he introduces himself ('You can call me Al', a reference to the notorious gangster Al Capone) the reader's trust in him is shaken. Can we honestly believe that an accidental sneeze led to the little piggies' demise? His feeble attempts to justify his actions simply do not stand up. The irony is made apparent in the dissonance between words and pictures. As the wolf appeals to his audience, the reader's attention is drawn to the little fluffy rabbit ears sticking out of a bowl of cake mix. While it is true that there is always more than one side to a story, all points of view are not equally valid.

Huck in Mark Twain's *The Adventures of Huckleberry Finn* is classic instance of an unreliable narrator. Though in this case the lack of reliability arises from Huck's inexperience and. It is a naïve viewpoint and thus at the other end of the scale of to B. B. Wolf's disingenuous narration. Huck's incomprehension is used to comic effect, particularly with regard to the behaviour of adults and their 'sivilized' ways. The effect is ironic. In some instances this is a verbal irony, for example when Tom tells Huck he may join his band of robbers if he goes 'back to the widow and be respectable'. There are also instances of dramatic irony, where the reader is more knowing than Huck about the events he has witnessed. For example, when he relates his experiences of seeing a drunk horseman at the circus, the reader knows that he has seen an acrobat.

In *Treasure Island*, the naïvety of Jim Hawkins's narration of the early chapters is gradually replaced by a more considered and experienced voice: 'I was a fool, if you like, and certainly I was going to do a foolish, over bold act; but I was determined to do it with all the precautions in my power'.

Interior monologue

Do you ever talk to yourself? Fortunately it is not a sign of madness; most of us have conversations running in our heads. But trying to represent a character's thoughts in fiction is quite a challenge. As already mentioned, credibility is tested if an omniscient third-person narrator is privy to the innermost thoughts of a character. Some writers reveal the hidden conversations by trying to represent the flow of thought in a first-person narration, a convention that we call interior monologue. A writer might employ this technique even if the story is being told largely in the third person.

ACTIVITY

In *Mighty Fizz Chilla*, Philip Ridley intersperses interior monologue with other forms of narration in order to explore the troubled mind of his protagonist, Milo Kick. Read these two extracts and then consider the effect of Ridley's style of narration.

> *Ocean, innit!*
> *Me – in middle.*
> *Not big, wet stuff full of fishes.*
> *It's where I live innit!*
> *Big concrete stuff full of people.*
> *But now … No people.*
> *Scary, innit!*
> *Heart – it's punching in me chest.*
> *Sweat – it's trickling down me face.*
> *Me – screaming, 'WHERE IS EVERYBODY? WHERE IS – '*

Dee Dee Six (to give 'Robot Woman' her full name) is sixty-five years old, tall, thin, and wearing pinstripe trousers (Bloke's stuff, innit), lace-up shoes (Bloke's stuff, innit). Her hair is grey and cut in a straight line (like a bowl on her head, innit). Her face is covered with countless tiny wrinkles (like a shattered windscreen, innit) and has small, beady eyes, round-rimmed spectacles, pencil-line eyebrows and a tiny, lipless mouth. (*Mighty Fizz Chilla* by Philip Ridley)

Commentary

The first passage is a dream sequence. Ridley uses short sections of italic print to show what is happening inside Milo's head. There are no accompanying explanations – this is *showing* rather than *telling*. The lines are short and reflect Milo's anxious state. The single punctuated words 'Heart', 'Sweat', 'Me', make the reader aware of the sensations that Milo is experiencing. In the second passage the reader meets a new character, Dee Dee Six. Her appearance is described factually by an objective narrator but Milo's hidden conversation revealed in parentheses provides an evaluative commentary which also provides information about his negativity.

Narrating in the past and present tense

Most commonly narrative is written in the past tense, relating things that have already happened but the present tense may also be used and it is interesting to consider what effects can be created by shifts in tense.

Read this extract from Gillian Cross's thriller, *Calling A Dead Man*. Then answer these questions:

- In which tense is the passage written?
- How does Cross's use of tense affect your reading and response to the passage?
- Rewrite the second paragraph in the past tense. What do you notice?

'What's he going to eat?' That was Yelena, of course.

'And who is he?' Nikolai prodded with his foot. 'Maybe the whole thing's a trap. If we take him into our houses, he'll steal everything we have.'

Irina Petrovna shook her head scornfully, but Yelena screeched and headed back to her cabin, hobbling as fast as she could move. The door slammed shut and they heard the bolt slide across.

'So many treasures,' the Kommendant said, sarcastic and weary. 'This is such a rich place for robbers to come to.'

Irina Petrovna walked forward, painfully. Her arthritis was always worst in the wet autumn weather. The stranger was still now and she stared down at his flushed face and the raw places where the ticks had been.

'He has nothing,' she said. 'And he is getting cold. What can we do but take him in?'

He is falling through nothing, exploding into a chaos of pain and dust and destruction. If he opens his eyes, light crashes over him like tumbling blocks of concrete, blowing his brains apart.

Voices pound into his ears at a million decibels, throbbing in his skull. Every touch on his burning skin scorches it with agony. His mouth is as dry as rubble, as dry as crumbling mortar in a desert wall, and his lips split open when he tries to speak.

There is no chance to think. No chance to wonder who he is, or where he is or how he got there. There's nothing except the pain, taking him from moment to moment. Drowning out everything else.

Commentary

A shift from past to present in this extract allows a move from an external perspective to an internal one. Although written in the third person, the effect is close to internal monologue. We are made aware of the man's state of consciousness and the sequence of thoughts that flash into his mind. This effect can only be achieved by moving into the present tense. This internal viewpoint makes the scene more immediate. But it would be too simplistic to suggest that the present tense always makes a scene more immediate. It has other uses as well. It can, for instance, be employed to describe habitual events that are common in both past and present, or an event that occurred in the past can be given a momentary illusion of continuing into the present.

In *The Foreshadowing* Marcus Sedgwick also employs shifts in tense for impact and to solve the challenge presented by writing an historical story written as though it is happening in the here and now. The story moves towards a future endpoint, which is really in the past. He explains, 'The diary format in the *continuous* present can create problems when you are talking about something that happened yesterday but from a more distant reflective stance. It did lead to some convoluted tenses when it changes into the past historic as it does in the dream sequences. Hopefully it works for the reader' (Marcus Sedgwick, *Write Away!*).

Experimental forms of narration

Writers are continually searching for new forms of narration that enable them to truthfully represent complex human experience. Finding new ways of telling enables writers to say new things. In his groundbreaking novel for young adults, *Breaktime*, Aidan Chambers experiments with a range of narrative techniques including third-person narration, interior monologues, letters, dialogue and images. Perhaps most startling is the way in which he presents main character Ditto's first sexual encounter. The page is divided into two columns. The right-hand column is Chambers's representation of the experience and the left-hand column reads like a report. It is the gap between the two columns that reveals the inadequacy of language for describing the experience.

Although used infrequently, a second-person narration (using the pronoun *you* instead of *s/he* or *I*) can be employed to create the impression of a personal relationship between the reader and the subject of a story. Writing an entire story in the second person is difficult to manage. Malachy Doyle uses this technique in his novel *Who Is Jesse Flood?* and in his text for the picture book *Cow*. Books of the Choose Your Own Adventure type, in which the reader makes choices about the plot by choosing options and jumping around the text also use this direct address through the second person.

Recently several writers, particularly in America and Australia, have experimented with the verse novel as a means of describing experience. Examples for teenage readers include Virginia Ewer Wolff's *Make Lemonade*, Sonya Sones's *Stop Pretending* and Margaret Wild's *Jinx*.

For younger readers, Sharon Creech's *Love That Dog* is a poignant story about a boy called Jack who is at first unimpressed by poetry

ROOM 105 – MISS STRETCHBERRY

September 13

I don't want to
Because boys
Don't write poetry.

Girls do.

I tried.
Can't do it.
Brain's empty.

but comes to find it a powerful means of expressing personal loss.

LOVE THAT DOG
(INSPIRED by WALTER DEAN MYERS)
By Jack

Love that dog,
Like a bird loves to fly
I said love that dog
Like a bird loves to fly
Love to call him in the morning
Love to call him

'Hey there, sky!'
(*Love That Dog* by Sharon Creech)

This book is an absolute must for teachers and students as it is an affirming story and testament to the power of good, sensitive teaching to turn children on to reading and in particular poetry. An interesting comparison can be made with another verse novel, Malorie Blackman's *Cloudbusting*. Sam, the first-person narrator uses a range of verse forms to communicate his feelings about his friend Davey and the bullying that goes on at school. Sam's encounter with Davey opens up all kinds of imaginative possibilities and when his teacher, Mr Mackie, suggests that the class write a poem, Sam knows that this is the perfect medium for what he has to say about his secret friendship.

ACTIVITY

Research: taking it further
Read a selection of the titles referred to in this section or review your personal collection of children's books. Make notes on the relative merits and weaknesses of the following:

- first-person narration;
- omniscient third-person narration;
- dual or multiple narration
- objective narration;
- interior monologue;
- epistolary narrative;
- second-person narration;
- unreliable narrator;
- diction;
- verse novel.

Selected Titles
Ahlberg, A. and Ahlberg, J. (1999) *The Jolly Postman*. London: Viking.
Banyai, I. (1998) *Zoom*. London: Puffin.
Blackman, M. (2005) *Cloudbusting*. London: Random House.
Boyne, J. (2006) *The Boy in the Striped Pyjamas*. London: David Fickling.
Browne, A. (1999) *Voices in the Park*. London: Random House.
Burgess, M. (2006) *Sara's Face*. London: Andersen Press.
Burnett, F.H. (1994) *The Secret Garden*. London: Puffin.
Chambers, A. (1995) *Breaktime*. London: Random House.
Creech, S. (2002) *Love That Dog*. London: Bloomsbury.
Gleitzman, M. (2006) *Belly Flop and Water Wings*. London: Puffin.
Haddon, M. (2004) *The Curious Incident of the Dog in the Nighttime*. London: Red Fox.
Hutchins, P. (2001) *Rosie's Walk*. London: Random House.
Doherty, B. (2001) *Dear Nobody*. London: Puffin.
Fine, A. (2006) *The Tulip Touch*. London: Puffin.
Kipling, R. (2004) *The Just So Stories*. London: Walker.
Marks, G. (2003) *Radio Radio*. London: Bloomsbury.
Morpurgo, M. (2003) *The Wreck of the Zanzibar*. London: Egmont.
Nesbit, E. (1995) *The Story of the Treasure Seekers*. London: Puffin.
Ridley, P. (2006) *Mighty Fizz Chilla*. London: Puffin.
Skelton, M. (2006) *Endymion Spring*. London: Puffin.
Sedgwick, M. (2005) *The Foreshadowing*. London: Orion
Snicket, L. (2003) *A Series of Unfortunate Events: The Bad Beginning*. London: Egmont.
Stroud, J. (2004) *The Amulet of Samarkand*. London: Random House.
Turnbull, A. (2003) *No Shame, No Fear*. London: Walker.

Narrative structure

Rearrange these statements to form a story. When you have done this, describe the function each statement serves in the story (e.g. establishes setting).

He returned home to his wife with the gold.
Once upon a time.
Gladly, the woodcutter shared his meagre meal of bread and cheese with her.
The woman looked hungry and tired and she asked if he could spare her a few crumbs.
One day, when their last penny had been spent, the woodcutter decided to go out into the wide world to seek his fortune.
A poor young woodcutter and his wife lived in a cottage in the forest.
And they lived happily ever after.
On his travels he met an old woman resting against a tree.
She told him to take his axe and chop at the base of the tree and to his delight he found a pot of gold.

Commentary

When I was at primary school, I recall being rebuked for writing a story that did not have a beginning, middle and end. I was rather perplexed by the criticism. As far as I was concerned the story started and therefore must have a beginning and, as I had finished writing, it must also have an ending. I felt sure that the middle was somewhere in between. My confusion arose from the fact that I did not understand what the teacher meant by those everyday terms – I did not understand the function of beginning, middle and end in stories. Standard narrative structure has been analysed and described in different ways. A simple description identifies four elements:

- Exposition: the scene is set and characters are introduced.
- Complication: the characters' lives become complicated in some way.
- Climax: this is the point in the story where suspense is at its highest.
- Resolution: provides a solution for the complication – though this is not necessarily a happy one.

Now let us look at the woodcutter story:

Once upon a time a poor woodcutter and his wife lived in a cottage in the forest. One day, when their last penny was spent, the woodcutter decided to go out into the wide world to seek his fortune. On his travels he met an old woman resting against a tree. The woman looked tired and hungry and asked if he would spare her a few crumbs. Gladly the woodcutter shared his meagre meal of bread and cheese with her. She told him to take his axe and chop at the bottom of the tree and to his delight he found a pot of gold. He returned home to his wife with the gold. And they lived happily ever after.

If you reconstructed the woodcutter story, you have demonstrated an implicit knowledge of story structure. Now we can use the four elements above to analyse this simple tale:

- Exposition: the first sentence tells us about the characters – the poor woodcutter and his wife, and the setting – a cottage in the forest.
- Complication: from the moment that we know that the last penny has been spent the story moves into the complication.
- Climax: suspense is at its highest when the old woman tells the woodcutter to take his axe and cut at the tree. The questions we ask at this point are: Why has

she asked him to do this? What is he going to find?

- Resolution: the woodcutter's money problems are solved when he finds the pot of gold. This story has a neat happy ending.

To think in terms of the four elements is more helpful than using the terms beginning, middle and end. But for a more complex analysis we can draw on Longacre's (1976) detailed framework.

Elements of standard narrative structure

- Aperture: the first few words before the real story begins. Most conventionally the fairy tale's 'Once upon a time' or 'Long, long ago in a land east of the sun and west of the moon there lived ...'. Apertures are commonly found in oral storytelling.
- Exposition: part of the story where the setting (time and place) and characters are introduced.
- Inciting moment: this is the moment in the story when the predictability of the exposition is broken, the point at which we know we are reading a story rather than a recount. In *Tom's Midnight Garden* the inciting moment occurs when Tom is sent away to stay with his Aunt and Uncle because his brother Peter has measles.
- Developing conflict: all narratives contain some form of conflict; this is what makes the story worth telling. At this point suspense is built. The reader wants to know what will happen next. This phase is described as the rising action of the plot.
- Climax: this is the part of the story where suspense is at its highest, a confrontation or final showdown becomes inevitable. Climaxes vary in intensity and proximity to the end of the story. In J.K. Rowling's *Harry Potter and the Goblet of Fire* the major climax, when Harry finally confronts and defeats Lord Voldemort, occurs two chapters before the end.
- Denouement: a crucial final event occurs, which makes the resolution possible. This might include the unravelling of the plot. The denouement occurs in the penultimate chapter in *Harry Potter and the Goblet of Fire*. From the denouement the plot enters a phase called the falling action.
- Final suspense: the moment in the story where the details of the resolution are worked out.
- Conclusion: a satisfactory ending is worked out. While the ending must be satisfactory in terms of the story it might not be happy. Conclusions can be open ended or closed with all loose ends tied up.

Longacre's (1976) framework is a refinement of the basic narrative stages outlined earlier. Stages 1–2 can be seen as filling the exposition function, 3–4 the complication, 5 the climax and 6–8 the resolution.

Coda

A further element of structure not accounted for in this framework is the coda, the reiteration of a story's moral. In Perrault's fairy tale collection *Histoires ou contes du temps passé* each story has a coda attached (though they are not usually included in modern editions). This one is from 'Le Petit Chaperon Rouge' (Little Red Riding Hood):

> One sees here that young children
> Especially pretty girls,
> Who're bred as pure as pearls,
> Should question words addressed by men.
> Or they may serve one day as feast
> For a wolf or other beast.

I say a wolf since not all are wild
Or are indeed the same in kind
For some are winning and have sharp minds.
Some are loud, smooth, or mild.
Others appear plain kind or unriled.
They follow young ladies wherever they go,
Right into the halls of their very own homes.
Alas for those girls who've refused the truth:
The sweetest tongue has the sharpest tooth.

In this explicit example Perrault clearly implies that the wolf represents men who prey on young girls but he also makes it clear that any young lady who fails to heed his advice is responsible for her own fate. Anne Fine writes a coda at the end of *The Tulip Touch* but in this instance it is embedded in the main narrative:

Yes, now I know that even back then, Tulip was going off to drown that poor kitten. But Dad was no older the day he pushed his grandfather's tortoise under the bush and left it there to die. You could say that Tulip was braver and kinder. And people aren't locked doors. You can get through to them if you want. But no one did. No one reached out a hand to Tulip. Nobody tried to touch her. I hear them whispering and they sicken me. 'Bus seats!' grumbles Mrs Bodell. 'Locker doors!' complain the teachers. 'Chicken sheds!' say the farmers. 'Greenhouses! Dustbins!' moan the neighbours. And Mum says, 'A lovely old hotel!'
    But what about Tulip?
    I shall feel sorry for Tulip all my life
And guilty, too.
Guilty.

Anne Fine was motivated to write *The Tulip Touch* after the James Bulger murder trial. The main theme is about the acquisition of moral responsibility. Throughout the novel her stance is antithetical to John Major's (1993) statement, 'We must condemn a little more and understand a little less'. And in the coda she reasserts the moral: we must understand a little more and condemn a little less. Guilty is the single word with which society condemns those who operate outside its moral codes and conventions. Fine encourages her young readers to consider what lies behind the word. Who should take responsibility for the burden of guilt? Natalie has been able to acknowledge her part in Tulip's tragic story but others with greater authority and power continue to attribute blame elsewhere. Fine challenges the view that redemption and reconciliation are not possible or desirable.

Story frame

A story frame may be placed around the main narrative. This is the case with Nina Bawden's *Carrie's War* which opens with the adult Carrie returning with her own children to visit the place where she was evacuated during the war. The novel concludes with her children finding the cottage at Druid's Bottom and she is reunited with her old friends, Hepzibah Green and Mister Johnny.

A story frame was added to the 1998 film version of *Tom's Midnight Garden* although Philippa Pearce had not written one. What is particularly interesting in this example is that the inclusion of a frame changes the implied audience. While the book is clearly written from a child's point of view, the film is intended for a family audience and has to build in appeal for adults. (This is not to suggest that adults cannot read and enjoy the book – many do).

ACTIVITY

> ## *Narrative structure*
>
> Read the story of 'Kate Crackernuts' reproduced in Appendix 3.3.
> Use Longacre's framework to analyse the structure of this traditional story.
>
> - Does the story fit this pattern?
> - Consider whether or not some sections were more difficult to analyse than others?
> - If so, why?
>
> More complex stories will also have sub-plots, though these are often limited in fiction that is written for children.

Story shapes

Short traditional stories often follow a standard narrative presentation (Figure 3.1) with rising action from the inciting moment through the development of conflict followed by the falling action of the denouement, final suspense and conclusion. However, not all elements are present in every story and in longer more complex narratives patterns may repeat or spiral through a series of conflicts and mini-climaxes before building to a final suspense and major climax. An example of an alternative pattern is the linear plot, which adheres to a strict chronological order and does not rise to a climax.

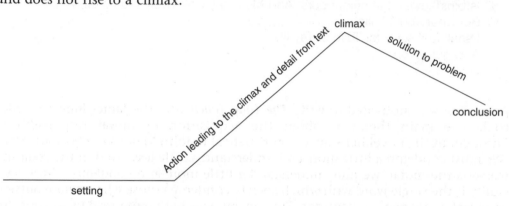

Figure 3.1 *Story Structure: Standard Narrative Presentation*

ACTIVITY

> Reading and analysing picture books can help you develop an awareness of different story shapes (see Figure 3.2).
>
> Read the following synopsis of Susan Hill's picture book, *Beware Beware*, or obtain and read a copy of the book.
>
> > In a cosy farmhouse kitchen a young mother is cooking while her daughter looks through the window at the winter scene and the woods beyond the bottom of the garden. She wonders, 'What's out there?' Then tentatively she steps outside. The woods are gloomy and forbidding but the girl is curious and she enters. In the woods strange things can be seen and heard, the girl runs from the woods just as her mother comes to find her. She comforts her daughter and they return home together. Night-time comes and mother and daughter are sewing at the kitchen table. The girl's head is turned to the window. 'What's out there?' she wonders.
>
> This story shape is a traditional home-away-home pattern but the ending suggests the start of another story rather than complete closure.
> We could draw the shape of the story like in Figure 3.2.
> Select a picture book. Read and then draw the shape of the story.
> Does the story conform to any of the patterns that have been discussed in this chapter?
> Can you identify any other stories that have the same pattern as the one you have drawn?

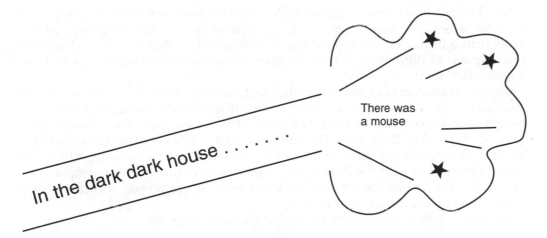

Figure 3.2 *This shows the shape of Ruth Brown's* 'A Dark Dark Tale'

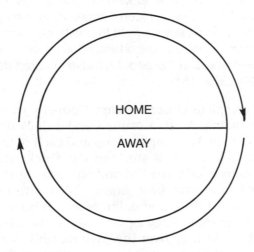

Fig 3.3 *The home–away–home structure*

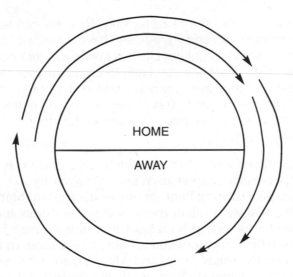

Figure 3.4 *A recurring home–away–home–away structure*

Perry Nodelman (1996, following Clausen, 1982) has argued that one of the ways in which plots of children's books differ from adult books is in the home–away–home structure (Figures 3.3 and 3.4). In adult literature 'you can't go home again' he explains. But 'characters in children's stories tend to learn the value of home by losing it and then finding it again. This *home–away–home* pattern is the most common plot of children's literature' (1996: 155).

Novels for children often take the form of the *Bildungsroman* or education story in which a central character moves from dependence to independence, adolescence into adulthood. A case in point is Tolkien's *The Hobbit*, which charts the development of Bilbo Baggins from unadventurous, home-loving hobbit to independent free spirit.

Younger readers may prefer stories that include some form of closure where the emphasis is on security and the restoration of normality. But strong closure is sometimes achieved at the expense of credibility. For example, the reconciliation scene at the end of E. Nesbit's *The Railway Children* has been criticized as unbelievable wish-fulfilment. And in Nina Bawden's *Squib* the ease with which the abused child, Squib, is rehabilitated into a new family may also seem implausibly optimistic. But it could be argued that these are adult responses and that young readers find such endings comforting.

For Berlie Doherty, reassuring a young audience is important:

> I think a children's writer has a dual responsibility – you must entertain the child, it must be something they enjoy reading – but I think also because we're adult and have had experiences we need to kind of show a way through what seems to be a hopeless tangle at times. I don't necessarily mean a happy ending, because happy endings aren't always right for the book, more often than not, but the possibility of a solution I think is important. I don't think it's fair to leave a child with a sense of hopelessness at the end, because children do get very involved with books. (in Carter, 1999: 151)

Not all stories have complete closure. Helen Cooper's *Pumpkin Soup* is a good example of a circular ending. A cat, a squirrel and a duck live in harmony. They like nothing more than to make pumpkin soup and each of them is assigned a special role in its preparation. All is well until one day Duck, who is in charge of the salt, decides that he wants to stir. The Cat and Squirrel object to the disruption of the status quo so Duck runs away from home. Filled with remorse, his companions search high and low for their friend, but when all hope is fading they return home to find him making soup. They agree to share the jobs and so they all live happily ever. Or do they? Turning over the page we find that Duck wants to play the bagpipes and so the argument starts again … This is the home–away–home structure with a twist. Author, Celia Rees, writes,

> Endings have to round off the story satisfactorily. Readers can feel cheated if a book doesn't end properly. An ending needs to have a sense of completion, but should also point forward to the future. Life is a continuum and carries on, and a book should reflect that. In a book you have to convince your reader that your characters are real, that they live in a real world and that real things are happening to them. In fiction everything has to stop at the end of the story – so you need to put across the sense that this is the end of the story, but another is just beginning. (in Carter, 2001: 99)

Another variation is the episodic story in which each chapter is a self-contained adventure. For instance each chapter in *Winnie-the-Pooh* by A.A. Milne, details a self-contained adventure featuring Pooh or one of his friends. Many of these chapters are so memorable that we think of them as separate stories and they have subsequently been marketed as such in both book and film formats. Further examples are Catherine Storr's delightful stories about Polly, a very modern Little Red Riding Hood, *Clever Polly and the Stupid Wolf*, and *My Naughty Little Sister* by Dorothy Edwards. Reinhardt Jung's *Bambert's Book of Missing Stories* is a delightful collection of 11 stories assembled within a framing narrative with the individual tales illuminating the connecting narrative. Episodic stories are more frequently found in books written for a young audience than adult literature.

Seven basic plots

Christopher Booker (2004: 5) identifies seven basic plots that occur in fiction:

It was not long before I began to make a startling discovery. Not only did it indeed seem to be true that there were a number of basic themes or plots which continually recurred in the storytelling of mankind, shaping tales of very different types and from almost every age and culture. Even more surprising was the degree of detail to which these 'basic plots' seemed to shape the stories they had inspired; so that one might find, for instance, a well-known nineteenth-century novel constructed in almost the same way as a Middle Eastern folk tale dating from 1200 years before; or a popular modern children's story with the structure of an epic poem composed in ancient Greece.

Booker's basic plots are:

1. overcoming the monster;
2. rags to riches;
3. the quest;
4. voyage and return;
5. comedy;
6. tragedy;
7. rebirth.

Stories about overcoming the monster detail a threat posed by a monstrous figure who is challenged and defeated by the hero/heroine. Legendary stories of this type include *Beowulf*. The pattern can also be observed in *Superhero* comics such as *Spiderman* and *Superman* stories and in the popular Harry Potter fantasy series. In rags-to-riches stories the interest is in seeing a character who is initially quite humble and disregarded raised to an elevated position. Well-known fairy tales of this type include *The Ugly Duckling* and *Cinderella*. An example from contemporary teenage fiction is Julie Hearn's *Ivy*. Orphan Ivy is adopted by her aunt and lives in poverty until she is recruited by 'skinner' Carroty Kate to coax wealthy children away from their nannies so that she can strip them of their valuable clothes. Years later Ivy escapes finding her way back to her adopted family where she finds respite in laudanum until she is spotted by a wealthy pre-Raphaelite painter and becomes his model. However, this too is another kind of imprisonment, and it is only when she finds a purpose in rescuing animals at Battersea Dog's Home that she can rise above her circumstances.

Comedy, Booker (2004) asserts, is a very special kind of story and it can't be explained as simply a 'funny story'. Although the plots are quite complicated, a general summing up identifies the essence of comedy as a story where:

- we see as a little world in which people have passed under a shadow of confusion, uncertainty and frustration, and are shut off from one another;
- confusion gets worse until the pressure of darkness is at its most acute and everyone is in a nightmarish tangle;
- finally, with the coming to light of things not previously recognized, perceptions are dramatically changed. The shadows are dispelled, the situation is miraculously transformed and the little world is brought together in a state of joyful union.

The basic comedy structure can be applied to *How to Train Your Parents* by Pete Johnson (2003). After moving to a new area Louis is horrified to discover his parents becoming ultra-competitive, wanting him and his younger brother to get straight As at school and join all sorts of after-school clubs like the other kids. At the outset he is alienated from his parents, uncertain and confused. In spite of developing a friendship with Maddy, who seems to have things sorted, things go from bad to worse. The nightmarish tangle arises when Louis unofficially takes time off school to attend an audition in London. Ultimately all parties learn something, including Louis, who realizes that the *laissez-faire* approach adopted by Maddy's parents is no more desirable than his parents' hot housing.

Tragedy is a story which ends in death. Drawing on five different patterns of tragedy (Icarus, Faust, Macbeth, Jekyll and Hyde, Lolita), Booker (2004) identifies structures that underpin all tragedy:

- Anticipation stage: the hero is in some way incomplete or unfulfilled and his thoughts are turned towards the future in hope of some unusual gratification. Some object of desire or course of action presents itself, and his energies have found a focus.
- Dream stage: he becomes in some way committed to his course of action and for a while things go almost improbably well for the hero. He is winning the gratification he had dreamed of, and seems to be 'getting away with it'.
- Frustration stage: almost imperceptibly things start to go wrong. The hero cannot find a point of rest. He begins to experience a sense of frustration, and in order to secure his position may feel compelled to further 'dark acts' which lock him into his course of action even more irrevocably. A 'shadow figure' may appear at this point, seeming in some obscure way to threaten him
- Nightmare stage: things are now slipping seriously out of the hero's control. He has a mounting sense of threat and despair. Forces of opposition and fate are closing in on him.
- Destruction or death-wish stage: either by the forces he has aroused against him, or by some final act of violence which precipitates his own death, the hero is destroyed.

This structure can be applied to Melvin Burgess's *Sara's Face* (2006). The story told through video diary and documentary is about a beautiful but vulnerable teenage who self-harms. Recovering in hospital after damaging her face with a hot iron, she allows herself to be drawn under the Svengali-like influence of a manipulative and ruthless pop-star. He plans a face transplant where he will take Sara's discarded face to replace his scarred and damaged one. Sara's boyfriend suspects that Sara has changed her mind and intervenes to stop the operation but it is too late. The book closes with a reclusive Sara reflecting on the course of events. The *anticipation* stage of this novel hints at Sara's unease and dissatisfaction. We learn that she was popular and beautiful but that she is an outsider, someone who doesn't quite fit, although she has the capacity to inspire the loyalty of those closest to her: 'She was too strong a taste for many of her contemporaries, but those who did love her loved her dearly and were loved in return'. The *dream stage* in this novel is brief. Sara develops a friendship, she is popular with boys but the sexual attention oversteps Sara's boundaries. In the *frustration* stage Sara embarks on a course of action which leads to an increasing incidence of self-harm and propels the narrative towards its tragic conclusion. In the *nightmare* stage Sara falls under the influence of Jonathan Heat a vain but fading pop-star and in spite of a rescue attempt gives her consent for the transplant (*destruction stage*) which leaves her a recluse without a face.

With reference to *The Snow Queen*, *A Christmas Carol*, *Crime and Punishment* and *Silas Marner*, Booker identifies an underlying structure in the rebirth story. This sequence is described as:

- a young hero or heroine falls under the shadow of a dark power;
- for a while, all may seem to go reasonably well, the threat may even have receded;
- but eventually it approaches again in full force, until the hero or heroine is seen imprisoned in the state of living death;
- this continues for a long time, when it seems that the dark power has completely triumphed;
- but finally the miraculous redemption.

In children's literature, C.S. Lewis's *The Lion, the Witch and the Wardrobe*, Catherine Storr's *Marianne Dreams* and Beth Webb's *Star Dancer* are versions of rebirth stories. The quest, and voyage and return structures are discussed more fully in Chapter 7.

Booker cautions that stories do not fit neatly with mechanical regularity into these patterns or indeed always exhibit the features of only one plot: 'There are extensive areas of overlap between one type of plot and another. Indeed, there are many stories which are shaped by more than one "basic plot" at a time (there are even a small number, including *The Lord of the Rings*, which include all seven of the plots ...) There are still other stories which are shaped only by part of such a plot' (2004: 6).

ACTIVITY

Review the titles listed in your reading log. Identify the basic plot of each story.

- Which of Booker's categories do they belong to?
- Do all stories fit one or more of the basic plots?
- How might this classification of plot be adapted to support your work with children?

Non-conventional structure

Recent picture-book makers have played with new ways of structuring narratives. Chris Van Allsburg's *The Mysteries of Harris Burdick* uses the artifice of an unsolved mystery to provide a context for a series of stunning, enigmatic black-and-white pictures. The pictures are apparently unconnected except by the device of the framing narrative and they do not need to be read in order. Each picture has a title and caption. One picture entitled 'The Seven Chairs' depicts a nun seated on a chair floating 20 feet above the ground. This bizarre image is situated in a medieval perpendicular gothic cathedral. The caption reads, 'The fifth one ended up in France'. The reader immediately wants to know the answer to the questions that are implied. Where are the other six chairs? Why did this one end up in France? What special powers do the chairs possess? Who is the nun in the picture? And so on. In effect some elements of the narrative are given but the reader must construct the story for themselves or be content to wonder at the possibilities.

Stephen King was so intrigued by one of the images in the book, *The House on Maple Street*, that he was inspired to write a short story based on it. Anthony Browne has also been directly influenced by Van Allsburg's work and he applies a similar concept in *Willy the Dreamer*. A series of separate images each with its own implied story is connected by the text device 'Willy dreams ...' and other unifying elements such as the banana motif and the appearance of characters that we recognize from the earlier Willy books.

Even more radical is David Macaulay's *Black and White*. Each double-page spread is divided into quadrants and each section depicts what appears at first to be a separate story. The style of each story is presented in a different illustrative style and printed in different fonts. As the reader progresses through the book the four strands start to connect and most readers at this stage start to look backwards and forwards in the text as they try to work out what is happening. *Black and White* is a non-linear text that subverts the standard presentation of narrative structure. Obtain a copy and read it for yourself. Raise your consciousness of what happens when you read it. If possible work in small groups with an observer taking notes of the strategies that are used in order for the book to make sense (see also picture book codes in Chapter 8).

Suspense and surprise

All narratives contain suspense, the means by which our curiosity and interest in the story is aroused and maintained. The word comes from the Latin *suspendere*, 'to hang'. And that's exactly what happens as we read; we are left 'hanging on', waiting to see how things will be resolved. Suspense creates both expectation and doubt. As we read, we ask questions about causality, such as Why did that happen? Why is this happening? What will happen next?

Foreshadowing is one device used to build suspense and to make the narrative more believable by preparing the reader for what is to follow. Hints, actions and setting can be used as clues to future events. Marcus Sedgwick's *The Foreshadowing* charts a journey towards a future that his protagonist, Alexandra, has already seen in her portentous dreams and visions. In the story, set in 1917, Alexandra wants to be a VAD nurse against the wishes of her father, a surgeon responsible for treating shell-shocked patients. When Alexandra's brothers enlist and travel to the Western Front, she begins to have premonitions about their fate. The convention of a dream sequence is used along with the motif of the raven, rich in literary allusion being associated with the Valkyries who in Norse myth selected the bodies of slain warriors and accompanied them to Valhalla, and also with the Celtic warrior goddess, the Morrigan. The mention of the black curtain may remind the reader of a funeral parlour. This is a scene which appears to foretell of death and the image of the gun confirms this:

> [L]ast night the raven came back to me in a dream.
> I heard the beat of its wings, drumming louder and louder.
> It came right up close to me.
> Its wing drifted across in front of my face – so close that I could see the barbs of each feather. The wing swung like a huge black curtain across the stage of a theatre, and lifted to reveal a thousand ravens swinging round the treetops of a blighted wood.
>   – The ravens parted, and I saw a gun.
>   – The gun fired, with a violent bang that shook me awake in an instant. (*The Foreshadowing* by Marcus Sedgwick)

Whose death is Alexandra witnessing in her dreams. As the visions become clearer Sedgwick sows seeds that suggest Tom is the victim and Alexandra herself believes this to be the case. She travels to the frontline in order to find and warn him. However, there are more surprises as the story unfolds and moves towards the final suspense:

> I've told the reader that Alexandra can see the future and knows what's going to happen. So I need to consider how I can keep some surprises for the reader. I came up with the resolution in which Alexandra shoots Tom very early on. Then it was just a matter of being careful about the way it was written all the way through. I'm so close to telling the reader what's going to happen. I even mention that she's the one holding the gun but it's like a double bluff that keeps the reader from realising that she's the one who's going to do it. When you read back you'll see that it makes perfect sense. (Marcus Sedgwick, in www. writeaway.org.uk)

Conflict

Most fiction has some form of conflict at the heart, which usually escalates towards the climax.

Commentary

Here are some of the conflicts that are present in children's books:

ACTIVITY

> Write the titles of a range of children's books that you know well. Now identify the main cause of conflict in each of the books. Review your list. Do any patterns of conflict emerge? Suggest how you might categorize the types of conflict you have identified.

Title	Source of conflict	Conflict type

Do you think that children's fiction has a different range of conflicts to those found in adult fiction?

Are there some conflicts that are more common in books for younger children and others that are more evident in writing for older children?

When you have made your notes read the commentary below.

Then review your list. Have you found sources of conflict not mentioned in the commentary?

Character against character

J.K. Rowling's *Harry Potter* stories are concerned with the struggle between Harry and Lord Voldemort, which can be interpreted as an archetypal battle between good and evil. This is a frequently occurring pattern in fantasy. Further examples include Susan Cooper's *The Dark Is Rising* sequence, Brain Jacques's *Redwall* and C.S. Lewis's Narnia books. You have probably noticed that in all of these books the main child character is representative of the good forces. For example, in the animal fantasy, *Redwall*, it is the young mouse Mathias, a child substitute, who eventually succeeds in defeating the dastardly Cluny the Scourge. Frequently the conflict in these books is resolved with a battle – a final showdown. That a child can be the vanquisher of evil serves to demonstrate that the meek can overcome the powerful providing right is on their side, a theme that has a strong tradition in Judaeo-Christian mythology.

The family is a frequent source of conflict in contemporary children's books. In Louis Fitzhugh's *Nobody's Family Is Going to Change*, Emma and her younger brother, Willy, take a stand against their authoritarian father. Fitzhugh questions whether children should obey their parents when parental decisions are not in the best interests of their children. This book was first published in the 1970s amid a growing concern for children's rights. Emma is aware of this political context: 'She found a book on children's rights, which she had discovered in the library on Saturday morning, difficult to read. It seemed to go on and on about how there weren't any'. In the more recently published *Bumface*, by Morris Gleitzman, Angus is in a permanent state of conflict with his irresponsible mother who seems to be more interested in pursuing an acting career than looking after her three children (all have different fathers). In a reversal of roles Angus takes care of his younger brother and sister and tries to prevent his mother from increasing his burden by having more babies. Conflict between parents and their children is particularly prevalent in the teenage confessional book. Writers of these books are usually firmly on the side of the young characters, but the extent to which they present insight into parental concerns varies. Quite often parents are marginalized and their viewpoints are dismissed as out of date, uncool or even mad.

Children's relationships with each other are another source of conflict. As society has become more aware of the damage caused by bullying, authors have started to explore this social problem from various angles. Sometimes the protagonist develops the self-confidence to confront a bully, as is the case in Michael's Coleman's *Weirdo's War*. In Jacqueline Wilson's *Bad Girls*, Mandy is made to look much younger than she really is because her older parents are out of touch and dress her in old-fashioned clothes. She is bullied on account of her appearance but, with the help of Tanya, a wayward 13-year-old, she overcomes these difficulties and her parents gradually acknowledge that they must let her grow up. Another common conflict arises between siblings. In Jacqueline Wilson's *Double Act*, twin sisters Ruby and Garnet are inseparable but, when Garnet wins a scholarship to a private school, Ruby's envy estranges them. Eventually they both girls learn to be independent and establish themselves as individuals.

Character against society

In some books the child character is at odds with society, as in Libby Hathorn and Gregory Rogers's *Way Home*. This picture book shows the reader a day in the life of an unnamed boy who has to cope with extreme poverty and the danger of living on the streets, his only companion a stray kitten. This picture book condemns a society that fails to protect children. *Rose Blanche*, a poignant picture book by Roberto Innocenti and Ian McEwan is set in war-torn Europe. Alarmed at the brutal treatment of a young Jewish boy, a young girl follows an army truck into the forest where she witnesses the horror of the concentration camp. Appalled by her discovery, Rose risks her own safety to smuggle bread to the prisoners. She symbolizes the struggle of those who choose to fight for their beliefs – the white rose was a symbol of the underground resistance in Germany during the Second World War. An important concern of children's literature is the conflict that arises from prejudice. The irrepressible heroine in *Amazing Grace* by Mary Hoffman and Caroline Binch overcomes her classmate's prejudice, aided by her wise grandmother:

> 'You can't be called Peter,' said Raj. 'That's a boy's name.'
> But Grace kept her hand up.
> 'You can't be Peter Pan,' whispered Natalie, 'he wasn't black.' (*Amazing Grace* by Mary Hoffman)

Grace proves them all wrong when she auditions and is chosen for the part.

Character against self

Commonly occurring conflicts centre on children's fears and emotions. Helen Cooper's *Bear Under the Stairs* is about a young boy who is convinced that a bear lives in the cupboard under the stairs. To pacify the bear, he feeds it everyday until the smell of rotting food becomes unbearable and his mother discovers what has been going on. Together they clean the cupboard and the boy confronts his fear. The conflict in Anthony Browne's *Changes* is an internal confusion. When Joseph's father tells him that things are going to change, he is unsure about what this can mean. His anxiety is manifested in the changes that take place around him. A shiny metallic kettle transforms into a soft, living cat. At the end of the book the reason for change is revealed when his parents introduce his new baby sister. Other books in which the child's emotional turmoil is at the centre of the book's conflict include Maurice Sendak's picture book classic *Where the Wild Things Are* and Satoshi Kitamura's *Angry Arthur*.

Technology against nature

Children are often regarded as having a close affinity with nature and a strong commitment to environmental concerns. So it is not surprising that many children's books have been written about green issues. Jeannie Baker's wordless picture books, *Window* and *Belonging* are fine examples. In the author's note she writes,

> We are changing the face of our world at an alarming and an increasing pace. From the present rates of destruction, we can estimate that by the year 2020 no wilderness will remain on our planet, outside that protected in national parks and reserves. By the same year 2020, a quarter of our present plant and animal species will become extinct each hour.

Window is a series of collages created from natural materials. The story follows a boy from birth to young adulthood, a period of 24 years. Each double-page spread shows the view through his bedroom window. At the outset we see a forest and wild birds, an outhouse suggests there is no plumbing. In the following image the boy is 2 years old, the setting is still rural but a garden has been cultivated and a mud track suggests that more vehicles are using the road. The subsequent images depict increasing urbanization and pollution until the young man eventually marries and moves to a new home in the countryside where already the surrounding land has been sold for building (see also 'Themes' in Chapter 4).

Key words

- Narrative: the telling of a series of connected events.
- Dialogic perspective: multiple viewpoints.
- Focalization: in third-person narration, the viewpoint from which we experience the story.
- Interior monologue: first-person narration that reveals the secret conversations inside the narrator's head.
- Intrusive narrator: a third-person narrator who addresses the reader directly and comments on the events and characters.
- Narrator: the persona that tells the story either in the first, second or third person.
- Omniscient narrator: a narrator who sees and knows all the characters' thoughts, feelings. The application of limited omniscience is more usual in contemporary fiction.
- Unreliable narrator: a narrator whose viewpoint is open to question. This may be due to the narrator's limited understanding or self-deception.
- Diction: the choice of words in speech or writing. Diction might be formal, informal or colloquial.
- Epigram: an inscription, sometimes used at the beginning of chapters.
- Foreshadowing: the presentation in a work of literature of hints and clues that hint at to what is to come later in the work.

In this chapter you have seen that:

- A story can be told in many ways. An author makes a choice when selecting a third person, second person or personal narrator.
- The choice of narrator influences the point of view, which affects the way in which the reader experiences the story.
- Stories are most usually narrated in the past tense but the present tense is sometimes used to make a scene more immediate, to give the impression of a past event continuing into the present or to create a momentary illusion of being in the present.
- Writers experiment with new forms of narration as they search for adequate ways of representing and commenting on human experience.
- Narratives are structured in different ways but basic structures recur across diverse fictions.

Further reading

Alvarez, A. (2005) *The Writer's Voice*. London: Bloomsbury.
Booker, C. (2004) The *Seven Basic Plots*. London: Continuum.
Grainger, T. (1997) *Traditional Story Telling in the Primary Classroom*. Leamington Spa: Scholastic.
Hardy, B. (1977) 'Narrative as a primary act of mind' in M. Meek, A. Warlow and G. Barton (eds), *The Cool Web: The Pattern of Children's Reading*. London: The Bodley Head.
Meek, M. (ed.) (1996) *Information and Book Learning*. Stroud: Thimble Press.
Wall, B. (1991) *The Narrator's Voice: The Dilemma of Children's Fiction*. London: Macmillan.

Appendix 3.1

Extract 1

Test your teacher on Tudors

Here are a couple of facts your teacher (or parents or friends) may *think* they know. Perhaps you'll catch them out if you ask …

You:　　　　Please Miss! (or Sir, or Fatface) Who had the first postal service in this country?

Teacher:　　I'm glad you asked me that … (Teachers are always glad when you ask them something – it makes them think you are interested.) … Of course everybody knows that the famous Victorian, Rowland Hill, invented the postal service.

You:　　　　[with a sigh] But my book on the Terrible Tudors says the first postal service was invented in the reign of Elizabeth the First!

Then go on to quote these facts …

Rowland Hill created the Penny post and postage stamps, not the postal service. Tudor Guilds and universities had private postal services. The government was worried about spies sending messages out of the country this way. So, they insisted that a service under the Master of Posts should carry all letters outside England – that way they could read them if they suspected something! (*The Terrible Tudors* by Terry Deary)

Extract 2

On a crisp, clear winter's morning, with no warning at all, a terrible earthquake ripped a giant hole through the city of Lisbon. As the people ran, screaming for their lives, a giant tsunami rose up over the coast and swept right over them. One hundred thousand people were killed. Many of them, and much of their city, had vanished without trace: flushed down into the bowels of the earth. Lisbon was completely destroyed.

As the new year of 1756 dawned, all of Europe was in a state of shock. There was a sense of change – a whiff of danger in the air. The Church had been ruling with its iron rod for centuries. Now people started to ask questions. If God ruled the world, why did He do that to Lisbon? Suppose He was just watching everything rather than actually running it? Perhaps the scientists could explain the earthquake better than priests? Should people start looking after themselves and each other, and stop leaving everything up to God? It was the beginning of what we now call The Age of Enlightenment – a time that changed everything, from politics to music.

In the pretty little Austrian city of Salzburg, a violin teacher called Leopold Mozart was anxious. He had a lot to feel anxious about. He was poor, and he was ambitious. He knew that the world around him was changing, and he was keen to understand it, 'We live in a century during which we will hear many new things,' he said. Whatever this new age was about, he – Leopold Mozart – planned to make his name in it. (*Wolfgang Amadeus Mozart: The Boy Who Made Music* by Gill Hornby)

A dark brown monk's habit comes into view, like a shadow warning of evil.

Again, all you can see inside the cowl is darkness. Does this stranger actually have a face? The hooded man stands next to the pair admiring the tomb, which is as tall as a two-story building. He raises one baggy sleeve and points to the large central figure. "Doesn't he look like the devil himself?" the hooded man asks, as if the only possible answer is 'yes'.

One of the noble gentlemen looks at him suspiciously, then leans backwards, as if he doesn't want to get too close.

"It's a statue of Moses carrying the tablets bearing the Ten Commandments," the first man says.

"His face reminds me of Master Michelangelo. I think he wanted to immortalise himself here," the other adds.

The long sleeve conceals a fist, which is raised threateningly. "Can't you see the horns on his head? Michelangelo has portrayed Moses as a figure from hell!"

The men just laugh contemptuously at this remark.

"That's not Michelangelo's fault. Many people have made the same mistake in translating the holy text. It states that Moses came down from Mount Sinai with the two tablets of testimony and rays of light beaming from his head, but it was mistranslated as 'horns on his head'. That's the only reason why Michelangelo carved him like that."

Infuriated, the hooded man turns away with a snort. He swishes off as if his feet aren't touching the ground.

The two men watch him go, shaking their heads, then they turn back to the tomb.

As he slowly disappears into the distance, you hear one of them say, "Many people are envious of someone as brilliant and successful as Michelangelo. How stupid to speak ill of the great artist."

Extract 3 Thomas Brezina (2006) *Who Can Open Michelangelo's Seven Seals?* pp. 78–9

Appendix 3.2

Extract 1

Friday, 20th November, 1942

Dear Kitty,

None of us really knows how to take it all. The news about the Jews had not really penetrated through to us until now, and we thought it was best to remain as cheerful as possible. Every now and then, when Miep lets out something about what has happened to a friend, Mummy and Mrs. Van Daan always begin to cry, so Miep thinks it better not to tell us anymore. But Dussel was immediately plied with questions from all sides, and the stories he told us were so gruesome and dreadful that one can't get them out of one's mind.

Yet we still have our jokes and tease each other, when these horrors have faded a bit in our minds. It won't do us any good, or help those outside, to go on being as gloomy as we are at the moment. And what would be the object of making our 'Secret Annexe' into a 'secret Annexe of Gloom'? Must I keep thinking about those other people, whatever I am doing? And if I want to laugh about something, should I stop myself and quickly feel ashamed that I am cheerful? Ought I then to cry the whole day long? No that I can't do. Besides, in time this gloom will wear off.

Added to this misery there is another, but of course it pales into insignificance beside all the wretchedness I've just told you about. Still, I can't refrain from telling you that lately I have begun to feel deserted. I am surrounded by too great a void. I never used to feel like this, my fun amusements, and my girl friends completely filled my thoughts. Now I either think about unhappy things, or about myself. And at long last I have made the discovery that Daddy, although he's such a darling still cannot take the place of my entire little world of bygone days. But why do I bother you with such foolish things? I'm very ungrateful Kitty; I know that. But it often makes my head swim if I'm jumped upon too much, and then on top of that have to think about all those other miseries!

Yours Anne

(From *Anne Frank's Diary*)

Extract 2

ONCE I walked as fast as I could towards the city to find Mum and Dad and I didn't let anything stop me.

Not until the fire.

I slow down, staring at the horizon.

The fire is miles away, but I can see flames clearly as they flicker in the darkness. They must by huge. If that's a pile of burning books, there must be millions.

I stop.

I wipe my glasses and try to see if any Nazis are over there. I can't. It's too far away to see people, let alone arm bands.

I can hear trucks, or cars though, and faint shouting voices.

Part of me wants to run away, just in case.

Another part of me wants to go closer. Mum and Dad might be there. This might be where all the Jewish book owners have been taken, so the Nazis can burn all their books in one big pile.

I go closer.

I don't want to stay on the road in case I bump into any Nazis who are running late, so I cut across some fields.

One of the fields has cabbages in it. As I get closer to the fire, the cabbages are starting to get warm, Some are starting to smell like they're cooking. But I don't stop to eat any.

I can see what's burning now.

It's not books, it's a house.

I still can't see any people, so I stuff the bread and water inside my shirt and take my hat off and pee on it and put it back on to keep my head from blistering and go even closer in case there are some people who need to be rescued. I wrote a story once about Mum and Dad rescuing an ink salesman from a burning house, so I know a bit about it.

Blinking from the heat and the glare, I reach the wire fence that separates the house from the fields. The wire is too hot to touch. I wriggle under it.

The lawn is covered with dead chickens. Poor things, they must be cooked. That's what I think until I see holes in them.

They've been shot.

The owners must have done it to put them out of their misery.

Then I see the owners.

Oh.

(From *Once* by Morris Gleitzman)

Appendix 3.3: Kate Crackernuts

Once upon a time there was a king and a queen as in many lands have been. The king had a daughter, Anne, and the queen had one named Kate, but Anne was far bonnier than the queen's daughter, though they loved one another like real sisters. The queen was jealous of the king's daughter being bonnier than her own, and cast about to spoil her beauty. So she took the counsel of the henwife, who told her to send the lassie to her next morning fasting.

So next morning early, the queen said to Anne, 'Go, my dear, to the henwife in the glen, and ask her for some eggs.' So Anne set out, but as she passed through the kitchen she saw a crust, and she took and munched it as she went along.

When she came to the henwife's she asked for eggs, as she had been told to do; the henwife said to her, 'Lift the lid off that pot there and see.' The lassie did so, but nothing happened. 'Go home to your minnie and tell her to keep her larder door better locked,' said the henwife. So she went home to the queen and told her what the henwife had said. The queen knew from this that the lassie had had something to eat so watched the next morning and sent her away fasting; but the princess saw some country folk picking peas by the roadside and being very kind she spoke to them and took a handful of peas, which she ate by the way.

When she came to the henwife's, she said 'Lift the lid off the pot and you'll see.' So Anne lifted the lid but nothing. Then the henwife was rare angry and said to Anne, 'Tell your minnie the pot won't boil if the fire's away.' So Anne went home and told the queen.

The third day the queen goes along with the girl herself to the henwife. Now, this time, when Anne lifted the lid off the pot, off falls her own pretty head, and on jumps a sheep's head.

So the queen was now quite satisfied, and went back home.

Her own daughter, Kate, however, took a fine linen cloth and wrapped it round her sister's head and took her by the hand and they both went out to seek their fortune. They went on, and they went on, and they went on, until they came to a castle. Kate knocked at the door and asked for a night's lodging for herself and her sick sister. They went in and found it was a king's castle, who had two sons, and one of them was sickening away to death and no one could find out what ailed him. And the curious thing was, that whoever watched him at night was never seen any more. So the king had offered a peck of silver to anyone who would stop with him. Now Katie was a very brave girl, so she offered to sit up with him.

Till midnight all went well. As twelve o'clock rang, however, the sick prince rose, dressed himself and slipped downstairs. Kate followed, but he didn't seem to notice her. The prince went to the stable, saddled his horse, called his hound, jumped into the saddle and Kate leapt lightly up behind him. Away rode the prince and Kate through the greenwood, Kate, as they passed, plucking nuts from the trees and filling her apron with them. They rode on and on till they came to a green hill. The prince here drew bridle and spoke: 'Open, open, green hill, and let the young prince in with his horse and his hound,' and Kate added, 'and his lady behind.'

Immediately the green hill opened and they passed in. The prince entered a magnificent hall, brightly lighted up, and many beautiful fairies surrounded the prince and led him off to dance. Meanwhile Kate, without being noticed, hid herself behind the door. There she saw the prince dancing, and dancing, and dancing, till he could dance no longer and fell upon a couch. Then the fairies would fan him till he could rise again and go on dancing.

At last the cock crew, and the prince made all haste to get on horseback; Kate jumped up behind, and home they rode. When the morning sun rose they came in and found Kate sitting down by the fire cracking her nuts. Kate said the prince had a good night; but she would not sit up another night unless she was to get a peck of gold. The second night passed as the first had done. The prince got up at midnight and rode away to the green hill and the fairy ball, and Kate went with him, gathering nuts as they rode through the forest. This time she did not watch the prince, for she knew he would dance, and dance, and dance. But she saw a fairy baby playing with a wand and overheard one of the fairies say: 'Three strokes of that wand would make Kate's sister as bonny as she ever was.'

So Kate rolled nuts to the fairy baby, and rolled nuts until the baby toddled after the nuts and let fall the wand, and Kate took it up and put it in her apron. And at cockcrow they rode home as before, and the moment Kate got home to her room she rushed and touched Anne three times with her wand and the nasty sheep's head fell off and she was her own pretty self again.

The third night Kate consented to watch, only if she could marry the sick prince. All went on as the first two nights. This time the fairy baby was playing with a birdie; Kate heard one of the fairies say: 'Three bites of that birdie would make the sick prince as well as ever he was.' Kate rolled all the nuts she had to the fairy baby until the birdie was dropped, and Kate put it in her apron.

At cockcrow they set off again, but instead of cracking her nuts as she used to do, this time Kate plucked the feathers off and cooked the birdie. Soon there arose a very savoury smell. 'Oh!' said the sick prince, 'I wish I had a bite of that birdie.' So Kate gave him a bite of the birdie, and he rose up on his elbow. By-and-by he cried out again: 'Oh, if I had another bite of that birdie!' So Kate gave him another bite, and he sat up on his bed. Then he said again: 'Oh! If I but had a third bite of that birdie!' So Kate gave him a third bite, and he rose hale and strong, dressed himself, and sat down by the fire, and when the folk came in next morning they found Kate and the young prince cracking nuts together. Meanwhile his brother had seen Anne and fallen in love with her, as everybody did who saw her sweet pretty face. So the sick son married the well sister, and the well son married the sick sister, and they all lived happy and died happy, and never drank out of a dry cappy.

(Collected in Joseph Jacob's (1890) *English Fairy Tales*. London: The Bodley Head)

Chapter 4

Aspects of Narrative: Character, Setting and Themes

In this section we shall see that:

- characters are representations of the author's values and beliefs;
- the heroes and heroines of children's literature are most commonly children or child substitutes;.
- characters are introduced by a variety of means that reflect ways in which we become acquainted with people in real life;
- setting can operate as a background or be integral to the story;
- the theme of a story is the underlying idea or meaning.

Aspects of narrative fiction

Narrative fiction can be read in different ways depending on which elements of the narrative the reader focuses on.

ACTIVITY

- Write a brief synopsis of Frances Hodgson Burnett's The Secret Garden or another story that you know well.
- If you are working in a group or with a partner, exchange your synopses.
- Are there any similarities or differences in the way you have chosen to summarize the story?

Commentary

If you have compared your synopsis with someone else's you may have found that you focused on different aspects. Here are some possible ways in which you might have chosen to summarize the story:

- Emphasizing character: *The Secret Garden* is a story about an unattractive and stubborn little girl, Mary, who is sent to live with her guardian, the brusque and elusive Archibald Craven. Mr Craven entrusts her to the care of his strict housekeeper, Mrs Medlock. However, Mary is befriended by a kindly young housemaid, Martha. Later she develops a friendship with Martha's brother, Dickon, who teaches her about the wildlife of the moors. Mary also discovers that she has a cousin, the petulant and sickly Colin, who spends his days and nights cooped up in his bedroom. With the help of Dickon and the old gardener, Ben Weatherstaff, Mary and Colin are restored to health.
- Emphasizing setting: Mary is brought up in India where she is cared for by her Indian *ayah*. When her mother and father die from an outbreak of cholera, Mary is sent to live at her uncle's house on the wild Yorkshire Moors. Her new home, Misselthwaite Manor, is a forbidding house reminiscent of Thornfield Hall in

Jane Eyre. Strange cries can be heard echoing through the corridors at night. She later discovers that these cries emanate from her cousin's darkened bedroom. Mary spends most of her time in the open air in Misselthwaite's gardens,which contrast with the claustrophobic house. She discovers a key that will unlock the door of the secret garden. The garden is neglected and overgrown but when winter turns to spring new growth appears and Mary works hard to restore it to its former glory.

- Emphasizing theme: *The Secret Garden* charts Mary Lennox's growth from dependence to independence, from sickness to health. Frances Hodgson Burnett suggests that real magic is to be found in the natural world and that a healthy body is the key to a healthy mind.

Was your synopsis similar to one of the examples or did you focus on a different aspect of the story? Perhaps you included a combination of elements?

Stories are grown from interaction of constituent elements but we must remember that a story is always more than the sum of the individual parts. Helen Cresswell expresses it like this, 'A plot is just a mechanical thing, whereas a story is organic – it actually grows out of ideas or characters or a combination of ideas and characters. And stories have meaning. A story will resolve itself. Stories connect and people can tune into them' (in Carter, 1999: 118).

Character

To be honest, plots don't interest me nearly as much as people. When I stop to chew the pencil, it's rarely to wonder what the characters will do now, or where they'll go. Far more often it's what are they thinking? Or how are they feeling? (Anne Fine, in Carter, 2001: 104)

ACTIVITY

In literature we use the term character to mean a participant in a story (human or nonhuman).

Think back to your childhood reading and make a list of your favourite characters. Now choose one from your list. Which of these statements match the character's appeal to you? Tick all that apply:

- the character has admirable qualities;
- this character is like you;
- you have experienced some of the problems faced by this character;
- you wish you were like this character;
- you hold similar opinions and share the same values as this character;
- the character plays an exciting role in the story;
- the character is presented in an unusual way;
- the character is presented realistically with human strengths and failings;
- other (specify).

Share your observations and discuss similarities and differences in your responses to your chosen character.

Commentary

Sharon Creech's novel *Walk Two Moons* takes its title from a native North American saying, 'Never judge a man until you have walked two moons in his moccasins'. It is a lesson that Salamanca Hiddle, the main character has to learn. But the phrase is also a metaphor for the way in which literature enables readers to 'walk two moons' with a host of different characters. Michael Cadnum explains, 'No other art form can so fulfillingly portray what it is like to be someone else, to learn patience, to learn how hard we have to work to achieve maturity, to take an interest in things outside ourselves' (Cadnum, *Books for Keeps*, January 1999, p. 10).

From an early age children respond to characters in fiction, They act out stories in which they adopt roles from books, television or computer games. Publishers and toy manufacturers know that characters appeal to young readers and all manner of goods can be purchased, from Thomas the Tank Engine lunchboxes to Bob the Builder colouring books and Harry Potter pyjamas. Indeed, there is an entire industry devoted to the marketing of character goods. Characters encountered in childhood reading can have a lasting impact. Children's author Julia Jarman recalls reading *Little Women*, 'From the first line "Christmas won't be Christmas without presents" the characters were so real. I was Jo when I read *Little Women* and the sequels. I wanted to be just like her – a good person despite all my faults, and a writer who tells the truth' (from www.writeaway.org.uk). She is not alone in her response. Many female readers have talked about the impact Jo March had on their awareness of self; she was a role model of independence to which many aspired.

Children respond to the subtleties and inconsistencies of personality. Recently on a visit to a school, I overheard a child talking confidentially to a friend about their teacher who seemed unusually irritable. 'I don't think Mr Peters is a very happy person', he whispered. His tone suggested that he understood that behaviour can reflect feelings. Children are also able to discriminate aspects of personality. They undoubtedly prefer the company of some adults to others and they seem able to detect genuine behaviour – the adult who puts on a child-friendly show to curry favour is quickly identified as a fraud. Of course, children do not have perfect judgement; they do not have a vast range of experience to inform those judgements. In this respect literature serves an important role. Stories enhance children's understanding of complex human behaviour and enable them to experience vicariously a diverse range of characters and relationships.

Character functions in children's literature

What types of characters are present in children's literature and what functions do they serve? Northrop Frye (1957) identified certain types of characters that appear in children's stories:

- The *protagonist* is the central character (person, animal, or personified object) in the plot's conflict.
- The *antagonist* is the force in conflict with the protagonist. It may be society, nature, or fate, as well as another person. It can also be the protagonist's own self, if he or she has an internal conflict.
- A *character foil* is a character whose traits are in direct contrast to those of the principal character. The foil therefore highlights the traits of the protagonist. The foil is usually a minor character, although if there are two protagonists, they may be foils of each other. Character development is showing the multitude of traits and behaviours that give the literary character the complexity of a human being. The amount of character development affects the quality of the story.
- A *flat character* is not fully developed; we know only one side of the character.
- A *round character* is fully developed, with many traits – bad and good – shown in the story. We feel that we know the character so well that he or she has become a real person.
- Character development is a continuum with perfectly flat characters at one end and very round ones at the other. Every character lies somewhere on this continuum. Round characters are usually considered an indication of literary quality. However, characters in folktales are almost always flat, and flatness is appropriate for minor characters in modern literature for children. A character foil is often flat, even if the protagonist is round.
  The amount of change in a character over the course of the story also affects its quality:
- A *static character* is one who does not experience a basic character change during the course of the story.

- A *dynamic character* is one who experiences a basic change in character through the events of the story. This change is internal and may be sudden, but the events of the plot should make it seem inevitable.

There is also a continuum of character change in a story, with very static characters at one end, and very dynamic ones at the other. Every character lies somewhere on this continuum. Dynamism in the protagonist is usually considered an indication of quality, but many characters, especially in stories for younger children, have only the mild amount of change which can be expected from growing and maturing from day to day.

A character may thus be round and dynamic, round and static, or flat and static. A flat character cannot usually be dynamic, because you do not know enough about the flat character to notice a change. If a character *seems* flat and yet *seems* to change, it is usually because the characterization is not well written.

Representation of character

It is easy to assume that the characters we meet in books are a reflection of people in real life; they give the illusion of being so. A reader might identify with a character they recognize as being 'just like me'. And sometimes we talk about characters as though they were real people justifying why we like or do not like them. An extreme instance is when actors receive letters addressed to the characters they play as though they were real people. However, writing is not a neutral or objective activity and characters are not real people. They are representations constructed by writers to reflect their values and beliefs. When a writer's value system is congruent with our own, we will not recognize the construction, but when they hold markedly different values it is made visible. We cannot therefore judge character in terms of authenticity and accuracy but only in relation to the values that it represents and the social implications.

When a representation is overworked and formulaic it becomes a stereotype. It is problematic when a main character is two-dimensional. Cynthia Voigt argues that the writer has a responsibility to convey the complexities of character: 'Teaching taught me to recognise that everyone has his or her own life and they tend to try and do well by it, and to sit there and write them off is no way to see what is true' (in *Books for Keeps*, January 1991, p. 12). The role that a character plays in the story influences the extent to which they need to be fully realized. We expect a main character to be rounded whereas secondary and minor characters do not have to be as developed.

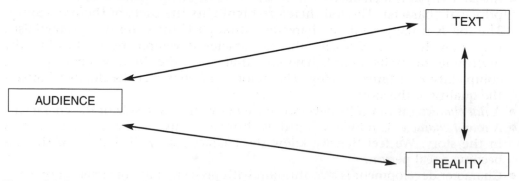

Figure 4.1 *Representation is a three-way relationship*

In order to evaluate character in children's fiction we should ask ourselves two questions. What does this representation mean to me? What will it mean to others? In the later half of the 20th century we became increasingly aware of representations that privileged some groups above others. For instance, before the publication of Eve Garnett's *The Family From One End Street* (1937), British children's literature favoured children from wealthy middle-class backgrounds Even those described as being 'poor' such as the family in E. Nesbit's *The Railway Children* were sufficiently 'comfortable' to employ a woman to help in the kitchen. Garnett was moved to write her story after a commission to illustrate a book called *The London Child* brought her into contact with London's working class. However, in spite of her good intentions, rereading *The Family From One End Street* today we can detect a patronizing authorial tone towards the Ruggles family:

> In spite of a wife and seven children (not to speak of Ideas) Mr Ruggles was a very contented sort of man. When the wind was in the East and blew bits of dirt from his dustbins and cart into his eyes and mouth he spat and swore a bit, but it was soon over. So long as he had his job and his family were well and happy, and he could smoke his pipe and work in his garden, see his Working Men's Club once or twice a week, dream about his pig, and have a good Blow Out on Bank Holidays, he wanted nothing more. (*The Family From One End Street* by Eve Garnett)

Because the values of the dominant culture in society have shifted we are able to view this book with a different gaze.

Lynn Reid Banks explains how she has developed a new awareness of her earlier writing: 'When I look at the books I wrote years ago I find stereotypical aspects I never intended. I myself seem to have been a victim of my upbringing and *My Darling Villain* may not have fully solved the problem of finding instantly recognizable signals without stereotyping' (Lynne Reid Banks, in *Books for Keeps*, March 1991, p. 13).

The term that we use to talk about the writer's system of values and beliefs is *ideology*. Peter Hollindale (1988) explains that in literature it operates at three levels:

- Explicit: when the writer wants to recommend and promote their social, moral and political beliefs to the reader. This is an intended surface ideology. Such views can be expressed didactically or can be more subtly conveyed by a skilled writer.
- Implicit: the writer's unexamined assumptions. Very often these values will be taken for granted, particularly if they are widely shared values.
- Dominant culture: all writers operate within a culture at a given point in time and place, and as such their books are products of the world in which they live.

Books express what Hollindale terms the 'commonalities of an age'. He asserts that, 'Our priority in the world of children's books should not be to promote ideology but to understand it, and find ways of helping others to understand it, including the children themselves' (1988: 10). He identifies questions that assist the reader in exposing the ideological content of a book. The following make specific reference to character:

- Are desirable values associated with niceness of character? What for instance constitutes a 'good' child? Are nice manners, good looks, and obedience desirable hallmarks or does the author celebrate imagination, independence and free spirit?
- Are undesirable values associated with unpleasant character? A criticism levelled at Roald Dahl, and more recently J.K. Rowling, is that a character's worth is associated with their physical attributes. Augustus Gloop and Dudley Dursley are presented as being inherently unpleasant and their fatness is inextricably bound up with personality.
- Is any character shown performing a mixture of roles? In Anthony's Browne's *Piggybook* Mrs Piggot breaks from the stereotyped pigeon-hole she has been placed in by her husband and sons. The last page shows a smiling Mrs Piggot working on the engine of the family car.
- Does any character belong as an accepted member of more than one sub-culture or group? For example, do child characters mix with both adults and other children or are the two always presented as separate and alien groups.
- Who are the people who do not exist in story? Are some groups downgraded? Which characters are not named? In 19th-century children's fiction the servants

with whom children would have had a great deal of contact are frequently downgraded or invisible, while in contemporary fiction it is interesting to look at the way in which adults, specifically parents and teachers, are depicted. And we should remain vigilant to the presentation or absence of minority groups. For example, what images of the disabled are present in children's fiction?

Child characters in children's literature

Are there any character types that recur frequently in literature for children? If we accept that there is a body of work that can be called children's literature then we must agree that it relates first and foremost to the interests of children. It is not surprising therefore that the protagonist is usually a child (or substitute child).

A common concern of children's fiction is growth of a child character into maturity or significant steps taken towards independence. Such change brought about during the duration of the story is called character development (see *Bildungsroman* (p. 66) in Chapter 3).

Different constructions of childhood are evident in the portrayal of child characters. It is widely acknowledged in contemporary studies that childhood is not a natural phenomenon related to stages of intellectual development or physical growth (Aries, 1973; Jenks, 1996; James and Prout, 1997). On the contrary it is largely accepted that childhood has been perceived differently throughout history and within cultural contexts. It is a dynamic social construct. At one end of the spectrum is the puritanical belief that children are born sinful with a natural propensity for evil, a prevailing view in 17th-century England. Corporal punishment was advocated as a means of teaching children right from wrong and helping them to live obedient and pious lives. The view is exemplified in the following verse:

> But if that in idleness you do delight,
> Refusing these lessons here plainly in sight;
> Look then for no kindness, no favour, nor love,
> But your master's displeasure, if thus him you move.
>
> Therefore be wary you do not offend
> Your parents, your master, nor injure your friend;
> Lest stripes do reward you, and make you to say,
> 'Your precepts I'll follow, your words I'll obey.' (from *A School Master's Admonition*, c. 1625, anonymous)

At the other end of the scale is the concept of a romantic or ideal childhood that espouses the child's natural goodness. In Romanticism it is society that has a polluting influence on the innocent child. The idea of the Romantic child has proved to be persistent and is still perhaps the most widely promulgated image of childhood presented through the media.

One of the problems, however, is that when children fail to match the expectations that are generated by this construction they are deemed to be acting in an unnatural manner. An extreme and tragic example of this was the public reaction to the James Bulger murder and trial, and in particular to the two boys responsible for his death. One of the ways in which their actions were rationalized was through the assertion that children who kill are anomalies who do not conform to the intellectual, social or moral development associated with normal children.

It is supposed to be the age of innocence, so how could these 10-year-olds turn into 'killers' (*Sunday Times*, 28 November 1993), 'evil freaks' (*Sunday Times*, 28 November 1993), 'the Satan Bug inside' (*Sunday Times*, 28 November 1993), 'the spawn of Satan' (*Guardian*, 27 November 1993), 'little devils' (*Sunday Times*, 28 November 1993) (all cited in Jenks, 1996)? In this way they come to be regarded as non-children thus allowing society to reaffirm its belief in ideal childhood.

Following the conviction of Robert Thompson and John Venables, Anne Fine was compelled to write *The Tulip Touch* in an endeavour to explore some of the issues arising from the case. The story opens with Natalie's family moving into their new home, a large country hotel. She befriends Tulip, an odd child who is shunned by the other children. But Natalie finds her strange behaviour exciting. Together they play bizarre, intimidating games, which become wilder and more sinister until Natalie realizes the implications of their delinquent behaviour. She abandons Tulip and the consequences are devastating. Fine rejects the view that a child is born with a propensity for evil: 'No one is born evil. No one', it says on the cover of *The Tulip Touch*.

Fine constructs Tulip's character so that the reader empathizes with her. She is capable of kindness particularly towards Natalie's younger brother and there are glimpses of appealing child-like behaviour:

> Tulip loved Christmas at the Palace …
> … 'And will there be some of those great long pink fishes on a dish?'
> 'Salmon, Tulip. Yes, there'll be salmon.'
> 'And wine jellies, like last year?'
> 'Yes, Wine Jellies.'
> 'And can I turn on the blinking lights?'
> Dad grinned.
> 'Yes, Tulip. You can turn on the blinking lights.'
> We all indulged her at Christmas. It was, my father said wryly, the only one time Tulip ever acted her age. Her eyes kept widening. Her mouth kept falling open. And once, like Julius, she was even found scrabbling under the tree, shaking all the empty wrapped boxes, just to be sure that what she'd been told was true, and they were really only there for show.

Here Fine makes ironic use of 'acted her age', a phrase that is usually used to admonish children for displaying behaviour associated with younger children. Signs of goodness are evident and this implies that there is always the possibility of redemption. Furthermore, Fine is interested in exploring causality. She implies that Tulip's violent father and her weak, battered mother are responsible for her deviant behaviour and that her violent graphic forms of expression are simply par-rotings of the verbal abuse that she has received.

The Tulip Touch is also about Natalie's developing moral judgement. Part One describes the early days of friendship. Natalie recalls some happy memories but in this part there is a darker note as the section ends with Natalie playing a sub-servient role to Tulip. It is suggested that Tulip has a fatal charismatic appeal which, in spite of herself, Natalie is unable to reject. Although Natalie's teacher attempts to prevent her from becoming too closely involved, 'I warn you, you'll come to no good as Tulip's hold-your-coat merchant', we observe that by the end of the chapter Natalie is left literally holding Tulip's coat. Part Two deals with the escalation of seriousness in games. It concludes with a climactic arson attack and Natalie's epiphany:

> The first few drops pattered through the whispering fronds. The dripping turned into trickles, but I didn't move. Let her call. Let her search for me.
> Let her give up and go home.
> A soft bead of rain ran over my forehead and in my ear, and I recalled Miss Golightly, years before, explaining a picture in Assembly.
> 'He's pouring the water over the baby's head to put her on the side of light.'
> Tulip crashed nearer, but my heart stayed steady.
> 'Go away,' I willed her silently, playing *The Tulip Touch* backwards for the very first time. 'Turn around. Go away. I don't want you anywhere near me.'
> Not fire. Light.
> She called a few more times, ever more hopelessly.
> And then she left. (*The Tulip Touch* by Anne Fine)

The writing resonates with religious significance as Natalie gazes into a fire she has started:

Everything about it was dark and furious, and every inch of it seemed to suck you in and swirl you round making you feel dizzy and anxious. And everywhere you looked, your eyes were drawn back, over and over to the centre, where, out of the blackness, two huge forlorn eyes stared out as usual, half-begging, half-accusing.

The fire symbolizes Natalie's choice: self-destruction or rebirth. She moves away from the darkness and chooses light, undergoing a moral baptism.

In the final part the novel focuses on Natalie's recovery and her rejection of Tulip. The consequences of that rejection are extreme and Natalie is left to confront her own part in Tulip's fall.

Age is an important factor; crucially Natalie is older at this point in the novel than the boys convicted of the murder of James Bulger and is only just beginning to develop the moral conviction to make choices based on her own judgements rather than the moral imperatives of others.

Fine's belief as expressed in this novel is that children have the capacity for good and evil but it is adults who set the example. Moral responsibility and conviction develop after a child can cite the difference between right and wrong. *The Tulip Touch* questions the view that redemption and reconciliation are neither possible nor desirable. This is underlined by Natalie's comment, 'And people aren't locked doors. You can get through to them if you want.'

ACTIVITY

Select two contrasting children's books and make notes on the different constructions of childhood that they present. Suggested titles:

A.A. Milne, *Winnie-the-Pooh* (Pooh Bear and Christopher Robin).
David Almond, *Clay* (Davie).
Lauren Child, *Clarice Bean, That's Me!* (Clarice Bean).
Beatrix Potter, *The Tale of Peter Rabbit* (Peter Rabbit).
Maurice Sendak, *Where the Wild Things Are* (Max).
Morris Gleitzman, *Bumface* (Angus Solomon).
Frank Cottrell Boyce, *Millions* (Damien).
Adam Guillain, *Bella Balistica and the Temple of Tikal* (Bella).
Philip Pullman, *Northern Lights* (Lyra).
Jacqueline Wilson, *The Story of Tracy Beaker* (Tracy Beaker).
Roald Dahl, *Charlie and the Chocolate Factory* (Charlie, Violet, Mike, Augustus, Veruca).
Cynthia Voigt, *Homecoming* (Dicey).
Frances Hodgson Burnett, *Little Lord Fauntleroy* (Cedric).
Lewis Carroll, *Alice in Wonderland* (Alice).
David McKee, *Not Now, Bernard* (Bernard).
Carl Hiassen, *Hoot* (Roy).

Adult characters in children's literature

It is revealing to consider the way adults are presented in contemporary literature for children and to compare this to literature of bygone times. Roald Dahl is noted for his unfavourable portrayal of adult female characters. These villainesses are often shown as subjecting children to abuse as Aunt Sponge and Aunt Spiker do in *James and the Giant Peach*; while in *The Witches*, Grand High Witch's sole purpose is to annihilate the children of Inkland.

While adults may once have been shown to be a source of moral authority, today they are often depicted as morally or emotionally weak, sometimes even dependent on their stronger children as in *The Illustrated Mum* by Jacqueline Wilson or

Bumface by Morris Gleitzman. They may be well-meaning but absorbed by their own problems leaving their children to rely on their own resources to overcome problems such as bullying, bereavement, homelessness and drug addiction. Adults may be noted by their absence, a frequent pragmatic choice allowing child characters to act with greater freedom and autonomy. A survey of the representation of particular groups of adults such as teachers, parents and grandparents is another interesting area for reflection.

Animals and toys in children's fiction

Animals, which rarely appear in adult literature with a few notable exceptions such as Richard Adams's *Watership Down* and some that verge on animal biography such as Henry Williamson's *Tarka the Otter*, have played a significant role in children's fiction.

The animal story has a long tradition that dates back to folk tales and the animal fables of Aesop and the Pantachantra. Early examples of animal stories in children's literature include Anna Sewell's *Black Beauty* (1877) which was subtitled 'The Autobiography of a Horse' and written for the didactic purpose to 'induce kindness, sympathy and an understanding treatment of horses'. Black Beauty is a well-bred horse who suffers a series of misfortunes enduring life as a London cab horse before he is rescued and spends his later years in comfort. The success of Sewell's book must in part be attributed to the way in which it elicits a compassionate response. The currently popular *Animal Ark* series is based on a similar principle.

The source of appeal in Rudyard Kipling's *The Jungle Book* (1894), Kenneth Grahame's *The Wind in the Willows* (1908) and Brian Jacques's *Redwall* (2006), is quite different. In these anthropomorphic stories the animals clearly represent facets of human personality and nature. For example in *The Jungle Book* a young boy, Mowgli, is found abandoned in the jungle by a pack of wolves who raise him as one of their own. Mowgli develops friendships with the jungle animals, Baloo the bear and Bagheera the black panther. John Rowe Townsend (1990: 99) writes, 'The world of the jungle is in fact both itself and our own world as well: the human jungle. The law of the jungle ... appears really to indicate how men must fend for themselves in a dangerous world: how they must hunt together and must be bold, but bold in obedience to their leaders'.

In the mid-20th century it became popular to write realistically about animals. Books from this period include Marjorie Kinan Rawlings's *The Yearling* (1938) and Felix Salten's *Bambi* (1926). The realisitic story had its antecedent in American writer Jack London's adventures *Call of the Wild* and *White Fang*. Sheila Burnford's *The Incredible Journey* (1961) is a realistic animal adventure about three pets that make a perilous journey across Canada to become reunited with their owners. Although the animals are clearly characters in the story, the objective point of view describes their observable behaviour. Burnford never ventures into ascribing thoughts or feelings to them.

Anthropomorphism can also be found in the nursery. In 1995 Disney released the computer-animated feature-length film, *Toy Story*, in which a young boy's toys come to life. A well-loved wooden cowboy is in danger of being superseded in the boy's affections by the current toy craze 'Buzz Lightyear'. Ultimately the toys learn that their owner has enough affection for both of them. *Toy Story* is also part of a long tradition in children's literature and media. In Jane Hissey's picture book stories about Old Bear and his friends the toys are an extended family, with Old Bear and Branwell Brown adopting a parental role and Little Bear the role of youngest child. In perhaps the best loved toy story of all time, A.A. Milne's *Winnie-the-Pooh*, some of the toys belong to the realm of childhood – Pooh, Piglet, Tigger – and others belong to the realm of adulthood such as Kanga and Rabbit, while Christopher Robin, the real child in the story, is an omnipotent being in the context of the storybook world.

ACTIVITY

Survey the range of animal stories available in the school or public library.
    Decide which of these headings describes each book (possibly more than one).

- Realistic animal story;
- Animal biography;
- Animal autobiography;
- Anthropomorphic – animals as parents and children;
- Anthropomorphic – animals as childish adults;
- Allegory;
- Animals as major supporting characters;
- Animals as archetypes;
- Animal fantasy;
- Other (write your own categories as necessary).

Consider the different ways in which animal stories might appeal to young readers.

ACTIVITY

Read and review some animal stories for your journal:
Selected Titles
Adams, R. (1973) *Watership Down*. London: Puffin.
Alborough, J. (2000) *Duck in a Truck*. London: Collins.
Atkinson, E. (2000) *Greyfriars Bobby*. London: Random House.
Avi (2002) *Poppy*. London: Simon & Schuster.
Bond, M. (2006) *The Tales of Olga da Polga*. Oxford: Oxford University Press.
Burnford, S. (2004) *The Incredible Journey*. London: Puffin.
Butterworth, N. (2005) *The Whisperer*. London: Collins.
Clement-Davies, D. (2002) *The Sight*. London: Macmillan.
Deacon, A. (2003) *Slow Loris*. London: Random House.
DeCamillo, K. (2003) *The Tale of Desperaux*. London: Walker.
DeCamillo, K. (2006) *The Miraculous Journey of Edward Tulane*. London: Walker.
Fine, A. (1996)*The Diary of a Killer Cat*. London: Puffin.
Fine, A. (2004) *The Return of the Killer Cat*. London: Puffin.
Grahame, K. (2000) *The Wind in the Willows*. London: Walker Books.
King-Smith, D. (2003a) *The Hodgeheg*. London: Puffin.
King Smith, D. (2003b) *The Sheep-pig*. London: Puffin.
Kipling, R. (2004) *Just So Stories*. London: Walker Books.
London, J. (1994) *The Call of the Wild*. London: Puffin.
McCall Smith, A. (2005) *Akimbo and the Elephants*. London: Egmont.
Milen, A.A. (1973) *Winnie the Pooh*. London: Heinemann.
Oppel, K. (2000) *Sunwing*. London: Hodder.
Philbrick, R. (2005) *The Fire Pony*. London: Usborne.
Potter, B. (2002a) *The Tale of Peter Rabbit*. London: Frederick Warne.
Potter, B. (2002b) *The Tale of Tom Kitten*. London: Frederick Warne.
Said, S.F.(2004) *Varjak Paw*. London: Random House.
Said, S.F. (2005) *The Outlaw Varjak Paw*. London: Random House
Salten, F. (2004) *Bambi*. London: Simon & Schuster
Sewell, A. (2005) *Black Beauty*. London: Usborne
St John, L. (2006) *The White Giraffe*. London: Orion
Strong, J. (1998) *The 100 Mile-an-hour Dog*. London: Puffin
Tomlinson, H. (2004) *The Owl Who Was Afraid of the Dark*. London: Egmont
Waddell, M. and Benson, P. (1994) *Owl Babies*. London: Walker
Waddell, M. and Oxenbury, H. (2002) *Farmer Duck*. London: Walker
White, E.B. (2003) *Charlotte's Web*. London: Puffin
Williamson, H. (1995) *Tarka the Otter*. London: Puffin

Building character

In life we come to know people in different ways. Judgements are made on the basis of accent and dialect, appearance, behaviour, what a person says and the opinions of others. We use evidence that is both valid and invalid. Characters in literature are developed in similar ways so that we get to know them for example through:

- names;
- description, appearance;
- action;
- thought and speech;
- placement in a specific setting;
- style, language, vocabulary choice;
- assessment and comment made by other characters;
- the author's personal assessment and comment.

What is in a name?

'But names are important!' the nursemaid protested.

'Yes,' said Quillam Mye. 'So is accuracy.'

'What's half an hour though? No one will know she wasn't born unti after sunset. Just think, born on the day of Goodman Boniface, a child of the Sun. You could call her Aurora, or Solina, or Beambath. Lots of lovely names for a daughter of the Sun.'

'That is true, but irrelevant. After dusk, that calendar day is sacred to Goodman Palpittle, He Who Keeps Flies Out of Jams and Butterchurns.' Quillam Mye looked up from his desk and met the nursemaid's gaze. 'My child is a bluebottle,' he said firmly.

The nursemaid's name was Celery Dunnock. She was born on the day sacred to Cramflick, She Who Keeps the Vegetables of the Garden Crisp. Celery had every reason to feel strongly on the matter of names. Her eyes were pale, soft and moist, like skinned grapes, but at the moment they were stubborn, resolute grapes.

Quillam Mye had a meticulous brain. His thoughts were laid out like the strands of a feather, and a single frond out of place felt like a tear in his mind. His eyes were dark and vague like smoked glass.

The twin grapes looked into the smoked glass and saw a mind full of nothing they could understand.

'Call it Mosca and have done with it,' Mye said. Mosca was rather an old-fashioned name for a fly-born but better than Buzzeltrice or Caddis. He returned his attention to the task of writing his treatise. It was a history of he times in which he, and now his infant daughter, lived. It was entitled 'The Shattered Realm: A Full and Clear Account of Our Kingdom of Rags and Tatters'. (*Fly by Night* by Frances Hardinge)

Unlike Quillam Mye in Frances Hardinge's award-winning *Fly by Night* (2006) parents usually exercise great care over the choice of a name, sometimes taking months of discussion and research before finally deciding on a name that is perfect for their baby. In fiction, naming characters requires similar care and attention. David Lodge (1993: 37) writes, 'In a novel names are never neutral. They always signify, if it is only ordinariness'. For fantasy writer Stephen Elboz finding the right name is an important part of realizing the character: 'An actress friend of mine says she knows she has found the character when she has the right pair of shoes; for me it's the name. When I have found the right name the character starts to come alive. I do lots of work on finding the name; I look through all the baby books of names!' (from www.writeaway.org.uk). Val Tyler talks about how the process of finding the right name works for her and the images that come ready attached to names: 'The name Sheldon Croe just popped into my head and with it an image of an angular adolescence with elbows that stuck out and big feet and piggy eyes, which I had to call beady eyes. I didn't want to write Crow with a "w" because I didn't want to say this is a bird, but I wanted it to have that feel without making it obvious, but he was a bit of a "rook" or a "crow"'. (www.writeaway.org.uk).

> Jot down a few ideas about the images conjured by these names. Which do you think are the villains?
>
> Draco Malfoy
> Constance
> Thomas Oakley
> William Beech
> Cluny the Scourge
> Blackhead
> Serafina Pekkala
> Plato Jones

Commentary

It is likely that you were able to decide without much difficulty which of the names listed belong to villainous characters (Blackhead, Draco Malfoy and Cluny the Scourge). Blackhead, a term in common usage describes an unpleasant facial blemish. It is the name given to an unsightly and greedy character in Stephen Elboz's *The House of Rats*. Draco Malfoy is Harry Potter's well-known adversary at Hogwarts. The name makes allusion to Draco the Athenian lawyer whose punitive laws give us the term 'draconian'. It is also comes from the Latin for dragon or serpent which is an apposite symbol for Slytherin House. The surname Malfoy is derived from the same root as malevolence (a desire to do harm) and malfeasance (a wrong doing). Cluny the Scourge is a dark-hearted pirate rat in Brian Jacques's *Redwall*. Full of evil intent he threatens to disrupt the peace of Redwall Abbey. A scourge is a whip used to inflict pain and refers directly to Cluny's whip-like tail, his most powerful weapon. Perhaps he also owes something to the Cluny of R.L. Stevenson's *Kidnapped*, another unsavoury character. Even if you did not recognize the literary allusions of these names you probably responded to the harsh sounds which clearly mark them as the bad guys.

Constance and Serafina Pekkala have more pleasant associations. Constance is the steadfast badger warrior in *Redwall*. She is, as her name suggests, reliable and dependable. Serafina is a witch in Philip Pullman's *Northern Lights*, one of Lyra's allies. Her name is derived from the Hebrew, Seraphim, the highest of the nine orders of celestial being.

The name Plato Jones suggests both the ordinary and extraordinary, Jones being a commonly occurring Welsh surname but unusually coupled here with the Greek name Plato which carries connotations of wisdom and learning. In fact, this perfectly sums up the character who appears in Nina Bawden's *The Real Plato Jones* and *The Outside Child* who, being half Greek and half Welsh, thinks that he belongs nowhere until he comes to accept that his dual cultural heritage is a blessing rather than disadvantage.

William Beech and Thomas Oakley are the main characters in Michelle Magorian's *Goodnight, Mister Tom*. Thomas is an ordinary name can be abbreviated to Tom; generally mono-syllabic names sound strong. It is not coincidental that the surnames of these characters are associated with trees. Oak trees grow strong and solid and live to an old age. Beech trees have a more flexible and malleable wood. Thus the names suit the old loner and the young abused boy who is evacuated and given over to his care.

Character through action, thought and dialogue

Characters are introduced and developed through a range of techniques and conventions. What do we learn about Pearl in the following extract from the opening of Morris Gleitzman's *Water Wings*?

'What I need,' said Pearl, as she started to slide off the roof, 'is a grandmother.'

There weren't any around so Pearl grabbed hold of the TV aerial instead.

Then a thought hit her.

She looked anxiously down at the driveway.

If she fell, she didn't want to fall on Winston.

He was the kindest, bravest guinea pig in the whole world, but if he tried to catch her he'd also be the flattest.

Pearl could see him directly below, a fluffy black and white blob, peering up at her, nose twitching with concern.

'Winston,' she called, 'shift over there next to the herb tub.'

Winston didn't move.

He gave her a few encouraging squeaks.

Pearl braced her feet against the tin roof, gripped the aerial as hard as she could and leant over the guttering so Winston could see her pointing at the clump of basil.

A gust of wind nearly blew her off.

'Winston,' she yelled, 'it's not safe. Move.'

Winston moved.

Pearl is involved in action that strikes us as dangerous – that a young girl should be on the roof of the house is extremely risky. But the situation is also funny; Pearl wants a grandmother but the nearest available object is a television aerial. So from the first two lines we might detect that Pearl is lively and has a sense of humour. Gillian Cross explains that the situation in which an author places the character is really important: 'I don't think of plot and character as separate. My characters express their personalities through the plot, the things that they do. I like to put them in extreme situations which highlight the moral choices they have to make. I think moral choices are important and I think children share that view' (Cross, in Carter, 1999: 105).

Although written in the third person, this scene is focalized from Pearl's perspective so we are getting to know the character from the inside. We wonder why 'a grandmother' seems to be the answer to the predicament in which she finds herself. Is she an orphan or very lonely? This could be further emphasized by her projection of human characteristics onto her pet guinea pig and his apparent importance in her life. In this instance Pearl's character is being built up from insight into her thoughts.

In addition to revealing their thoughts a character can be developed through very careful selection of what they say and how they say it. For Graham Marks writing dialogue is central to his character-led stories: 'Dialogue is really important to me because our lives are driven by conversation, it makes things happen in the real world. The trick is to listen to people talking and to find your own way of transcribing what you hear' (from www.writeaway.org.uk).

Megan McDonald expresses a view held by many writers when she talks about getting the dialogue 'right': 'Dialogue is probably the most important thing to me. It really puts me off when I read a book and the kids sound as though they are adults – that's the adult writer coming through … When I'm in a restaurant or riding a bus I'm quiet myself but listen to what people say and how they say it. To me the most important thing is hearing the character's voice in my head' (from www.writeaway.org.uk).

It has been suggested that young readers like books that contain dialogue as this assists the reading process for them. In fact, the degree of textual difficulty can be influenced by the way in which speech and thought are presented. Basically there are four forms of presentation:

- Direct speech/thought shows the reader what has been said or thought, for example 'I have to go'. The actual words that are spoken are placed within quotation marks.
- Indirect speech/thought tells the reader what has been said or thought, for example. She said she would have to go, or He thought it was time to leave the party. In this case speech and thought are embedded in the narration and no quotation marks are used.

- Tagged speech or thought is presented with a tag or attribute, for example she said, he thought, they argued noisily.
- Free speech or thought does not possess a tag.

The level of control that an author has over the reader's response is partly reflected in the way in which speech and thought are presented. The greatest control is exercised by using indirect-tagged speech: 'She whispered quietly to the prince that she would have to go', which gives the reader a lot of information and consequently places limits on interpretation. Direct free speech (e.g. 'I have to go') provides the least information so the reader has to work harder at interpretation. In order to work out how this is said and to whom, the reader has to use the surrounding context. The more that character is built up through action the less necessary it becomes for a writer to add a lot of attribution to the dialogue. Usually speech is presented in direct-tagged mode, while thought is presented in indirect-tagged mode. To present thought directly is the most artificial, as one person cannot know precisely what another is thinking.

Commentary

In the first extract we are given some important information about Minty. We know that she has a gift for seeing things in the spirit world, and a strength of character is implied because she accepts this as normal. We also learn that her father has died. We have some indication of the way Minty is feeling: 'The weekends, once *oases*, were now *deserts*'. The image used is a reflection of her state of mind. The dialogue between Minty and her mother serves to illuminate their relationship. The untagged direct comment 'Post me off like a parcel?' is ambiguous. Is Minty entering into jocular banter with her mother, do they seem to have a close relationship? Or does it mask deeper feelings; now that her father is no longer around does she need more than ever to be close to her mother? In fact both these explanations can exist alongside each other as the untagged direct speech allows for interpretative freedom. Minty's name may also give us more information about the character. It is unusual and has an old-fashioned quality, Minty suggesting freshness and mint canes being an old-fashioned sweet. It sounds informal and friendly. We later we learn that Minty is an abbreviated version of Araminta.

The second extract is more visual than the first one; we are given more information about physical appearance. Lexical clues such as 'hangman's rope' and 'brain-fever' indicate that this is from a period story. We learn that Smith is very dirty, as even the infectious diseases are afraid of catching something from him. He is a 'sooty spirit', very black dirt associated with chimney places which makes him blend into the sooty surroundings of London. Accompanying the grime is an unpleasant odour, 'a powerful whiff'. Speed is a quality that is emphasized several times. Smith obviously has a good survival instinct. The hangman's rope is not quick enough to catch him and he is described as having 'a turn of speed that was remarkable, and a neatness in nipping down an alley or vanishing in a court that had to be seen to be believed'. The simile 'A rat was like a snail beside Smith' is another indicator of Smith's speed as well as likening him to the grimy sewer rats, creatures that have the ability to disappear inside small nooks and crevices. We only learn his surname, which is indicative of his social status, he has no titles and no childish pet name. He is to be treated like an adult in a harsh and cruel world.

In the final extract we have one character's appraisal of another. While ostensibly we are finding out about Plato, we are at the same time picking up important clues about the speaker, Jane. Plato is not physically strong or imposing but he is good with words as we are told in the opening sentence he has invented his own label, 'outside child', to describe himself and Jane. His idiosyncratic knowledge extends beyond that of most 12-year-old boys (knowledge of old Bisto advertisements) which is described in romanticized terms. Jane is honest, she confides to the reader that she is sometimes embarrassed to be seen with Plato, but she clearly respects him, at the same time repeating the things he has told her, 'That is what Plato Jones calls me', 'He says we are both like the Bisto Kids ...'.

Read the following character introductions reproduced below:
What impressions have already begun to form about these characters?
What techniques have these authors used to convey character?
Consider which of the following are evident in these extracts:

- names;
- description, appearance;
- action;
- thought and speech;
- placement in a specific setting;
- style, language, vocabulary choice;
- assessment and comment made by other characters;
- the author's personal assessment and comment.

Even before she came to Belton, Minty Cane had known that she was a witch, or something very like it. She had known since she was tiny, for instance, about the cold pocket of cold air on the landing stairs. (Though she could not have known that a man had hanged himself there.) She knew, too, that she shared her bedroom. She had woken at night to see shadowy presences gliding across the floor. She had never spoken to them, merely watched, sensing that they were on some silent business of their own. At other times she had seen blurred faces hovering over her, and pale hands floating like blossoms in the dark. There had been invisible footsteps, breathings.

She did not talk about these things for the simple reason that they did not strike her as remarkable. Their appearance was as commonplace to her as that of the milkman. The only difference was that the milkman did not cause her spine to prickle. During the past year Minty had occasionally heard her father's voice and that she knew was remarkable, because he was dead.

Now she and her mother were living in a different, smaller house, and her mother was working full-time at the hospital. Minty came home from school and found the house empty. The weekends, once oases, were now deserts.

'And when it comes to the summer holidays, we shall have to do something about you,' her mother said.

'What?' demanded Minty. 'Post me off somewhere, like a parcel?'

'That's an idea,' said Kate. 'Registered, of course.'

'Wonder what it'd cost,' Minty said. 'What stamp you'd have to put on me? And where would you stick it? On my forehead?'
(*Moondial* by Helen Cresswell)

He was called Smith and was twelve years old. Which, in itself, was a marvel; for it seemed as if the smallpox, the consumption, brain-fever and even the hangman's rope had given him a wide berth for fear of catching something. Or else they weren't quick enough. Smith had a turn of speed that was remarkable, and a neatness in nipping down an alley or vanishing in a court that had to be seen to be believed. Not that it was often seen, for Smith was a rather sooty spirit of the violent and ramshackle Town, and inhabited the tumble-down mazes about fat St Paul's like the subtle air itself. A rat was like a snail beside Smith, and the most his victims ever got of him was the powerful whiff of his passing and a cold draught in their dextrously emptied pockets. (*Smith* by Leon Garfield)

I am an outside child. That is what Plato Jones calls me.

Plato is my best friend in the world, even though I am a bit ashamed to be seen with him sometimes. He is a year younger than I am, only twelve, and small and thin for his age. He wears braces on his teeth that make him spit when he talks, and huge goggly glasses, and he can't run or play games because of his asthma. He says, 'Only another outside child would put up with me.' He says we are both like the Bisto Kids – raggedy kids in an old advertisement, standing out in the cold and peering in through a window at a warm kitchen where someone's mother is cooking. (*The Outside Child* by Nina Bawden)

ACTIVITY

> Make a detailed study of a main character from a book you are currently reading or have recently read.
>   Consider:
>
> - the techniques the author applies in developing the character;
> - the extent to which the character changes or develops;
> - the relationship of character to the overall message or theme of the book;
> - the values that the character represents.
>
> Investigate whether children have favourite characters from their reading. In what ways do these characters appeal (e.g. identification, empathy, entertainment etc.)?

Setting

Commentary

The setting is the time and place in which the action occurs. In some stories the setting is incidental, simply providing a backdrop for the action. For example, in *Rosie's Babies*, a picture book by Penny Dale, Rosie comes to terms with the arrival of a new baby aided by imaginative play with her toys and a supportive mother. The illustrations set the story in a pastoral idyll: Rosie plays in the orchard. But the story is not dependent upon place; it would be essentially the same story if it had been set in an urban tower block, or suburban terrace. This is not, however, to say that the setting is insignificant. While it does not alter the story, it certainly affects the mood and, depending on the reader's orientation, will elicit different responses. I have worked with students who have extolled the virtues of the natural, relaxed setting and others who have rejected it as unrealistic and irrelevant to most of the children in their classes.

Stories that are primarily concerned with a character's thoughts and feelings – an inner landscape – are not dependent on setting. However, we often find that locations are used to provide clues to a character's mood or as a means of externalizing inner turmoil. In *The Baby Who Wouldn't Go to Bed* by Helen Cooper, a weary mother tries to put her lively baby to bed. He drives around in his little car while the mother insists that it is time for bed. The baby's response is an emphatic 'No!' Surreal over-sized images of his soft toys and the paraphernalia of bedtime dominate the scene, emphasizing the battle of wills between the mother and her toddler.

In other stories the setting is integral; if you change it you have a fundamentally different story. Fantasy writer Stephen Elboz explains the importance of place in his work,

> When I was young I wanted to be an architect and I liked looking at books about buildings. I do like a building to become a character in my stories. In *The Byzantium Bazaar*, the old department store is like a character and in the 'Magic' books it is London takes on the role of a character. I have a strong sense of the visual and think about the book in terms of the pictures that are created. I'm also very aware of the atmosphere of places especially old houses and the things they suggest to me. (from www.writeaway.org.uk)

An example of a novel that has a setting as character is Louis Sachar's *Holes*. Set in the scorching desert, the realization of location creates a physical intensity. One of the sources of conflict in this story sets humans against the environment. *Holes* is, at one level, a story of survival against the odds:

> There is no lake at Camp Green Lake. There once was a very large lake here, the largest lake in Texas. That was over a hundred years ago. Now it is just a dry, flat wasteland.
>
>   There used to be a town of Green Lake as well. The town shrivelled and dried up along with the lake, and the people who lived there.

Books in which the story is contingent upon setting may incorporate the place name in the title:

Anne Fine, *The Road of Bones*
Helen Dunmore, *Ingo*
Anita Desai, *The Village by the Sea*
Jeanette Winterson, *Tanglewreck*
Michael Morpurgo, *Kensuke's Kingdom*
Robert Louis Stevenson, *Treasure Island*
Lewis Carroll, *Alice's Adventures in Wonderland*
Elizabeth Laird, *A Little Piece of Ground*
Frances Hodgson Burnett, *The Secret Garden*
Philippa Pearce, *Tom's Midnight Garden*
Kenneth Grahame, *The Wind in the Willows*
Marcus Sedgwick, *Floodland*
Richard Adams, *Watership Down*
Clive King, *Stig of the Dump*.

Can you think of any other children's books that have the name of the setting in the title? How does the title reflect the themes of the book?

Carefully realized settings can develop a reader's belief in the story through the inclusion of details that provide clues to place or period. In historical fiction, for instance, the setting might add authentic detail or at least the illusion of authenticity (see Chapter 4). Similarly, high fantasy is dependent on the believable creation of a secondary world and science fiction requires successfully realized futuristic settings (see Chapters 6 and 7). But setting is not always used realistically; it can also operate at a symbolic level. For example, in traditional stories such as *Hansel and Gretel*, the forest can be interpreted as the manifestation of anxiety or a place where the characters can grow from dependence to independence. Anthony Browne's picture book of this Grimms' tale emphasizes the psychological symbolism.

Film and television adaptations of books realize setting differently to text, which rarely describe the minute detail that the location and prop teams need in order to create *mise-en-scènes*. In film a location may be changed from the original in the book. For example, the settings for film versions of Mary Norton's *The Borrowers*, Anne Fine's *Madam Doubtfire* and Lynn Reid Banks's *The Indian in the Cupboard* were all changed from Britain to America. Young readers can discuss the impact this has on the stories and be encouraged to consider why such decisions are made.

Setting and symbolism

> Obtain a copy of Anthony Browne's *Voices in the Park* and make some notes about the symbolic use of setting.

ACTIVITY

Commentary

In his picture book, *Voices in the Park*, Anthony Browne uses the seasons symbolically to represent a facet of each character's personality. Mrs Smythe is associated with autumn, season of death and decay; as she exits the park, a trail of shrivelled brown leaves is left in her wake. Mr Smith is placed in a wintry setting; gloomy, heavy skies operate as a pathetic fallacy, reflecting his mood – he is unemployed and depressed, and is shown looking despairingly at the newspaper, searching for jobs. But after the trip to the park with his daughter the scene has changed; it is still winter but the things associated with Christmas are visible: bright lights, Father Christmas, the injection of a different colour palette. Charles is associated with spring, his feelings are very tender and his encounter with Smudge awakens new possibilities – spring has the conventional association of Hope. Smudge is associated with summer in all its glory and bright colours; she is joyful and active.

Browne's symbolism is derived from the Romantic tradition. The other main sources of symbolism in western literature are Christian and classical.

ACTIVITY

> Select a book that you have read recently in which setting was integral to the story. Re-read passages where the setting is described. How has the writer captured a sense of time and place?
>
> Select a novel in which setting is important and where a film version of the book exists.
>
> Read the list of contrasting moods and themes that have been explored in fiction.
>
> Choose one from the list and describe two settings real or imaginary that are suggested by the words:
>
> - loneliness and companionship;
> - secrecy and honesty;
> - death and life;
> - ancient and modern;
> - nature and technology;
> - science and art;
> - freedom and imprisonment;
> - destruction and regeneration;
> - dependence and independence.
>
> Where did your images come from? For example, from stories you have read? Personal experience? Or films?

Subject and theme

Subject and theme are words that describe what the story is about. First, we can distinguish between the two related terms. In Susan Hill's *Beware Beware* a young girl escapes from the watchful gaze of her mother and sets out to explore the wood at the very edge of her garden. This is the subject of the story, whereas the theme, or central unifying idea, might be described as a story about growth from dependence to independence. The subject of a book may be deceptively simple and yet have a profound theme, as is the case with Eric Carle's *Draw Me a Star* which can be enjoyed by pre-school children but still provides food for thought for readers of 11 years and older.

Explicit themes are directly revealed in the text, as in Margaret Shaw's *Walking the Maze* where Annice observes, 'The trouble with books ... is that books change people. The trouble is that you are never quite the same person at the end of a book as you were at the beginning'. Other themes are implicit in the story as in *Beware Beware*. Comparing two books that have similar themes but different subjects can help to reveal to the young readers the deeper, underlying messages. Picture books provide an excellent means of achieving this as the entire narrative can be read/viewed in one session and as the themes are often challenging. This complexity of theme is one of the reasons that picture books should continue to be a part of children's reading experience long after they have 'learnt to read'. Some commonly occurring themes in children's fiction are:

- facing and overcoming fear (Helen Cooper, *The Bear Under the Stairs*; Anthony Browne, *The Tunnel*);
- good versus evil (J.K. Rowling, *Harry Potter and the Goblet of Fire*);
- coping with bereavement (Michael Rosen, *Sad Book*);
- acquisition of wisdom (Philip Pullman, *The Firework Maker's Daughter*);
- growth from dependence to independence (*Hansel and Gretel*, *The Secret Garden*);
- self and selflessness (Frances Hodgson Burnett, *The Secret Garden*);

- conflict of nature and urbanization (Colin Thompson, *The Paradise Garden*);
- the power of the imagination (Colin Thompson, *Once Upon an Ordinary School Day*);
- abandonment (Cynthia Voigt, *Homecoming*);
- secrets (Lauren St John, *The White Giraffe*);
- search for social or cultural values (John Marsden, *The Rabbits*);
- the nature of heroism (Pete Johnson, *The Hero Game*);
- insight into different cultures (Daniel Pennac, *The Eye of the Wolf*);
- development of moral responsibility (Anne Fine, *The Tulip Touch*);
- interpersonal relationships (Helen Cooper, *Pumpkin Soup*);
- do not judge others too readily (Sharon Creech, *Walk Two Moons*);
- war and peace (Nikolai Popov, *Why?*);
- the discovery of self-identity (Randa Abdel-Fattah, *Does My Head Look Big in This?*).

This list is not exhaustive. You will notice that Frances Hodgson Burnett's *The Secret Garden* is listed as having more than one theme; this is because many books have multiple themes. Furthermore recognition and identification of theme – what the book means – is largely contingent upon personal experience and response. Young readers may well recognize different themes to the ones already identified.

ACTIVITY

> What other themes have you identified in the children's books that you have read?
>   Are there any subjects or themes that you consider unsuitable material for children?

In this chapter you have seen that:

- characters are not authentic images of real people but representations that
- reflect the values and beliefs of their creators;
- different constructions of the concept of childhood are evident in the way child characters are presented;
- some characters such as animals and toys appear more frequently in children's fiction than in writing for adults;
- the role played by setting ranges from providing a backdrop to being an antagonist in the plot;
- the themes of children's literature are challenging and complex. Readers' perceptions of themes are contingent upon their life and book experiences.

Key words

Anthropomorphism:	ascribing human behaviour to a non-human (e.g. animal, toy, machine).
Dialogue:	the conversational element of the narrative.
Direct speech/thought:	shows the reader what was said or thought. The actual words are written in quotation marks.
Indirect speech/thought:	shows the reader what was thought or said. Quotation marks are not used.
Ideology:	a system of concepts, values and beliefs that are held by individuals or groups. See above for Hollindale's explanation of the three levels of ideology present in literature.
Pathetic fallacy:	human feelings are ascribed to the inanimate. For example, when the weather appears to reflect the mood of character.

Representation:	a textual construction that creates an image or likeness of the real world. Representations are not accurate images of reality as they reflect the cultural world of the writer.
Stereotype:	an oversimplified image or attitude held in common by members of a group.
Symbol:	the word derives from the Greek *symbolon* meaning mark, emblem, sign or token. In literature a symbol is an object (animate or inanimate) which stands for something else (e.g. a red rose for love, a dove for peace, etc.).

Further reading

Hollindale, P. (1988) *Ideology and the Children's Book*. Stroud: The Thimble Press.
Hollindale, P. (1997) *Signs of Childness in Children's Books*. Stroud: The Thimble Press.
Jenks, C. (1996) *Childhood*. London: Routledge.

Chapter 5

Traditional Stories and Fairy Tales

In this chapter we shall:

- explore the origins of traditional stories and some of their characteristic features;
- consider the relevance of traditional stories and fairy tales to the repertoire of children's literature;
- suggest some ways in which children can engage with traditional stories and fairy tales.

Traditional stories

'Traditional story' is an umbrella term that encompasses all stories that originated from the oral tradition, the verbal method of cultural transmission from one generation to the next. In this section we look at some of the different stories that are considered traditional, highlighting those features that distinguish them from other types of tale.

ACTIVITY

Can you define each of the following types of tale?
What are the characteristic features of each story type?

- myth;
- legend;
- fable;
- folk tale;
- trickster tale;
- aetiological story;
- fairy story.

From this list of traditional stories can you identify to which of the categories listed above each belongs? List some reasons for your choices.

- Thor's Hammer;
- Robin Hood and the Sheriff of Nottingham;
- Pandora's Box;
- Yggdrasill the World Tree;
- Story of St Christopher;
- Anansi Hunts with Tiger;
- How the Leopard got his Spots;
- Beauty and the Beast;
- Paikea, The Whale Rider;
- The Epic of Gilgamesh;
- The Hare and the Tortoise;
- The Happy Prince;
- The Death of King Arthur;
- Altjeringa: The Aboriginal Dreaming;

▶

- The Little Mermaid;
- Little Red Riding Hood;
- Noah and the Flood;
- Brer Rabbit and the Tar Baby;
- Sedna, Goddess of the Sea;

It is not always possible to distinguish between the different types of traditional story. In many cases myth and legend are treated as one entity as can be witnessed by the many titles on the bookshelf that include the words 'Myth and Legend of ...'. And in truth both myth and legend are often intertwined in a single narrative where it is difficult to unravel the elements that can be attributed to mythic or legendary origins. This is the case in stories of *The Odyssey* and the Celtic tales of King Arthur. Fairy stories also have an earlier mythic provenance. Folk tales cannot easily be disentangled from their literary counterparts the fairy tales. Nevertheless, with this proviso, it is still interesting to consider the distinctive features of each type of story and reflect on their origins.

Myths

Myths are the oldest stories. They were originally told to explain how the world came into being and to account for natural phenomena such as the seasons, or the cycle of night and day. They were a means of conveying the belief system and ideals of the culture from which they originated and would have been passed orally from generation to generation rather than written down. Importantly, they would have been told as if true. 'Myth is set in a cosmological time at the very dawn of the world: Burning ice, biting flame; *that is how life began*' (from 'The Creation', *Viking! Myths of Gods and Monsters* by Kevin Crossley-Holland, emphasis added).

Creation myths usually have an omnipotent being who brings the world into existence. In Japanese Shinto mythology, the deities of heaven commanded Izanami and Izanagi to shape the earth, which they did by stirring the waters of the ocean with a jewelled spear. This stirring of the waters to create earth is a recurring motif in world mythologies. Another example is found in a Hindu creation myth that tells how the gods decided to churn the ocean in order to find the elixir of immortality.

As they churned, the ocean turned to butter bringing forth 'fourteen precious things' including the sun and moon. In contrast, the Australian Aboriginal creation stories do not have one omnipotent being. Instead they tell of the Ancestors, who rose from below the earth and were absorbed into various parts of nature including animal species, rock formations and rivers. The Aboriginal mythic time or dreamtime does not lie in the past but is an eternal present that can be accessed through ritual. Common themes and motifs can be found in myths from all over the world. Flood stories, for example have variants from all continents. The Mesopotamian *Epic of Gilgamesh* tells how Utnapishtim was the only man to survive the flood, being warned of the tempest by the gods. He was instructed to build a boat onto which he was to take two of every creature. After seven nights the boat came to rest on top of Mount Nisir. Utnapishtim sent forth a dove, a swallow and, finally, a raven to see whether the waters were receding and when the raven failed to return he knew it had found a resting place. The similarity with the Judao-Christian story of Noah and the deluge is striking.

Typically in mythology gods are manifestations of natural phenomena. For example, Helios, is the Greek sun god, Thor, the Norse god of thunder and Yemaya, the Yoruban goddess of the seas. Often myths feature conflicts between the gods as a vehicle for depicting a universal conflict between good and evil. In Norse myth conflict arises from Loki's attempts to undermine Odin, while in Greek mythology Hades is set up in opposition to Zeus, and in Yuman mythology Kokomaht fights for good against his evil counterpart, Bakotaht. However, the line between good and evil is rarely simply drawn and even the all powerful are flawed, possessing traits such as jealously and greed. Mythological stories are concluded in a way that explains why things are as they are: when Pandora opens the forbidden box all evils are brought into the previously untainted world and only hope remains inside.

There are moral implications to consider when teaching myths. While we may no longer believe in the Olympian gods, some myths still hold spiritual truth for the cultures from which they originate and it is important not to trivialize them. Perry Nodelman (1996: 264) writes: 'For those of European background to treat stories of Gloocap or Nanabozho as entertaining literature is exactly like a publisher in Iran producing a book about the magical exploits of a fictional hero Christ for the entertainment of Muslim children'. However, an alternative viewpoint is offered by Mavis Reimer:

> The logical consequence of the view that we ought *not* to read as fiction that which is true to someone else is that we finally read nothing that doesn't confirm our own system of beliefs, a view that is egocentric in the extreme ... As a Christian I have no objection to Iranian children hearing of Christ as a magic hero; I suspect that the only Christians who would are extreme fundamentalists. (quoted in Nodelman, 1996: 265)

> With a partner discuss the implications of the viewpoints expressed by Nodelman and Reimer. Make notes in your reading journal.

ACTIVITY

Not originally intended for the entertainment of children, myths (and legends) find their way into children's literature via a number of routes:

1. Retellings: these are straight retellings that can be written for any age but, perhaps most commonly, for children. Such retellings might employ the transferred storyteller mode of narrative with a direct address to the reader employing little dialogue.
2. Reimaginings: these use elements of character and plot but transporting them to an updated setting often to underline the contemporary relevance of the universal themes. Examples include Marcus Sedgwick's *The Foreshadowing*, which borrows themes and character from the story of Cassandra bestowed with the gift of foretelling the future and cursed by being disbelieved. Sedgwick's story is set during the Great War. Alexandra (his Cassandra) foretells of great tragedy and, like her predecessor, her words are not empowering. Sedgwick uses the original story as a touchstone but is not constrained by its outcome. Alexandra must decide whether fate dictates what will become of her or whether free will has a part to play. Another recent example is David Almond's Clay, which draws on the thematic content of the Golem of Prague and *Paradise Lost* in this story of friendship and betrayal, good and evil, power and control.
3. Thematic influence: The universal themes of myth and legend may also inspire writers to create new stories.
4. Created mythologies: Some writers have set out with the intention of creating their own internally coherent mythic worlds. Perhaps the most celebrated example of this is J.R.R. Tolkein's *The Lord of the Rings*.

Review your existing knowledge of myths from a range of cultures.

> Of which of these do you already have some knowledge? List some of the stories that you know next to each of the cultural traditions:
>
> - Australian Aboriginal;
> - Celtic;
> - Chinese;
> - Egyptian;
> - Greek;
> - Hindu;
> - Japanese Shinto;
> - Norse;
> - Roman;
> - Yoruba;
> - Native North American (various).
>
> Read myths from a variety of cultural sources and add details to your book records.

ACTIVITY

▶

Research one of the world mythologies listed here, using a range of fictional and factual sources. Prepare a presentation for your colleagues.

Selected titles

Coats, L. (2003) *Atticus the Storyteller*. London: Orion.
Cottrell, A. (1986) *Dictionary of World Mythology*. Oxford: Oxford University Press.
Crossley-Holland, K. (2002) *Viking! Myths of Gods and Monsters*. London: Orion.
Fanelli, S. (2006) *Mythological Monsters*. London: Walker Books.
French, F. (1999) *Lord of the Animals: A Miwok Indian Creation Myth*. London: Frances Lincoln.
Lee, A. (illus.) and Guest, C. (trans.) (2000) *The Mabinogion*. London: Voyager Collins.
McCaughrean, G. (2003) *Gilgamesh, the Hero*. Oxford: Oxford University Press.
McCaughrean, G. (2003) *The Orchard Book of Roman Myths*. London: Orchard.
Maddern, E. and Kennaway, A. (1996) *Rainbow Bird: An Aboriginal Folk Tale from Northern Australia*. London: Frances Lincoln.
Moore, C. and Balit, C. (1997) *Ishtar and Yamuz: A Babylonian Myth of the Seasons*. London: Frances Lincoln.
Riordan, J. (2000) *The Coming of Night: A Yoruba tale From West Africa*. London: Frances Lincoln.
Swindells, R. and Lambert, S. (2003) *The Orchard Book of Stories from Ancient Egypt*. London: Orchard.
Williams, M. (1994) *Greek Myths*. London: Walker Books.

Myth in children's fiction

Myths have proved fertile ground for ideas among writers of children's fiction. Those most frequently used are the classical myths of Ancient Greece and Rome, Egyptian, Celtic and Norse.

ACTIVITY

Explore the way in which myth has been used as a source of inspiration for writers of contemporary fiction.

● Consider how these retellings breathe new life into the old stories.
● In what way does the mythic content of these stories bear relevance to the lives of the characters or the world in which they live?

The plot structure and themes of myths can be used as a stimulus for children's writing, providing a supportive frame while giving sufficient scope for individual interpretation. Children can be invited to write their own updated versions.

Selected titles

Deary, T. (2006) *The Fire Thief*. London: Kingfisher.
Druitt,T. (2005) *Corydon and the Island of Monsters*. London: Simon & Schuster.
Harvey, G. (2006) *Orphan of the Sun*. London: Bloomsbury.
Riordan, R. (2005) *Percy Jackson, the Lightning Thief*. London: Puffin.
Riordan, R. (2006) *Percy Jackson and the Sea of Monsters*. London: Puffin.

DVD

Miyazki, H. (2003) *Spirited Away*. Studio Ghibli.

Legends

Legends, unlike myths, are set in historical time and there is often debate as to whether they have some basis in fact. In a sense they preserve the past in exaggerated form. As Carlo Gebler explains when talking about *The Bull Raid,* his retelling of the Hound of Ulster Cycle, legends involve the 'retelling of human truths in fantastical or superhuman context, which is there for the purpose of adding interest because when things are bigger they are more interesting to listen to' (from www.writeaway.org.uk).

The word 'legend' (deriving from the Latin *legenda* – things to be read) was first applied to narratives about the lives of the saints that were read aloud in medieval Christian church services. A well-known legend of this type is the story of St Christopher. Christopher (whose name means bearer of Christ) is reputed to have been a Canaanite, and an intimidating giant. According to legend he served the devil but when he realized that his master was afraid of the cross, he switched allegiance and was instructed in the Christian faith by a hermit. One day a child asked for help crossing the fast-flowing river close to Christopher's home but as he carried the child on his shoulders he found his burden grew heavier and heavier until he was bowed down by the weight. When he reached the other side the child told him that he had been instructed by Jesus Christ to plant his staff in the ground. The next day it produced flowers and dates as a sign that the child had spoken the truth.

Today the term 'legend' is most usually applied to the hero tales; stories about humans with super-human powers and great physical strength. *The Iliad*, the classical epic poem about the Trojan wars, tells of the exploits of the major Greek heroes: Menelaus, Agamemnon, Achilles, Odysseus, Nestor, Ajax and Diomedes. At the birth of the greatest hero of them all, Achilles, son of the mortal Peleus and the Nereid, Thetis, it was prophesized that Troy would not be overcome unless he fought for the Greeks. According to legend his mother dipped him into the River Styx to make him invulnerable. Only his heel, where he had been held, was unprotected. Paris, son of the Trojan king, Priam, eventually killed Achilles with an arrow that pierced his heel, giving rise to the phrase 'Achilles' heel', to mean a person's weak spot. Like Achilles, many of the heroes were reputedly born of a union between mortals and immortals and the gods often play a part in directing the course of events, blurring the boundaries between myth and legend.

The heroes of legends are often raised in obscurity by surrogate parents. For instance, the young King Arthur is rescued by Merlin and raised by his surrogate father, Sir Bors, and Jason is raised by the centaur Chiron. It is interesting to conjecture why these patterns emerge. Perhaps the circumstances of their upbringing set these heroes apart from their fellow men but perhaps, as underdogs fighting against unjust powers, they are more acceptable champions of the people.

Other folk heroes achieve notoriety and acquire legendary status through outwitting unjust authority such as the outlaw of medieval England, Robin Hood. The ballads of Robin Hood tell how he robbed 'the rich to give to the poor' outwitting his adversary, the Sherriff of Nottingham. However, the theory that these were two separate classes of aristocracy (Norman and Saxon) owes more to Walter Scott's romanticized version than documentary evidence. Scholars have attempted to historicize Robin Hood but there is no record from medieval historians to confirm his existence. It is more likely that the exploits of more than one person led to the creation of the legendary figure in green.

Although heroes in the traditional European legends are rarely female, women have strong and important supporting roles. Nimue, The Lady of the Lake, is able to overcome Merlin with her powerful magic entombing him in stone (sometimes a hawthorn tree) so that he is unable to aid King Arthur in the final battle. In Greek legend, Medea (meaning cunning), daughter of King Aietes of Colchis and wife of Jason, possesses a powerful magic which she uses to help him win the golden fleece and overthrow the usurper, Pelias. Historical female figures who have taken on legendary status include Joan of Arc and Lady Godiva.

Fantastic beasts such as unicorns, chimeras, dragons and winged horses are common in legend. Information about animals, real or imagined, was recorded in the Bestiaries of the early Christian period. It is thought that stories often originated after rare sightings of unusual animals. The unicorn, for instance, may owe something to the Narwhal, a horned sea mammal. Metaphor might also partly account for the beasts in some legends, so that a dragon might simply mean a very fierce opponent. In the transmission of the tale the original use of the word is forgotten.

ACTIVITY

Investigating legendary heroes

- Survey the range of heroes that are present in the legends of different cultures.
- Are there any common characteristics?
- Why do you think these patterns of heroism emerged?
- Find examples of legends in which women are the heroes (e.g. Joan of Arc). Do they possess the same or different characteristics to the male heroes?
- To what extent do you think the heroes of legends are relevant to the modern age?
- You might for instance compare the exploits of legendary heroes with political activists who have worked to overcome repression through peaceful demonstration (Gandhi and Mandela for example). Or consider what the expression 'search for the hero inside yourself' means.
- Compare the heroes of traditional legends with super-heroes. What qualities do they share? What are the differences in the qualities these heroes possess? Carlo Gebler observes, 'Superman has two Achille's heels: Krypton, the substance out of which he was born and Lois Lane. In contrast, the characters in the Táin have Shakespearean weaknesses, they are evil, covetous, libidinous, wily, greedy and callous' (from www.writeaway.org.uk). Do you agree with the view that legendary heroes are extreme versions of ourselves, while super-heroes are an unobtainable and somewhat sanitized ideal?

Review legends from a wide range of sources and add details to your book records:

Selected titles

Almond, D. (2005) *Clay*. London: Hodder.
Burgess, M. (2001) *Bloodtide*. London: Puffin.
Burgess, M. (2005) *Bloodsong*. London: Andersen Press.
Crossley-Holland, K. (2001) *The Seeing-stone*. London: Orion.
Crossley-Holland, K. (2005) *King Arthur's World*. London: Orion.
Daly, I. and Willey, B. (2000) *Irish Myths and Legends*. Oxford: Oxford University Press.
Farmer, N. (2004) *The Sea of Trolls*. London: Simon & Schuster.
Fisher, C. (2002) *Corbenic*. London: Random House.
Fisher, C. (2003) *The Oracle*. London: Hodder.
French, F. (2006) *Canticle of the Sun: A Hymn of St Francis*. London: Frances Lincoln.
Gebler, C. (2005) *The Bull Raid*. London: Egmont.
Geras, A. (2001) *Troy*. London: Scholastic.
Geras, A. (2005) *Ithaka*. London: Random House.
Henderson, K. and Ray, J. (2006) *Lugalbanda*. London: Walker Books.
Leeson, R. (2001) *My Sister Shahrazad*. London: Frances Lincoln.
Lively, P. (2001) *In Search of a Homeland*. London: Frances Lincoln.
McCaughrean, G. (2003a) *Heroes: Odysseus*. Oxford: Oxford University Press.
McCaughrean, G. (2003b) *Heroes: Persues*. Oxford: Oxford University Press.
McCaughrean, G. (2003c) Heroes: Theseus. Oxford: Oxford University Press.
Masson, S. (2004) *In Hollow Lands*. London: Hodder.
Mayo, M. and Ray, J. (illus.) (2001) *The Orchard Book of the Unicorn and Other Magical Animals*. London: Orchard.
Morpurgo, M. (1997) *Arthur: High King of Britain*. London: Mammoth/Egmont.
Sedgwick, M. (2005) *The Foreshadowing*. London: Orion.
Sutcliff, R. (2000) *Black Ships Before Troy*. London: Frances Lincoln.
Tomlinson, T. (2003a) *The Forestwife*. London: Corgi.
Tomlinson, T. (2003b) *The Moon Riders*. London: Corgi.
Tomlinson, T. (2004) *The Voyage of the Snake Lady*. London: Corgi

Folk tales

From memory, without reference to the library or your personal book collection, make a list of the folk tales that you remember.

Compare your list noting any similarities and differences with a partner.

Can you account for the similarities and differences?

Commentary

Perry Nodelman (1996) explains that on the occasions that he has asked his students to engage in a similar activity, they always list the same tales:

Little Red Riding Hood;
The Three Little Pigs;
Goldilocks and the Three Bears;
Hansel and Gretel;
Jack and the Beanstalk;
Snow White and the Seven Dwarfs;
Sleeping Beauty;
Cinderella.

How closely did your list resemble this one? Given the vast numbers of traditional stories, why is it that a limited repertoire has come to be produced in collections for children? To understand this situation we need to look at the history of the folk tale, its transformation from the oral to the written form and the means by which the stories have been distributed and appropriated into collections for children.

As the term suggests, 'folk tales' are stories 'of the people' passed down from generation to generation, for example Little Red Riding Hood.

Explanations of the origins of folk tales vary. Some believe they originated hundreds of thousands of years ago in the 'childhood of humankind', arising spontaneously in different parts of the world whenever humans arrived at a particular stage in their development. Others claim that they are of Aryan origin, having passed from India around the world thus accounting for the many versions of one tale found in different countries. Folklorists have researched the similarities of tales from around the world and developed systems of classification. The most comprehensive is offered by Stith Thompson (1992) who divides oral stories into 2499 distinct types of which type 510 is a 'Cinderella' type story, defined as a story of a young girl who is mistreated by her family and with magical aid transforms her fortune by securing a good marriage. Neil Philip collected examples of type 510 in *The Cinderella Story* (1989) which contains what is considered to be the oldest recorded version, the Chinese *Yeh-hsien*. Philip cautions that although looking at universal patterns is interesting and illuminating, 'each version should stand and be considered on its own, as well as for its relation to the "cycle"' (1989: 4).

It is in the final decade of the 17th century that we encounter versions of folk stories that have a lasting impact in the context of children's literature. Best known of the French writers was Charles Perrault whose *Histoires ou Contes du Temps Passé* 1697, (first published in English in 1729) was a collection of oral stories told and refined in the literary salons. Perrault imbued the tales with his own values adding a rhymed moral to emphasize his patriarchal message (see 'Moral Coda' in Chapter 3). The language, humour and detail of his tales reflect the values of upper-class and court society that was his millieu. Perrault's collection included tales that we recognize as nursery favourites today: *Le Petit Chaperon Rouge* (Little Red Riding Hood), *La Belle au Bois Dormant* (Sleeping Beauty), *Cendrillon* (Cinderella), *Le Mâtre Chat* (Puss in Boots), *Le Petit Poucet* (Tom Thumb).

Jack Zipes (1995) has shown that, although Perrault's stories have endured, they are not representative of the French salon tales, which were largely told by independent and unconventional women: Madame d'Aulnoy, Catherine Bernard and Gabrielle Suzanne de Villeneuve. The women emphasized romantic love and the freedom to choose a marriage partner rather than modest behaviour advocated by

Perrault. Madame De Beaumont (1711–80) was the first to explicitly write fairy tales for children. *Beauty and the Beast* and *The Three Wishes* were reproduced in her repertoire of stories (printed in London in 1756). Her stories were written in a plain colloquial style and it is her economical version of Beauty and the Beast that most frequently forms the basis of modern retellings.

In Germany Jacob Grimm (1785–1863) and Wilhelm Grimm (1786–1859) have exerted a strong influence on the repertoire of stories that are included in children's collections, though their interest was scholarly rather than infant entertainment. The Grimms recognized the importance of acknowledging the sources of the tales, and recorded observations about their significance. However, Jack Zipes has shown that the Grimms did not, as was once thought, objectively record the stories but infused them with their own values, often altering the moral messages of the earlier stories. In the 17 different editions that they produced between 1812 and 1858 editorial intervention is evident and frequent emendations change the tales to reflect the social and moral values of 19th-century middle-class culture. The Grimms' collections included *Snow White*, *Hansel and Gretel* and *The Twelve Dancing Princesses*, as well as some interesting but less well known stories: *King Grisly Beard*, *The Juniper Tree*, *Mother Holle* and *Cat-skin*.

Andrew Lang (1844–1912) and Joseph Jacobs (1854–1916) were the foremost collectors of tales in Great Britain. Lang came from the border regions of Scotland and was particularly steeped in ballads and folklore of that area. His first collection of folk tales, *The Blue Fairy Book*, was published in 1889. It was an eclectic volume containing 37 tales translated from Madame d'Aulnoy, Perrault and Grimm as well as Scottish, English and Norse folk tales. More colour books were published ending with *The Lilac Fairy Book* in 1910. Lang's early books focused on the folklore of Europe, while the later books included material from Africa, America, South America and Asia. In 1890 Jacobs began writing a collection of folk tales for children. His expressed intention was to write 'as a good nurse will speak'. *English Fairy Tales* (1890) was followed by a second collection, *More English Fairy Tales* (1893). Jacobs also collected tales from Scotland, Ireland and Wales, assiduously recording the sources, variants and parallels of the tales in his collections and in so doing demonstrating that the Celtic oral storytelling tradition had a provenance to rival the Russian folk tale.

ACTIVITY

> Read the story of 'Kate Crackernuts' presented in Appendix 3.3.
> Identify those features that you think are typical of the folk tale.
> Do any aspects of this story challenge your expectations?
> Consider:
>
> - plot;
> - character;
> - setting;
> - theme;
> - motif;
> - language.

Commentary

The plot of the folk story is fast moving. Within the space of a few hundred words the story arouses suspense and builds to a climax dealing briefly and to the point with existential dilemmas. The telling is simplified and details, unless they are important, are eliminated. In folk tales characters are either good or bad and are not believable by ordinary standards. Evil is as omnipresent as virtue and both are personified. Evil is often temporarily in ascendancy as it is in 'Kate Crackernuts' when Anne is bewitched. Bettelheim (1988) argues that moral choices in these stories are made not on the grounds of choosing between good and evil but through the reader making choices about which character they want to identify with. The question for the child is not 'Do I want to be good?' but 'Who do I want to be like?'.

Folk tales are often charged with the sin of reproducing stereotypical characters, but the tales are more complex than this. As mentioned earlier, some collectors and retellers of the folk tales in the 18th and 19th centuries tended to collect versions of the stories with passive girls and active men (e.g. Perrault). But versions of the tales do exist which include active women, 'Kate Crackernuts' being one example. In recent years this imbalance has been addressed by compilers such as Alison Lurie (*Clever Gretchen and Other Forgotten Folktales*) who have endeavoured to resurrect some of the stories of strong, courageous and resourceful heroines. Furthermore, characters in folk tales are archetypal, representing ideas rather than attempts at realistic characterisation. They are generic so that the name Jack simply means lad. Kate Crackernuts, Snow White and Goldilocks are simply named for their associated characteristics. Many stories work equally well if they have male or female heroines: the gender of characters can often be transposed without affecting the moral purpose of the story.

Stock characters are common in the folk tale. The queen in '*Kate Crackernuts*' is a typical wicked stepmother who showers preferential treatment on her own child. Bettelheim (1988) argues that the stepmother in *Hansel and Gretel* represents a facet of the natural mother that the child resents, an interpretation that is implied in Anthony Browne's illustrated version of the story.

One of the distinctive features of setting in this story is the fairy kingdom under the hill. This occurs frequently in stories that have their origins in Celtic and Welsh folklore; *King Herla* is another example. The setting of the classic tales reflect a bygone age, the henwife's cottage in the glen for instance.

The conventional folk tale pattern of three is evident in this story. Three times Anne is sent to the henwife and for three nights Kate takes care of the prince. The number 3 has mystical associations. Pythagoras called it the perfect number and trinities are important in diverse religions and mythologies, for example, in the Christian faith God, Son and Holy Spirit and in Hinduism, Brahma, Vishnu and Shiva. There are also pragmatic reasons relevant for narrative structure. Three is the most economical means of making the point. If an event occurs only once it is nothing out of the ordinary; if it occurs twice than it is a matter of chance. If, however, an event occurs three times and on the third occasion something special occurs, it emphasizes the uniqueness of the third way. For an event to occur four times would be an unnecessary elaboration. So three is the perfect number.

Folk stories are seldom sentimental. The phrase 'just like a fairy tale', misrepresents the spirit of the tales (though sentimentalized versions of them are produced). Kate wins her prize by using her wits and because she cares about her sister. In folk tales virtues such as presence of mind, kindliness and willingness to listen to advice are rewarded with wealth, comfortable living and ideal partner. The resolutions of the tales restore things to their proper state. In this example Anne's beauty is restored and the enchantment is reversed.

Stories may be simply told but themes are deep. The principal message of the tales is that life involves a struggle and difficulties can be severe. Readers are confronted with basic human predicaments such as jealousy, envy, abandonment, betrayal and death. Bettelheim (1988: 10) suggests that the fairy story is important because existential anxieties are taken seriously and children are offered solutions that they can understand, 'and they lived happily ever after does not fool the child into thinking eternal life is possible but helps to make reality more acceptable'. In '*Kate Crackernuts*', the language of oral storytelling is in evidence – 'they all lived happy and died happy, and never drank out of a dry cappy' – reflecting the way that stories told around the kitchen hearth or in the local inn would have been concluded. The dialect of the henwife is also typical in tales recorded from the oral tradition, 'go home to your minnie and tell her to keep her larder door better locked'.

Fractured Fairytales

There is an abundance of rewritings of old stories. Often these modern versions subvert the ideological content of the older stories asserting contemporary values, as can be seen in Jon Sciezska and Lane Smith's *The True Story of the Three Little Pigs* and Eugene Trivisaz and Helen Oxenbury's *Three Little Wolves and the Big Bad Pig*. In Sciezska's story, B.B. Wolf relates his side of events from his prison cell. But this is not simply a story told from another point of view. We quickly discover, aided by clues in the pictures (rabbits' ears sticking out of the beefburger), that although there may be more than one side to every story not all points of view are equally valid: B.B. Wolf is an unreliable narrator.

The justice system of the traditional tale is challenged in Eugene Trivizas's *Three Little Wolves and the Big Bad Pig*. In the traditional version Big Bad Wolf comes to a sorry end having tried to eat the Three Little Pigs. In Trivizas's version the pig threatens the little wolves but when the little wolves refuse to respond with violence, he is converted to a more peaceful life building his house of flowers instead. It can be argued that the story shows that there is potential for redemption. Nodelman (1996: 263), however, detects irony in this resolution: 'I suspect it makes fun of anyone impractical enough to pretend to believe that flowers might be stronger than armor-plate'. These stories are enjoyable for adults and children alike but full enjoyment is probably contingent upon knowledge and experience of the original versions. Certainly without this background much of the humour and intentional irony will be lost.

ACTIVITY

> Review a range of folk tales from different cultural sources and add details to your book records. Make a note of countries, regions that are underrepresented by the books available in your local library of bookshop.
>
> You might extend this investigation to work with children.
>
> Carry out a survey of the folk tales that children know at different ages. Are the tales in Nodelman's list included? Are there any surprises? How did the children encounter these stories (somebody told the story? Picture book? Film?).
>
> Assemble a collection of folk tales from the class library. Identify the origin of each story placing a marker on a large world map.

Today, children's earliest encounters with traditional stories may well be through the medium of film and most likely in DVD small-screen format. Disney's first feature length cartoon, *Snow White* (1937) established many of the features that have become synonymous with the Disney fairy tale formula. Because most of his sources were short and emblematic, additional material needed to be added to lengthen the plot and sustain interest in the characters. For characterization Disney relied upon the formula of early movies, which themselves drew from 19th-century melodrama: the innocent heroine, the gallant hero, the evil villain, and comic relief in the form of the clown (Zipes, 2000). In recent years the formula has been subjected to critical analysis which has drawn attention to the racial and gender stereotyping of Disney characters. The formula has been parodied by the Dreamworks studio notably, *Shrek* – note the resemblance of Lord Farquaad's castle to the iconic Sleeping Beauty castle of Disney's theme parks.

Selected titles:

Clayton, S.P. and Herxheimer, S. (2004) *Tales Told in Tents*. London: Frances Lincoln.
Crossley-Holland, K. (1999) *The Old Stories*. London: Orion.
Doyle, M. and Sharkey, N. (illus.) (2000) *Tales from Old Ireland*. London: Barefoot Books.
Gatti, A. (1997) *Tales from the African Plains*. London: Belitha Press.
Jarvie, G. (ed.) (1997) *Scottish Folk and Fairy Tales*. London: Penguin.
McCaughrean, G. (1999) *One Thousand and One Arabian Nights*. Oxford: Oxford University Press.
Mayhew, J. (2000) *The Kingfisher Book of Tales from Russia*. London: Kingfisher.
Souhami, J. (2006) *The Leopard's Drum: An Asante Tale from West Africa*. London: Frances Lincoln.
Naidu, V. (2000) *Stories from India*. London: Hodder Wayland.

Yep, L. (1997) *The Dragon Prince: A Chinese Beauty and the Beast Tale*. London: HarperCollins.

Fractured Fairytales

Ahlberg, A. (2003) *Each Peach Pear Plum*. London: Viking.
Briggs, R. (1973) *Jim and the Beanstalk*. London: Puffin.
French, F. (1989) *Snow White in New York*. Oxford: Oxford University Press.
Hawkins, C. and Hawkins, J. (2005) *The Fairytale News*. London: Walker.
McGee, M. and Beck, I (2006) *Winston the Book Wolf*. London: Bloomsbury.
Scieszka, J. and Smith, L. (1991) *The True Story of the Three Little Pigs*. London: Puffin.
Trvizas, E. and Oxenbury, H. (1993) *Three Little Wolves and the Big Bad Pig*. London: Mammoth.

Collect and compare different versions of the same tale. You might want to include some film versions.

Suggested questions for comparison

Consider these general questions:

- Who is the implied reader in each of the tales?
- How do the characters compare in the different versions?
- Do characters change or develop?
- Do the stories convey a moral message and does the message vary in the different versions?
- What values do the tales appear to be promoting? To what extent do you think these are the values of the time in which the tale was written?
- To what extent is social and psychological realism evident in the tales? You will also need to construct specific questions for the tale you are studying (e.g., 'Is Red Riding Hood warned not to go into the forest and does this affect the moral and ideological content of the story?').

Talk to children about the versions of the tales with which they are familiar.

Suggestions:

Red Riding Hood
Blundell, T. (1993) *Beware of Boys*. London: Puffin.
Browne, A. (1997) *The Tunnel*. London:Walker.
Dahl, R. (2001) *Revolting Rhymes*. London: Puffin.
Forward, T. and Cohen, I. (2005) *The Wolf's Story: What Really Happened to Little Red Riding Hood*. London: Walker.
Grimm, J. and Grimm, W. (1995) 'Little Red Cap' in *Grimm's Fairy Tales*. London: Penguin.
Hill, S. and Barrett, A. (illus.) (1995) *Beware Beware*. London: Walker.
Perrault, C. (2000) 'Little Red Riding Hood' in Perrault's *Complete Fairy Tales*. London: Puffin.
Zwerger, L. (1995) *Little Red Cap*. London: North South Books.

Cinderella
Allan, N. (2002) *Cinderella's Bum*. London: Red Fox.
Perrault, C. and Koopmans, L. (illus.) (2002) *Cinderella*. London: North South Books.
Steptoe, J. (1997) *Mufaro's Beautiful Daughters*. London: Puffin.
Cole, B. (1997) *Prince Cinders*. London: Puffin.
Onyefulu, O. (1995) *Chinye*. London: Frances Lincoln.
Walt Disney (1951) *Cinderella*. Walt Disney Home Video.
Roberts, L. and Roberts, D. (2001) *Cinderella: An Art Deco Love Story*. London: Pavilion.

Fables

A fable is a short story that makes a moral point while at the same time entertaining the reader. Animal characters and inanimate objects are used to satirize the characteristics of human behaviour. The best-known teller of fables is Aesop whose own life has acquired legendary status. Reputedly a slave in the 6th century BC, he had a misshapen body and was dumb until given the power of speech by the goddess Isis, after which he acquired an impressive wit which ultimately earned him his freedom. Aesop's fables include the story of the Sour Grapes. A fox tries to obtain some grapes but when his efforts come to nothing he claims that the grapes were sour.

An even older collection of stories is the Hindu classic the *Pantachantra*, or five tales. Regarded as a guide on how to live wisely: 'Vishnu Sharman said, "Oh King, listen to my pledge. A hundred villages do not tempt me to vend learning. Count six months from today. If I do not make your children great scholars, you can ask me to change my name".' The most famous fabulist after Aesop is French poet Jean de la Fontaine who published three volumes of fables in the second half of the 17th century. He reworked Aesop's tales in order to satirize the French court and bourgeoisie.

In common with other tales from the oral tradition, fables are told in a direct manner, superfluous details are not included as they would slow the pace and the tales would lose their impact. The narrative structure includes a short exposition with one conflict often arising out of a choice between a good and bad course of action. The resolution usually occurs in a single event and a concluding moral proverb might be added to clarify the message. It is believed that this convention was added to the fable around the 1st century. Although the fable is often regarded as a separate genre, it is also rendered through other genres such as folk tales for example *Little Red Riding Hood,* and aetiological narratives such as *How the Leopard Got His Spots.* The influence of fable can be seen in modern children's literature. Roald Dahl's *Charlie and the Chocolate Factory* contains the simple moral message about 'undesirable' behaviour such as watching too much television and eating chewing gum.

ACTIVITY

Study the following list of animals. What characteristics do you associate with each of them? Obtain and read a selection of fables from different traditions to find out how these animals are represented in the fables. Were there any surprises?

● fox;
● crocodile;
● crow;
● goose;
● monkey;
● dog.

Review fables from different sources for your records.
Extend this activity to your work with children. Invite them to write a modern fable. Suggest some modern messages that could be conveyed through the fable, for example do not throw litter, exercise for a healthy lifestyle and so on. Some children might write parodies.

Selected titles:

Aesop, and Temple, R. (trans.) (1998) *The Complete Fables.* London: Penguin.
French, V. and Paul, K. (1999) *Aesop's Funky Fables.* London: Puffin.
La Fontaine, J. and Chagall, M. (illus.) (1997) *The Fables of La Fontaine.* New York: New Press
Sama, V. (2005) *The Panchatantra.* New Delhi: Penguin.
Ward, H. (2007) *Aesop's Fables.* Dorking: Templar.
Zwerger, L. (2006) *Aesop's Fables.* London: North South Books.

Trickster tales

The trickster is a character who appears in folk stories from all over the world. He (and it is almost always *he*) is a clever deceiver, greedy and selfish, both cunning and ultimately stupid. He is anthropomorphized or possesses shape-shifting abilities so that he may be both man and creature such as Anancy the spider man.

In North America the trickster hare of east, central and southern Africa has become well known in his manifestation as Brer Rabbit. Stories featuring the cunning rabbit were recorded by Joel Chandler Harris (1848–1908) in *Uncle Remus, His Songs and His Sayings* (1880) and *Night with Uncle Remus* (1883). Chandler was working as a printer on a plantation in South Georgia when he first became familiar with the stories that were to be the basis of his collections. His motivation for writing them down was to preserve what he believed was a dying culture and to aid relations between black and white Americans after the Civil War. Of the 220 stories that Harris recorded, over one-half originated in Africa. Other tricksters are the Coyote and Raven in Native North American culture, while in the Caribbean and South America it is Anancy whose roots can be found in the folklore of West Africa. The European tradition of tricksters is derived from Reynard the Fox.

ACTIVITY

Review trickster tales from a range of cultural sources and add details to your records.

Selected titles:

French, F. (1992) *Anancy and Mr Dry Bone*. London: Frances Lincoln.

Hasting, S. and Percy, G. (illus.) (1993) *Reynard the Fox*. London: Walker Books.

Lester, J. and Pinckney, J. (2006) *The Tales of Uncle Remus: The Adventures of Brer Rabbit*. New York: Puffin.

McDermott, G. (1993) *Raven: A Trickster Tale from the Pacific North-West*. New York: Harcourt.

Naidoo, B. (2006) *The Great Tug of War and Other Stories*. London: Frances Lincoln.

Patten, H. (2003) *Clever Anasi and the Boastful Bullfrog*. London: Frances Lincoln

Literary fairy stories

'Fairy story' is a general term often used to include folk tales. In their collection of *Classic Fairy Tales*, Iona and Peter Opie (1980: 18) note that the term 'fairy tale' is comparatively modern. The term originated in France in 1698 with the publication of Madame d'Aulnoy's, *Contes des Fées*. Although a fairy tale does not necessarily feature a fairy, it does contain an enchantment or other supernatural element that is clearly imaginary. Tolkien called this an element of 'faerie', which can perhaps be best described as a supernatural or magical element. Literary fairy stories follow traditional patterns and owe much to earlier stories for their themes and motifs, but unlike folk tales they are the imaginative expression of a single writer.

Hans Christian Andersen (1805–75)

In May 1835, Andersen published a small 64-page booklet, *Tales Told for Children* (first printed in Britain in 1846), which included *The Tinder Box*, *The Ugly Duckling*, *The Little Mermaid* and *The Princess and the Pea*. Andersen, unlike the Grimms, was a creator not a collector. He had a humble background and the oral tradition was very much part of his background. Typically, Andersen's stories do not have a 'Once upon a time' beginning and, although many of his stories include kings, queens, princes and princesses, they speak in colloquial language and perform menial tasks. Andersen's narrative voice often makes a direct address to the reader as though he were telling the tale orally. On the whole his stories do not contain conventional morals and his melancholic view of life can be seen in those stories with tragic endings such as *The Steadfast Tin Soldier* and *The Little Matchgirl*. The following story is typical of Andersen's oevre.

The Flying Trunk

After squandering his inheritance, a young man is given a trunk, which turns out to be a magic flying trunk. He flies to Turkey where he falls in love with a princess but in order to win her as his bride he must tell a tale with a moral to impress the queen and with humour to make the king laugh. So he begins:

> Once upon a time there was a bundle of matches. They were extremely proud and haughty because they came of such high beginnings. Their family tree – the one they had all been part of – was once a tall and ancient pine tree in the forest. Now the matches lay on a kitchen shelf between a tinder box and an old iron pot, and they told these neighbours all about the time when they were young.
>
> 'Ah yes,' they said, 'we were on the top of the world when we were on that tree. Every morning and every evening we had diamond tea – they call it dew – and all day we had sunshine (when there *was* any sunshine) and all the little birds had to tell us stories. We could easily see that we were grander than the rest; we could afford green clothes all the year round, while the poor oaks and beeches wore leaves only in summer time . . .'
>
> Soon all the kitchen pots and pans want to tell their stories each vying to be the best until the kitchen maid returns and strikes the matches. 'Now,' they thought, 'everyone can see that we are the top people here. No one can shine like us – what brilliance! What a light we throw on dark places!'

And then they were all burnt out. (*The Flying Trunk* by Hans Christian Andersen. Translated by Naomi Lewis)

In this story everyday objects become protagonists, an invention of Andersen's that influenced the later development of the genre (and has become ubiquitous in Disney animations). His multi-layered stories appealed both to adults and children. The tone of Andersen's stories is ironic and it is important to find an edition that captures the humour of the original. The early translations failed to do this, hence the accusations of sentimentality leveled at him. This translation by Naomi Lewis captures the tone and colloquial expression that were characteristic of Andersen's writing, making it challenging for translators to do justice to his work. Collections by Naomi Lewis and Brian Alderson are particularly recommended.

Oscar Wilde (1854–1900)

Irish writer Oscar Wilde's childhood was steeped in stories from the oral tradition. His mother, Lady Jane Wilde, wrote what Yeats considered to be the finest books about Celtic fairy faith and his father was also a collector of folklore. Wilde's fairy story collections, *The Happy Prince* (1888) and *A House of Pomegranates* (1891), include memorable tales such as *The Selfish Giant, The Remarkable Rocket*, and, of course, *The Happy Prince*. The stories were written 'partly for children and partly for those who have kept the childlike faculties of wonder and joy'.

Influences from Grimm and Andersen can be detected in Wilde's stories, which both amplified and subverted the morals of the earlier tales. Wilde's *The Remarkable Rocket* bears some resemblance to Andersen's *The Flying Trunk* and *The Nightingale and the Rose* is a direct allusion to another Andersen's tale, *The Nightingale*. In Andersen's story all ends well when the emperor realizes that an artificial nightingale is no replacement for the real thing. Wilde's story has no such happy ending, his nightingale makes the ultimate sacrifice for the sake of a student she believes to be a true lover. The student laments that his sweetheart will not dance with him unless he gives her a red rose but only white ones grow in his garden. The nightingale searches for a red rose to give the student. The rose tree tells her that there is only one way to make a red rose she must press her breast against a thorn so that her blood will give new life to the damaged tree. It is a high price to pay but the nightingale prizes love above life:

And the marvellous rose became crimson, like the rose of the eastern sky. Crimson was the girdle of petals, and crimson as a ruby was the heart.

But the nightingale's voice grew fainter and her little wings began to beat, and a film came over her eyes. Fainter and fainter grew her song, and she felt something choking in her throat.

Then she gave one last burst of music. The white moon heard it, and she forgot the dawn, and lingered on in the sky. The red rose heard it, and it trembled all over with ecstasy and opened its petals to the cold morning air. Echo bore it to her purple cavern in the hills, and woke the sleeping shepherds from their dreams. It floated through the reeds of the river and they carried its message to the sea.

'Look, look!' cried the Tree, 'the rose is finished now.'; but the Nightingale made no answer, for she was lying dead in the long grass, with the thorn in her heart.

Sadly, her sacrifice is in vain. The girl prefers the jewels proffered by the Chamberlain's son and the student throws the rose into the street where it is trampled by a cart. In this extract we can see the elegant language that is a hallmark of Wilde's writing. Most of the stories end on a painfully sad note though in some stories such as *The Happy Prince* it is made explicit that the worthy characters attain a higher form of happiness in Paradise.

Select and compare two literary fairy stories.
Consider the way in which the writers have adapted traditional patterns and use language to convey their messages.

Suggested writers:

- Hans Christian Andersen;
- Oscar Wilde;
- George MacDonald;
- Michael Ende;
- Diana Wynne Jones;
- William Goldman;
- Vivian French;
- Joan Aiken;
- Susan Price;
- Robin McKinley;
- Donna Jo Napoli;
- Shannon Hale.

Selected titles:

Aiken, J. (1998) *Moon Cake and Other Stories*. London: Hodder.
Ende, M.(1985) *The Never Ending Story*. London: Puffin.
French, V. (1998) *The Thistle Princess*. London: Walker Books.
Goldman, W. (1999) *The Princess Bride*. London: Bloomsbury.
Jung, R. (2002) *Bambert's Book of Missing Stories*. London: Egmont.
Lewis, N. (1981) *Hans Andersen's Fairy Tales*. London: Puffin.
MacDonald, G. and Hughes, A. (2001) *At the Back of the North Wind*. London: Everyman Children's Classics, Orion.
Wilde, O. (1994) *The Happy Prince and Other Stories*. London: Puffin.

Now that you have explored the range of traditional stories and their sources, identify and discuss some of the issues related to the selection of tales for children.
For example, should children experience the oldest versions of the stories even though the ideological content may not reflect modern values?
Can new versions of old tales be appreciated without knowledge of the old ones?

Further reading

Armstrong, K. (2006) *A Short History of Myth*. Edinburgh: Canongate.

Bettelheim, B. (1988) *The Uses of Enchantment*. London: Penguin.

Tatar, M. (1998) *The Classic Fairy Tales*. New York: W.W. Norton.

Thompson, S. (2006) *The Folktale*. Whitefish, MT: Kessinger Publishing.

Warner, M. (1995) *From the Beast to the Blonde: On Fairy Tales and Their Tellers*. London: Vintage.

Zipes, J. (1995) *Fairy Tales and the Art of Subversion*. London: Routledge.

Chapter 6

Fantasy and Realism

In this chapter we will:
- explore the modes of fantasy and realism;
- look at the connections and contrasts between them.

Fantasy and realism are often described as distinct genres of fiction. The *Continuum Encyclopedia of Children's Literature* defines fantasy as 'a special case of fiction that breaks one or more of the rules that govern "real" life as we ordinarily define it and so invents an altered reality that must be true to rules of its own'. While realism is defined as 'the term used to describe stories that could have actually occurred to people or animals. The possibility exists that the events or similar events could have taken place. Fictional characters react to a situation in the same way that real people might react'. How accurate or useful is this distinction?

Fantasy

Manlove (1975) defines fantasy as a literary genre in which non-rational or 'magical' phenomena play a significant part. That is to say that the events in a fantasy story do not obey the rules of nature. He writes that fantasy 'is a fiction evoking wonder and containing a substantial and irreducible element of the supernatural with which mortal characters in the story or the readers become on at least partially familiar terms' (1975: 1). It is, he acknowledges in his recent book *From Alice to Harry Potter: Children's Fantasy in England* (2003), a contestable definition but nevertheless workable as a rule of thumb. Other critics have attempted to provide more schematized definitions.

Rosemary Jackson (1981: 33) developing the taxonomy proposed by Todorov (1973) argues that it is useful to 'define the fantastic as a literary *mode* rather than a genre, and to place it between the opposite modes of the marvellous and the mimetic'. The marvellous being the wonder tales of traditional story and the mimetic being those fictions that 'imitate an external reality'.

She goes on to explain, 'Fantastic narratives confound elements of both the marvellous and the mimetic. They assert that what they are telling is real – relying on the conventions of realistic fiction to do so – and then proceed to break that assumption by introducing what – within those terms – is manifestly unreal' (1981: 34). In this model fantasy and realism are not represented as distinct genres but modes of narrative, with fantasy occupying the central territory. Jackson's continuum (Figure 6.1) challenges us to think more carefully about the casual oppositional pairing of fantasy and realism.

Manlove (2003) argues that Jackson's definition is too narrow and fails to to embrace the full range of fantasy fictions. Instead he advises a broad definition like the one offered by Kathryn Hume (1984): 'Fantasy is any departure from consensus reality'.

MARVELLOUS	FANTASY	MIMETIC

Figure 6.1 *Jackson's literary modes*

ACTIVITY

To what extent do you agree with these statements about fantasy writing? Make notes in your journal or discuss in a group.

- Fantasy has nothing interesting or relevant to say about the modern world.
- You cannot have a concept of fantasy without a concept of reality.
- Fantasy is all about dungeons, dragons and wizards. It's a great escape from the mundane and ordinary.
- Young children really enjoy fantasy stories but grow out of them in the teenage years.
- All fiction is fantasy.
- Fantasy stories should not be read to very young children as they might confuse what is real with what is not.
- The gender roles in fantasy are stereotypical and outmoded.
- The best writers of fantasy tackle important issues.
- Fantasy is just as real as realism.
- Most fantasy espouses middle-class values
- Fantasy offers poor role models for young people. Problems are always solved through fighting, and good and evil are presented as unproblematically black and white.
- The alternative worlds in fantasy fiction are most frequently utopian.

Commentary

The penchant for fantasy in English children's literature has its roots in the 19th century. Charles Kingsley's *The Water Babies* (1863) is an early example of fantasy writing for children. Tom Grimes, a sweep's boy travels to the Other-end of Nowhere and Back. In the episodic submarine narrative, Tom encounters characters that help him on his moral journey. Although Kingley's story may be too didactic for modern taste, its language and wit foregrounded the literary nonsense that established Lewis Carroll's *Alices's Adventures in Wonderland* as a firm nursery favourite.

Robert Louis Stevenson's *Treasure Island* (1883) is a breathtaking adventure that has endured well and has been the blueprint for many subsequent adventures. The characterization of Long John Silver and his unsavoury crew of pirates is still able to produce a frisson of fear. Though the depiction of disability may not be politically correct, who can forget the menacing Blind Pew, Black Dog, or Israel Hands?

At the beginning of the 20th century several seminal fantasies were published, which continue to be read to and by children today. Interest in these books has been regenerated through film, television, theatre and multimedia versions. Edith Nesbit's *Five Children and It* (1902) is an episodic story about five children who discover a sand fairy who must grant them the first thing they wish for each day. Nesbit's writing was notable at the time for her attempt to address the child without heavy moral interjections. Kenneth Grahame's *The Wind in the Willows* (1908) is a prototype for the anthropomorphic animal story. Mole, Ratty, Badger and Toad continue to enchant children and the descriptions of life on the river bank create an idyllic picture. For the very young Beatrix Potter's animal stories (*The Tale of Peter Rabbit*, *The Tale of Tom Kitten*, *The Tale of Jeremy Fisher*, etc.) are as fresh as when they were first published, especially in their original format and language; Potter's insistence on the small format that could fit into a child's hand was inspired. Perhaps it is her unsentimental approach to her cast of 'naughty' but lovable characters and her fine observations of animal and human behaviour that collide in these stories, which give them their timeless appeal. An animal story of a different kind, Rudyard Kipling's aetiological *Just So Stories* (1902) with distinctive transferred storyteller voice, patterned refrains and memorable stories ('The Elephant's Child', 'How the Leopard Got His Spots' 'The Beginning of Armadillos') also stands up well today. Notable fantasies of the 1920s and 1930s included A.A. Milne's *Winnie the Pooh* (1926) and John Masefield's *The Midnight Folk* (1927) and *The Box of Delights* (1933). It's interesting to observe that fantasies of this period tended to be about the adventures of a solitary child. This shifted in the post-war years as more fantasies included the child in a social group. Great fantasies of this period include *The Lord of the Rings* (1954–5), *The Lion, The Witch and the Wardrobe* (1950) and *Tom's Midnight Garden* (1958) (see Chapter 8).

In the 1960s and 1970s fantasy moved from predominantly rural settings to more urban landscapes. Alan Garner's *Elidor* (1965) is an electrifying story set in the post-Second World War slum clearance sites in Manchester, and Clive King's *Stig of the Dump* (1962) is the story of a boy who finds a Stone Age cave-dweller living in a rubbish dump. Roald Dahl was the most anarchic fantasy writer of the period. *James and the Giant Peach* (1976) and *Charlie and the Chocolate Factory* (1964) dispense with the view that adults know best, characters are grotesque and the plot contains a good deal of horror: disagreeable children are discarded on a whim and dreadful aunts get their comeuppance.

Diana Wynne Jones emerged in the 1980s as one of the most inventive fantasy writers. The multiple worlds of her Chrestomanci series constantly rub against a reality that we can recognize, an idea that has been taken up by a number of contemporary writers. She writes,

> The world of Chrestomanci is not the same as this one. It is a world parallel to ours, where magic is as normal as mathematics, and things are generally more old-fashioned. In Chrestomanci's world, Italy is still divided into numbers of small states, each with its Duke and capital city. In our world, Italy became one united country long ago. (from www.leemac.freeserve.co.uk/questions.htm)

Welcome recent additions to the series are *Conrad's Fate* (2006) and *The Pinhoe Egg* (2006) *Howl's Moving Castle* (1985), animated by Miyazaki (2004) and its sequel, *Castles in the Air* (1990). These are comic, meta-fictive masterpieces.

Since the publication of *Harry Potter and the Philosopher's Stone* (1997) fantasy novels have been in the ascendancy with a burgeoning of fantasy novels and ubiquitous trilogies filling bookshop shelves. The enthusiastic reception of two recent film sequences, *Harry Potter* (2001–5) and sequels and *The Lord of the Rings Trilogy* (2001–4), has shown that fantasy has a widespread appeal, which crosses age and gender boundaries. But in spite of its popularity, some still regard fantasy as being inferior to other types of literature. Peter Hunt (Hunt and Lenz, 2001) explains that it is often criticized on the grounds of being formulaic, childish and escapist. While there may be a proliferation of second-rate 'sword and sorcery fiction', there is also a wealth of original fantasy writing: imaginative stories with compelling plots which confront the reader with sophisticated ethical and philosophical issues.

A good fantasy is deeply rooted in human experience. Indeed many fantasy authors write what might be termed the 'literature of ideas': stories which explore profound ideas. Peter Dickinson (1986: 39) warns of the problems of fantasies that do not have their roots in reality:

> Finally let me point out the obvious, which is that, as with all other literary forms, there is a great deal of dud fantasy around. A lot of books which don't really do the trick, many are devoid of new ideas. They are as repetitious as pony books. Space gymkhanas. Ponies for Boys. In fact this matters more than with other forms because an old idea is a dead idea and as fantasy is fundamentally about ideas, a dead idea is a dead book.

Philip Pullman, author of *His Dark Materials* echoes this view:

> I think of *His Dark Materials* as stark realism. The trouble with pigeon-holing books by genre is that once they have a particular label attached they only attract readers who like that sort of label. Fantasy is particularly affected by this. I very much want to reach readers who don't normally read fantasy at all. I don't like fantasy. The only thing about fantasy that interested me when I was writing this was the freedom to invent imagery such as daemon but that was only

interesting because I could use it to say something truthful and realistic about human nature. If it was just picturesque or ornamental I wouldn't be interested. (www.randomhouse.com)

Dickinson's and Pullman's novels are far from escapist, though they are resoundingly good stories which are both emotionally and psychologically 'real'. The protagonist of Dickinson's *Eva* has her brain transplanted into the body of a chimp when an accident leaves her paralysed. The consequences are disturbing. *Eva* is a startling novel, which raises questions that are relevant to current concerns about transplant surgery and animal experimentation. Pullman's *His Dark Materials* trilogy is a triumph of the imagination, an epic quest which takes two children, Lyra and Will, on a perilous journey to liberate the ghosts from the land of the dead and ultimate triumph over oppression. Though the story is paramount, *His Dark Materials* is a reflection on religion and science, at one level a reworking of Milton's *Paradise Lost*, but it also about what it means to be human, to grow up, to suffer, and to learn'.

This complexity is not limited to longer novels; the blurring of the boundaries between fantasy and realism occurs in many pictures books too. For example, in Maurice Sendak's classic *Where the Wild Things Are* (1963), Max is sent to bed without any supper after behaving badly and his room transforms into the imaginary land of the Wild Things. He becomes their king and leads them in a wild rumpus. But growing tired of their antics, he wants to return to where he is loved most of all. He travels back 'into the night of his very own room' and finds his supper waiting for him. Max's fantastic adventure also serves as a metaphor for his emotions. His antics with the Wild Things are a manifestation of his rage and when he enters the calm phase of his tantrum he realizes how much he wants his mother's love. More recently Helen Cooper's *Pumpkin Soup* (1998) and *The Baby Who Wouldn't Go to Bed* (1996) blend fantastic landscapes with keenly observed behaviour, which will be familiar to any parent of very young children.

ACTIVITY

- Make a list of the children's fantasy titles with which you are familiar.
- Do the books on your list share the same characteristics?
- Try classifying the books into different types of fantasy.
- Do any questions emerge from this exercise?

Commentary: the range of fantasy fictions

Fantasy fiction has been categorized and described in different ways. One classification divides fantasy into two major types:

- low fantasy, which takes place in the primary world (our world);
- high fantasy, which takes place in alternative worlds.

These are sometimes referred to as secondary or imaginary worlds. Peter Hunt (Hunt and Lenz, 2001) prefers 'alternative' to 'secondary', which he points out is a term derived from a misreading of Tolkien's *Tree and Leaf* (1964).

Low fantasy

In low fantasy, non-rational happenings occur in the rational world. This is the case in E. Nesbit's *Five Children and It*. While they are playing in a gravel pit close to their home, the Bastable children excavate a sand fairy or Psammead. Somewhat reluctantly, he grants them a series of wishes, always taking their requests literally, with disastrous results for the children. It is a fantasy story in which magic is used to educate the children to think more carefully about what they wish for, as wishes may well come true. With the exception of this one magical happening the children lead ordinary lives in rural Kent.

The supernatural element is more sinister in Jenny Nimmo's *The Snow Spider* trilogy and Susan Cooper's *The Dark Is Rising Sequence*. In these novels the landscape is steeped in myth and magic and the age-old battle between good and evil is fought in the English and Welsh countryside. Cooper explains, 'You walk those mountains and the awareness of the past is all around you. And I intend to write from that kind of awareness. The magic if you like is all around' (from www.thelostland).

It can be doubly disconcerting when the dark forces are abroad in a countryside that is recognizably Buckinghamshire, Wales or, in the case of Alan Garner, Cheshire. Garner (1968: 25) is aware of the potential potency of the supernatural impinging on the real world:

> If we are in Eldorado, and we find a mandrake, then OK, so it's a mandrake: in Eldorado anything goes. But by force of imagination, compel the reader to believe that there is a mandrake in a garden in Mayfield Road, Ulverston, Lancs, then when you pull up that mandrake it is really going to scream; and possibly the reader will too.

High fantasy

In high fantasy the alternative world can be entered in different ways:

1. *The primary world does not exist.* In this type of fantasy the reader is transported directly to the alternative world. For example, Middle-Earth of J.R.R. Tolkien's *The Lord of the Rings* or Terry Prachett's *Discworld*. Maps of imaginary lands are often included to help build the reader's belief in the fantasy world. In books by Tolkien and Ursula Le Guin the geography of their worlds is described in precise detail creating an illusion of authenticity. This is the case in Tolkien's prologue for *The Lord of the Rings* which provides a detailed historical and geographical context for his story. He creates a chronology of Middle-Earth and a record of significant historical events:

> There for a thousand years they were little troubled by wars, and they prospered and multiplied after the Dark Plague (S.R.37) until the disaster of the Long Winter and the famine that followed. Many thousands then perished, but the days of Dearth (1158–60) were at the time of this tale past and the Hobbits had again become accustomed to plenty. The land was rich and kindly though it had long been deserted when they entered it, it had been well tilled, and there they had once had many farms, cornlands, vineyards and woods. (*The Lord of the Rings* by J.R.R. Tolkien)

Although the fantasy worlds of Tolkien and Le Guin can be called 'alternative', they are nevertheless based on recognizable features of the world we inhabit and may even be symbolic representations of the primary world. Tolkien's Middle-Earth is, for instance, a mythic Middle England – a time forgotten by history – and the Shire is clearly identifiable as rural Oxfordshire, according to his biographer Humphrey Carpenter.

Similarly, the Oxford of Philip Pullman's *Northern Lights* is both familiar and strange. On first reading the reader might be prompted to ask: is this Oxford in another time? Does the story take place in the past? Or the future? Pullman explains in his preface that it is set 'in a universe like ours, but different in many ways'.

> Jordan College was the grandest of all the colleges in Oxford. It was probably the largest too, though no one knew for certain. The buildings which were grouped around three irregular quadrangles, dated from the early Middle Ages to the mid-eighteenth century. It had never been planned; it had grown piecemeal, with the past and present overlapping at every spot, and the final

effect was one of jumbled and squalid grandeur. (*Northern Lights* by Philip Pullman)

Several writers have chosen to set their fantasies in alternative versions of well known places: Stephen Elboz's *A Handful of Magic* in London, Mary Hoffman's *Stravaganza* and Kai Meyer's *Stone Light* in Venice.

2. *The alternative world is entered through a portal in the primary world.* This type of fantasy enables the writer to make a direct comparison between the two worlds. Probably the best-known examples are the rabbit hole that Alice falls down in Lewis Carroll's *Alice's Adventures in Wonderland;* and the wardrobe through which Lucy, Peter, Susan and Edmund enter the magical land of Narnia in C.S. Lewis's *The Lion, the Witch and the Wardrobe*. Doors, rings, mirrors, paintings and electricity pylons have all been used as portals to alternative worlds.

3. *The alternative world is a world-within-a-world, marked off by physical boundaries.* This seems to most closely match the world of Hogwarts in the Harry Potter novels. Although there is an invisible barrier that Harry has to pass through in order to board the Hogwarts Express, the school is still in our world. Muggles and wizards inhabit the same space, although there are some areas that Muggles cannot access because they do not have the necessary powers.

Features of alternative-world fantasy

Many of the characteristics of alternative-world fantasy follow the motifs and conventions of traditional stories.

Narrative structure

Two commonly occurring narratives are the quest and voyage/return Booker (2004).

The quest

A common structure for alternative-world fantasy is the journey or quest, which Booker (2004) describes as a story in which 'the hero and his companions go through a succession of terrible, often near-fatal ordeals, followed by periods of respite when they recoup their strength, receiving succour and guidance from friendly helpers to send them on their way'. Tolkien's *The Lord of the Rings* is one example that follows this pattern. The quest typically begins 'on a note of most urgent compulsion'. The threat in *The Lord of the Rings* is signalled by Gandalf's portentous return to the Shire, where he reveals to Frodo the dark threat imposed by Bilbo's ring, the lost ring of power craved by the dark lord Sauron so that he may bring all under his power and control. In quest stories typically the quest is undertaken by 'the hero and his companions' rather than a solitary hero/ine. Booker suggests that the selection of companions indicates four different types of relationship:

- the hero's companions may be a random selection and many may not even be named;
- the hero may have an alter-ego whose main characteristic is his/her fidelity;
- the hero may have a subtler alter-ego who displays qualities that are opposite to those possessed by the hero;
- the hero's companions are given distinct characteristics which complement each other.

In the first book of *The Lord of the Rings* trilogy, aptly entitled '*The Fellowship of the Ring*' the company neatly fits the fourth type of companionship. Frodo is accompanied by representatives from the different beings that inhabit Middle-Earth, each of them possessing the qualities for which their kind are known, for example Legolas the elf for speed, agility and bowmanship and Gimli the dwarf for his abilities to travel underground in the dark and to wield an axe. However, in the later stages of the quest the nature of the companionship changes. Frodo leaves the surviving companions and is accompanied solely by Sam Gamgee – an alter-ego who remains fiercely loyal to his 'master'. To some extent Gollum, who guides them temporarily as they make their way through Mordor, might also be regarded as an alter-ego embodying contrasting qualities to Frodo while at the same time representing what Frodo may become if he does not resist the ring.

Essentially the quest includes a succession of ordeals: the terrain is often hazardous as it is in *The Lord of the Rings* where there are forests and labyrinths, mountains and wastelands which must be traversed before the goal is reached; also there are the requisite battles with monsters such as Orcs, trolls and the giant spider Shelob; often the hero will have to resist a great temptation. For Frodo temptation comes from the Ring of Power which grows heavy and burdensome around his neck, willing him to slip it over his finger, which will make him visible to the dark lord.

Typically on the quest the hero will encounter helpers on the route. Frodo is guided by the wise wizard Gandalf and the beautiful but terrifying Elvin queen, Galadriel. Ultimately, a final ordeal tests the hero. Frodo must climb to the top of Mount Doom and throw the ring into the heart of the volcano. Escaping from death Frodo's sacrifice assures the renewal of Middle-Earth. Frodo, however, is called to make a final journey with Gandalf and Bilbo across the sea to the west.

Voyage–return or home-away-home

> You know, coming home and finding things all right, though not quite the same.
> (Sam Gamgee, in *The Lord of the Rings*)

In common with the quest, the voyage and return story is also based on a journey, but unlike the former, the hero/ine may stumble unexpectedly into the new world. The journey may take characters to an imaginary or magical realm as it does in *Alice's Adventures in Wonderland*. Essentially the hero or heroine travels away from familiar surroundings, the journey usually includes a threat or entrapment and in the final stages of the story the hero/ine escapes and returns to the familiar world. Typically voyage-and-return stories include an anticipation stage where the character 'falls' into the other world. This happens literally to Alice when she stumbles down the rabbit hole. Often in this stage of the story the hero/ine exhibits bored or reckless behaviour. This is followed by an initial fascination or dream stage. Indeed Alice's reponse to her new surroundings is to declare them 'curiouser and curiouser'. Wonderland is puzzling and unfamiliar; the characters do not respond as she expects them to. At first this is amusing but as the story progresses the mood changes.

In the frustration stage the hero/ines experience increasing difficult. Alice finds it increasingly frustrating to communicate with the creatures that she meets and they become increasingly aggressive. Finally at a croquet match organized by The Queen of Hearts, Alice is taken away to be tried for treason on the whim of the Queen.

The nightmare stage poses a serious threat to the hero/ine's survival. Alice finds herself in the dock tried by an incompetent King and a succession of witnesses who make no sense. But she finds her courage and voice. Accusing them of being nothing more than a pack of cards she breaks the spell and the dream dissolves. Alice awakes by the river bank, leaving the reader to ponder whether it had all been a dream. This structure is fairly common and is found in children's fantasies as diverse as *The Tale of Peter Rabbit, Treasure Island, Peter Pan* and *The Lion, The Witch and the Wardrobe.*

Character

In alternative-world fantasies heroes and heroines are often portrayed on the side of light and adversaries from the dark side. Stock characters may abound, such as the wise wizard or the hapless youth. Diana Wynne Jones (1996: 49) parodies this tendency to include archetypal and stereotyped characters:

> **Companions** are chosen for you by the Management. You will normally meet them for the first time at the outset of the Tour. They are picked from among the following: BARD, FEMALE MERCENARY, GAY MAGE, IMPERIOUS FEMALE, LARGE MAN, SERIOUS SOLDIER, SLENDER YOUTH, SMALL MAN, TALENTED GIRL, TEENAGE BOY, UNPLEASANT STRANGER and WISE OLD STRANGER.

Most parties will have at least one of these and may occasionally include one or two of the Other Peoples, usually small ones.

Main characters often have noble characteristics though these may be hidden under the guise or ordinariness, as they are with Aragorn in *The Lord of The Rings* and Adaon in Lloyd Alexander's *The Black Cauldron*:

> Adaon, Taran saw, was tall, with straight black hair that fell to his shoulders. Though of noble bearing, he wore the garb of an ordinary warrior, with no ornament, save a curiously shaped iron brooch at his collar. His eyes were grey, strangely deep, clear as flame, and Taran sensed that little was hidden from Adaon's thoughtful and searching glance. (*The Black Cauldron* by Lloyd Alexander)

Recent fantasies may explicitly challenge the expectations we have of character types. For instance, Eoin Colfer's recent *Artemis Fowl* series features an anti-hero. Ursula Le Guin, Tanith Lee and Terry Pratchett have written fantasies in which characters do not conform to type.

Setting

> Find the Map. It will be there, No Tour of Fantasyland is complete without one. It will be found in the front part of your brochure, quite near the page that says
> For Mom and Dad for having me ... (Wynne Jones, 1996: 9)

Fantasy is often dependent on the convincing realization of setting (see Chapter 4). Space or futuristic fantasy, a sub-genre of fantasy, is defined principally by setting. *Star Wars*, for instance, has much in common with high fantasy but the alternative world is futuristic. It can often be read as a fairy tale in which space suits replace suits of armour and space ships replace horses.

Language

For Le Guin (1992) fantasy language is of central importance to fantasy writing. Writers of fantasy fiction find different ways of using language to help the reader 'suspend their disbelief' and become absorbed in the alternative worlds they create. Some invent special languages for their created worlds.

High fantasy requires a style of writing that supports the status of the characters and gravity of the theme. Writers often achieve this by adopting an elevated style. The extent to which this is successful is variable. Tolkien claimed that *The Lord of the Rings* was a study in language and the seriousness of his endeavour is evident in his epic style:

> The Balrog reached the bridge. Gandalf stood in the middle of the span, leaning on the staff in his left hand, but in the other hand Glamdring gleamed cold and white. His enemy halted again, facing him, and the shadow about it reached out like two vast wings. It raised the whip, and the thongs whined and cracked. Fire came from its nostrils. But Gandalf stood firm.
>
> 'You cannot pass,' he said. The orcs stood still, and a dead silence fell. 'I am a servant of the Secret Fire, wielder of the flame of Anor. You cannot pass. The dark fire will not avail you, flame of Udun. Go back to the shadow! You cannot pass.'
>
> The Balrog made no answer. The fire in it seemed to die, but the darkness grew. It stepped forward slowly on to the bridge, and suddenly it drew itself up to a great height, and its wings were spread from wall to wall; but still Gandalf could be seen, glimmering in the gloom; he seemed small, and altogether alone: grey and bent, like a wizened tree before the onset of a storm. From out of the shadow a red sword leaped flaming. Glamdring glittered white in answer. There was a ringing clash and a stab of white fire. The Balrog fell back and its sword flew up in molten fragments. The wizard swayed on the bridge, stepped back a pace and then stood still.
>
> 'You cannot pass!' He said.' (*The Lord of the Rings* by J.R.R. Tolkien)

Tolkien uses an elevated register: vocabulary such as 'avail' and 'wielder' recreates an impression of a medieval language. Names are used as incantation, 'servant of the Secret Fire, wielder of the flame of Anor, flame of Udun'; the magic is literally in the language. The pace and rhythm are finely tuned and the epic effect is achieved through the use of a combination of long, descriptive compound sentences punctuated by Gandalf's short repeated commands, 'You cannot pass!' To see how important the selection and ordering of each word is try rewriting, 'The Balrog made no answer' in as many ways as possible (for example, 'The Balrog didn't reply'). Think about how these changes affect the impact of the passage. While Tolkien's language matches the grandeur of his scheme it is less effective in Alan Garner's first novel *The Weirdstone of Brisingamen:*

> 'Long years ago,' said Cadellin, 'beyond memory or books of men, Nastrond, the Great Spirit of Darkness rode forth in war upon the plain. But there came against him a mighty king, and Nastrond fell. He cast off his earth-shape and fled into the Abyss of Ragnarok, and all men rejoiced, thinking that evil had vanished from the world forever; yet the king knew in his heart that this could never be.'

As Neil Philip (1981: 29) has pointed out, '*The Weirdstone* suffers from the artificial, formal, hieratic language into which the narration lapses ... "here lay a knight comlier than all his fellows" ... This language similar to the high "epic" style affected by Tolkien at crucial points of *The Lord of the Rings* tends to sound either ponderous or precious'. In his later books (e.g. *The Stonebook Quartet*), Garner moved away from using an elevated style in favour of writing dialect as a means of showing the continuity between past and present.

Themes

The fantastic mode frequently depicts a conflict between good and evil. Ursula Le Guin (1992: 79) writes, 'Fantasy is the natural, the appropriate language for recounting of the spiritual journey and the struggle of good and evil in the soul'. In each of the *Harry Potter* books, Harry faces the dark forces, which are embodied by his adversary, Lord Voldemort. This is chillingly realized in *The Goblet of Fire*. At a wizarding gathering, which bears some resemblance to a Ku Klux Klan rally, Harry is forewarned about imminent danger from the dark forces by a sign that appears in the sky:

> And then without warning, the silence was rent by a voice unlike any they had heard in the wood; and it uttered, not a panicked shout, but what sounded like a spell.
>   'MORSMORDRE!'
>   And something vast, green and glittering erupted from the patch of darkness Harry's eyes had been struggling to penetrate: it flew up over the treetops and into the sky.
>   'What the –?' Gasped Ron as he sprang to his feet again, staring up at the thing that had appeared.
>   For a split second, Harry thought it was another leprechaun formation.
>   Then he realised that it was a colossal skull, composed of what looked like emerald stars, with a serpent protruding from its mouth like a tongue. As they watched, it rose higher and higher, blazing in a haze of greenish smoke, etched against the black sky like a new constellation.

One of the criticisms levelled at fantasy is the unproblematic way in which good and evil are presented in opposition to each other with, for the most part, characters falling into the camp of either allies or adversaries. It can be argued that this does little to help readers understand complex human motivations. Pratchett for example has talked about the patriarchal, classist and racist values that are promoted in traditional fantasies. Speaking about Tolkien's *The Lord of the Rings*, he has pointed out that evil characters are always black and reside at the easternmost edges of Tolkien's map. Contemporary writers challenge the ideology of earlier books. Pratchett's *Discworld* novels, for example, undermine the class-based, patriarchal societies of earlier fantasy:

> This is a story about magic and where it goes and perhaps more importantly where it comes from and why, although it doesn't pretend to answer all or any of these questions. It may, however, help to explain why Gandalf never got married and why Merlin was a man. Because this is also a story about sex, although probably not in the athletic, tumbling, count-the-legs-and-divide-by-two sense unless the characters get totally beyond the author's control. They might. (*Equal Rites* by Terry Pratchett)

Ursula Le Guin's *Earthsea* novels resist simplistic notions of good conquering evil. Her vision is one where the balance of opposing forces – good and evil, light and dark, life and death – must be achieved for restoration of harmony. The conflict her protagonist, Ged, faces is essentially the shadow of himself. Reflecting on the value system of her alternative world, Le Guin felt it did not accurately reflect her values and beliefs. This prompted her to write a further book, *Tehanu*, to combat some of the inequalities of the earlier books. Millicent Lenz writes that in *Earthsea* there is 'a class society, hierarchical and patriarchal in structure, headed by a king in Havnor, to whom wizards give the heart's gift' of fealty; in *Tehanu*, however, a questioning of rigidly defined male and female roles and leanings towards gender equality' (Hunt and Lenz, 2001: 73).

Philip Pullman has also challenged the values of traditional fantasy in the *His Dark Materials* trilogy which questions received ideas about the nature of good and evil, innocence and experience. The trilogy is a multi-layered text; a compelling fantasy adventure and a thesis arguing for a Republic of Heaven. Pullman has in this respect been compared to C.S. Lewis, though the views expressed in Pullman's books are antithetical to Lewis's doctrine. While young readers may not grasp the subtext of these books they can often apprehend deeper levels of meaning.

ACTIVITY

Make a collection of alternative-world fantasies.

- How are the alternative worlds set apart from our world?
- Why do you think Oxford, London and Venice have inspired settings for alternative-world fantasy?
- Do any of the books have portals into alternative worlds? What sorts of objects function as portals?
- What associations does each of these objects have that make them ideal connectors between two worlds? What comparisons (implicit or explicit) are made between the primary and alternative worlds?
- What other characters types frequently occur in alternative-world fantasies?
- What roles do women and old people play in these stories?
- Who holds power and how do they maintain it?
- Find a recent example of a quest fantasy and analyse its structure.
- Find a recent example of a voyage-and-return fantasy and analyse its structure.

Identify some ways in which you might explore fantasy fiction with children at different ages:

- You might invite children to write an alternative-world fantasy based on the place they live. What would remain the same? What would change?
- Invite children to observe and handle a special object, such as an old key, a decorative mirror, a music box and orally create a class story about how the object is an opening to an alternative world.
- Read an alternative-world fantasy novel or story with a class/group of children. Progressively build a map of the imagined world adding new features and notes as the story develops. The map might be a record of a quest, or illustrate the voyage and return.

To classify fantasies as either low or high is just one way in which commentators have chosen to describe the genre. Ruth Nadelman Lynn (1983) suggests alternative categories:

- allegory and fable: Ted Hughes, *The Iron Man*;
- animal story: Brian Jacques, *Redwall*; Richard Adams, *Watership Down*; Beatrix Potter, *The Tale of Peter Rabbit*;
- ghost story: Penelope Lively, *The Ghost of Thomas Kempe*; Antonia Barber, *The Ghosts*; Cliff McNish, *Breathe*;
- humorous fantasy: Terry Pratchett, *Discworld* novels; Dominic Barker, *Blart*;
- imaginary beings: Tove Jansson, *Finn Family Moomintroll*; Val Tyler, *The Greenwich Chronicles*; Steve Augarde, *The Various*;
- magic adventure: E. Nesbit, *Five Children and It*; P.L. Travers, *Mary Poppins*;
- secondary worlds: J.R.R. Tolkien, *The Lord of the Rings*; Tanith Lee, *Queen of the Wolves*;
- time travel: Helen Cresswell, *Moondial*; H.G.Wells, *The Time Machine*;
- toys: A.A. Milne, *Winnie-the-Pooh*; Jane Hissey, *Old Bear*;
- witchcraft and wizardry: J.K. Rowling, *Harry Potter and the Philosopher's Stone*; Diana Wynne Jones, *The Lives of Christopher Chant*; Stephen Elboz, *A Handful of Magic*.

ACTIVITY

Are the categories proposed by Ruth Nadelman Lynn comprehensive?

- Are these categories exclusive? (What about a humorous fantasy set in a secondary world? Or a magic adventure with an imaginary being?)
- Are there any forms of fantasy not included on this list (e.g. historical fantasy such as Joan Aiken's *The Wolves of Willoughby Chase*, space fantasy such as *Zathura*)?
- Is it helpful to categorize books in this way?
- What are the advantages? What are the disadvantages?
- Develop a personal classification system for fantasy.

Dream fantasies

'Oh, I've had such a curious dream!' said Alice, and she told her sister, as well as she could remember them, all these strange Adventures of hers that you have just been reading about; and when she had finished, her sister kissed her, and said, 'It was a curious dream, dear, certainly: but now run in to your tea; it's getting late.' So Alice got up and ran off, thinking while she ran, as well she might, what a wonderful dream it had been. (*Alice's Adventures in Wonderland*)

Since the publication of Alice in 1865, dreams have been one convention used in children's literature to explore alternative realities. Wonderland is a realm in which the manners and mores of Victorian England are subverted by Alice's encounters with the creatures she meets there.

In *Marianne Dreams* by Catherine Storr, Marianne is ill and confined to bed. She draws a picture of a house and a young boy and then she starts to have strange, lucid dreams in which she is drawn into the world she has created. In this deeply unsettling world she discovers that she has the capacity to harm others:

'Then her eyes fell on her drawing book. She snatched it up. It opened at her page of the drawing of the house, with the boy, who had been Mark in her dream, looking out. Marianne picked up the pencil, which had been lying beside the book and scored thick lines across and across and up and down over the window.

'I hate Mark,' she was saying to herself under her breath. 'I hate him, I hate him, I hate him. He's a beast, and he's spoiled my present. I hate him more than anyone else in the world.'

The next time Marianne enters her dream world she finds Mark trapped in the house with bars across the window preventing him from looking out. As a psychiatrist, Storr was interested in isolation and rejection, and exploring the inner world of the child. At one level Marianne's menacing dream world is a manifestation of her state of mind, a way of describing what Storr called, 'different faces of reality'.

In *Come Away from the Water, Shirley* and *Time to Get Out of the Bath, Shirley,* John Burningham draws explicit attention to the divide and connection between fantasy and dream worlds; the dreams in this instance are daydreams or inner play. Both books share a common structure. Each double-page spread depicts on the left-hand page a picture of 'reality', while the facing page shows Shirley's imaginative world. *In Come Away from the Water, Shirley*, Shirley's parents complain but on the right-hand page she fights pirates and finds treasure. The text makes no reference to what is happening in Shirley's head, the reader is left to infer the connection and fill the writerly gap.

Each of these three examples shows that dreams are used to reveal a state of mind or connect inner and outer realities. Manlove (1999) argues that 'dream fantasies' are not true fantasy as the dream is a function of realism in the text.

Ghost stories

Although ghost stories have their roots in traditional tales, Philippa Pearce (1995) notes that the children's ghost story is a relatively recent addition to the body of children's literature, making its first appearance at the beginning of the 20th century but increasing in popularity throughout the century and flourishing in contemporary writing. It was in the second half of the 20th century that the ghost story for children became very popular. Leon Garfield's *Mr Corbett's Ghost* (1969) tells the tale of a young apprentice, Benjamin, who is cruelly treated by Mr Corbett, his employer. Benjamin wishes Mr Corbett dead but when his wish is granted he finds himself haunted by the man he most hated. Philippa Pearce (1995: 342) has commented that while Garfield's stories are full of suspense and have the capacity to make the reader shudder they also 'probe deeply into human motivation and morality'. In fact, as Ruskin Bond notes, ghost stories often have important things to say about the way we live our lives: 'The ghostly always represents some shadow of truth'. This is true of Robert Westell's *The Watch House* (1977), the story a lonely girl who becomes obsessed by the old Life Brigade's Watch House. Set in Garmouth this is a tale about the presence of restless spirits of long-dead sailors and the brooding suspense of being watched from the windows of the Watch House. Robert Westell writes, 'perhaps I use the supernatural as a viewpoint to comment on the inner world of psychology' (in Pearce, 1995: 343).

This applies equally to a more recent novel, *Breathe* by Cliff McNish, (2006). Jack has an affinity with the spirits of the dead and when he and his mother move to an isolated house, following the death of his father, Jack immediately senses the presence of spirits reaching out to claim him. At the heart of the house is the Ghost Mother – long dead, but still mourning her daughter. She has intercepted the passage of four children from the living world to the afterlife and draws her strength by leeching their souls. Jack's encounter with ghosts leads him to the terrifying Nightmare Passage. His survival depends on his own powers, his understanding of the Ghost Mother's guilt, his contact with her dead daughter, and the resolution of his own grief. While *Breathe* is a chilling novel, not for the fainthearted, other ghost stories provide comedic opportunities. For example, in Penelope Lively's Carnegie medal winner, *The Ghost of Thomas Kempe* (1973) a 17th-century sorcerer materializes with the intent of turning a young boy into his apprentice. There is much humour in the bad-tempered poltergeist's antics. Lively's ghost story reveals her interest in peeling back layers of time, the persistence of history and tradition in landscape and the mingling of past and present. Ghosts are not always sinister and in Berlie Doherty's picture book, *Jinnie Ghost* (2005) Jinnie whispers dreams to children while they sleep so that they awake in the morning with new wonder.

ACTIVITY

Read a selection of ghost stories. Make some notes in your journal. You might want to consider some of theses questions.

- How do the ghosts function in the stories?
- Do they provide a reference point for reflecting on the world the characters inhabit?
- Is an explanation for the ghost's presence offered or is it left unexplained?
- What tone is created in the story and how is this achieved?

Selected titles:

Almond, D. (1999) *Kit's Wilderness*. London: Hodder.
Arnold, L. (2005) *Invisible Friend*. London: Hodder.
Barber, A. (1972) *The Amazing Mr Blunden*. London: Puffin.
Bowler, T. (2005) *Blood on Snow*. London: Hodder.
Burgess, M. (2002) *The Ghost Behind the Wall*. London: Puffin.
Crowly, B. (2002) *Step into the Dark*. London: Hodder.
Doherty, B. and Ray, J. (2005) *Jinnie Ghost*. London: Frances Lincoln.
Garfield, L. (2000) *Mr Corbett's Ghost*. Oxford: Oxford University Press.
Gordon, J. (2001) *The Midwinter Watch*. London: Walker.
Ibbotson, E. (2002) *Dial a Ghost*. London: Macmillan.
Kemp, G. (2004) *The Clock Tower Ghost*. London: Faber.
Lively, P (2006) *The Ghost of Thomas Kempe*. London: Egmont.
McNish, C. (2006) *Breathe*. London: Orion.
Westall, R. (2002) *The Watch House*. London: Macmillan.
Westall, R. (2004) *Ghost Abbey*. London: Random House.
Wilde, O. (2004) *The Canterville Ghost*. London: Usborne.
Wynne Jones, D. (2001) *The Time of the Ghost*. London: Collins.

ACTIVITY

Review a range of fantasy titles for your book records.

Selected titles:

Picture books
Burningham, J. (1992) *Come Away from the Water, Shirley*. London: Random House.
Burningham, J. (1994) *Time to Get Out of the Bath, Shirley*. London: Random House.
Browne, A. (1999) *Voices in the Park*. London: Random House.
Browne, A. (2000) *Willy the Dreamer*. London: Walker Books.
Browne, A. (2002) *Gorilla*. London: Walker Books.
Cooper, H. (1997) *The Baby Who Wouldn't Go to Bed*. London: Random House.
Deacon, A. (2006) While You Are Sleeping. London. Random House.
Knapman, T. and Stower, A. *Mungo and the Picture Book Pirates*. London: Puffin.
Sendak, M. (2000) *Where the Wild Things Are*. London: Random House.
Thompson, C. (1998) *How to Live Forever*. London: Random House.
Thompson, C. (2002) *Falling Angels*. London: Random House.
Van Allsburg, C. (1997) *The Mysteries of Harris Burdick*. London: Houghton Mifflin.

Novels
Adams, R. (1973) *Watership Down*. London: Puffin.
Aiken, J. (2004) *The Wolves of Willougby Chase*. London: Random House.
Alexander, L. (2005) *The Black Cauldron*. London: Usborne.
Augarde, S. (2004) *The Various*. London: Random House
Babbit, N. (2002) *Tuck Everlasting*. London: Bloomsbury.
Brennan, H. (2004) *Faerie Wars*. London: Bloomsbury.
Carroll, L. (2003) *Alice's Adventures in Wonderland*. London: Penguin.
Colfer, E. *Artemis Fowl*. London: Puffin.
Cooper, S. (1984) *The Dark Is Rising Sequence*. London: Puffin.
Cresswell, H. (2003) *The Bongleweed*. Oxford: Oxford University Press.
Funke, C. (2004) *Inkheart*. Frome: Chicken House.
Dahl, R. (2001) *James and Giant Peach*. London: Puffin.

▶

Dahl, R. (2001) *Charlie and the Chocolate Factory*. London: Puffin.
Doherty, B. and Ray, J. (illus.) (2005) *Jinnie's Ghost*. London: Frances Lincoln.
Dunmore, H. (2006) *Ingo*. London: Collins.
Fisher, C. (2002) *Corbenic*. London: Random House.
Gaiman, N. (2003) *Coraline*. London: Bloomsbury.
Garner, A. (2002) *The Owl Service*. London: Collins.
Hardinge, F. (2005) *Fly by Night*. London: Macmillan.
Hearn, L. (2002) *Across the Nightingale Floor*. London: Macmillan.
Hoban, R. (2005) *The Mouse and His Child*. London: Faber.
Hoffman, M. (2004) *Stravaganza: City of Masks*. London: Bloomsbury.
Jansson, T. (1970) *Finn Family Moomintroll*. London: Puffin.
Jacques, B. (1987) *Redwall*. London: Puffin.
Le Guin, U. (1993) *The Earthsea Quartet*. London: Puffin.
Mahy, M. (1999) *The Haunting*. London: Puffin.
Masefield, J. (1994) *The Midnight Folk*. London: Mammoth, Egmont.
Meyer, K. (2006) *The Stone Light*. London: Egmont.
Milne, A.A. (1973) *Winnie-the-Pooh*. London: Heinemann.
Nesbit, E. (1996) *Five Children and It*. London: Puffin.
Nix, G. (2003) *Sabriel*. London: Collins.
Nix, G. (2004) *Mister Monday*. London: Collins.
Norton, M. (1993) *The Borrowers*. London: Puffin.
Pratchett, T. (2001) *Amazing Maurice and His Educated Rodents*. London: Doubleday.
Pullman, P. (1998) *Northern Lights*. London: Scholastic.
Reeve, P. (2002) *Mortal Engines*. London: Scholastic.
Rowling, J.K. (1997) *Harry Potter and the Philosopher's Stone*. London: Bloomsbury.
Somper, J. (2005) *Vampirates*. London: Simon & Schuster.
Stewart, P. and Riddell, C. (2005) *Corby Flood*. London: Random House.
Storr, C. (2000) *Marianne Dreams*. London: Faber.
Stroud, J. (2004) *The Amulet of Samarkand*. London; Random House.
Westall, R. (2002) *The Watch House*. London. Macmillan.
Wynne Jones, D. (2000) *Howl's Moving Castle*. London: Collins.

Further reading

Hunt, P. and Lenz, M. (2001) *Alternative Worlds in Fantasy Fiction*. London: Continuum.
Jackson, R. (1981) *Fantasy: The Literature of Subversion*. London: Routledge.
Manlove, C. (2003) *From Alice to Harry Potter: Children's Fantasy in England*. Cybereditions Cooperation.
Tolkien, J.R.R. (2001) *Tree and Leaf*. London: HarperCollins.
Tucker, N. (2003) *Darkness Visible: Inside the World of Philip Pullman*. Cambridge: Wizard Books.

Realism

Realism in fiction means that everything in the story including characters, setting and plot could happen to real people living in our world. People act like people and animals behave like animals. There has long been a debate of just how realistic children's fiction can be. Truthful explication of society's problems, the inclusion of authentic language and exploration of taboo subjects may conflict with popular concepts of the child as an innocent in need of protection. Sometimes the best way to deal with a crisis may be through the use of fantasy and the imagination. Fairy tales, with their stories of human relationships and families go a long way towards helping children learn about human nature, and at the same time the child's imagination is enriched with the beauty of the images and metaphors. Susan Smith (1996: 354) writes,

> By their status, children are often helpless. As childhood becomes more complex and short in its life span – because of the problems of modern family life – it's more important than ever to give children heroes, someone to look up to. If a large number of children are coping with hunger, perhaps it is too much to dish up reality in all its harshness as bedtime reading.

The writer of realism employs very different techniques to the writer of fantasy. While fantasy uses imaginary elements that are contrary to reality and consequently need to create an internal consistency in order to encourage the suspension of disbelief, realism depends on relevant subjects and everyday occurrences. However, employing the labels 'realism' and 'fantasy' to describe genres of fiction is problematic. We have already suggested that fantasy must contain elements of realism in order to make any kind of meaning for the reader and, conversely, novels that we call realistic are of course fictions and by their very existence cannot be entirely 'real'. A novel may appear to be written in the realistic mode but have a strong element of wish fulfilment or adventure. For instance John Rowe Townsend's *Gumble's Yard* is a serious exploration of the effect of incompetent parenting on a family of children written in a mode that can be described as social realism but the sub-plot is a conventional fantasy adventure.

Everyday life

For young children realistic fiction tends to be about everyday experience. The conflicts in these stories are often concerned with developing independence or growing up. Shirley Hughes's *Alfie's Feet* features a pre-school child in a story about buying new wellington boots and learning how to put them on the correct feet, and in *Dogger*, also by Shirley Hughes, a young boy loses and eventually finds a favourite toy.

Families

> We begin in families. It's the thing we all have in common. A mother, adequate or otherwise. A father, absent or present. Brothers and sisters, or lack of them. Some place to sleep at some sort of base. A jumble of people wished upon us from birth. (Hilary Mckay)

The family story has a long tradition in children's literature but the concept of family and its representation has changed dramatically since the nineteenth century. Jo March in Louisa May Alcott's *Little Women* (1869) asserts that 'I do think families are the most beautiful things in all the world'. Contemporary writers however tend to focus on family problems which range from the normal conflicts that are attendant with growing up, to serious issues such as abandonment and abuse. Wise supportive parents in fiction for older children are in short supply but, on a positive note, a greater diversity of family situations is now evident in children's literature.

Unlike fantasy stories which tend to centre on adventure or epic quests, family stories deal with domestic issues and, most importantly, relationships. American writer Betsy Byars is renowned for her sympathetic portrayal of single-parent families and her sensitive depiction of relationships, particularly between mothers and sons. She has also written bleaker stories such as *The Cartoonist* (1978) in which she dispels the notion that parents love their children equally, and *Cracker Jackson* (1985) which is uncompromising in its depiction of physical abuse.

Jacqueline Wilson, currently one of Britain's most popular writers, does not patronize her young readership, believing that most issues (sexual abuse excepted) can be written about for children providing the writer is sensitive to the reader's potential vulnerability. *The Illustrated Mum* (2000) tells the story of an unconventional mother, Marigold, and her two children, Star and Dolphin. Marigold is covered with tattoos and her children think she is the brightest and most beautiful mother in the world. But things are not right, Marigold is deeply depressed and alcohol dependent:

'I'm going to Marigold,' I said, climbing out of bed. 'We had such a great time today. You just wind her up and make her worse. She's fine with me.'

Star said nothing. I was forced to pad on out of the bedroom. I went very slowly along the hall, putting the heel of my foot in front of my toes so that I only moved one foot length at a time. The kitchen light was still on. I went very slowly towards it. Marigold was sitting at the table in her T-shirt and jeans but she was fast asleep, her head slumped, her mouth slightly cupped round her glass but it was empty. So was the bottle.

'Marigold?' I whispered. 'Marigold, I've had a bad dream.'

I took hold of her by the arm. She was very cold.

'Marigold, come to bed. Please.'

Marigold groaned but didn't answer. Her eyes were half open and not focusing. I knew there was no point persisting. I went and got her quilt and wrapped it round her. Then I patted her icy hand.

In this deeply sad scene, Wilson does not retreat from showing how bad things can be for children and their families, but if the story were written entirely at this level of intensity it would be too depressing for her young readership. Wilson employs humour to diffuse tension and to reassert the loving relationship between Marigold and her children. Nicholas Tucker writes, 'This is writing that both entertains and educates, within which joy sometimes gives way to sorrow and where a character's problems, once expressed, are never allowed conveniently and sentimentally simply to fade away' (Tucker and Gamble, 2001: 74).

ACTIVITY

Review a range of stories that reflect the diversity of family, for children aged 0–4, 5–7, 8–11 and 12–14.

To what extent do you find the depiction of family realistic?

Make notes and add bibliographic details to your book records.

Selected titles:

Abdel-Fattah, R. (2006) *Does My Head Look Big in This?* London: Marion Lloyd Books.

Alcock, V. (1995) *The Cuckoo Sister*. London: Mammoth.

Alcott, L.M. (1994) *Little Women*. London: Puffin.

Almond, D. (1998) *Skellig*. London: Hodder.

Boyce , F.C. (2004) *Millions*. London: Macmillan.

Cleary, B. (2004) *Ramona the Pest*. Oxford: Oxford University Press.

Daly, N. (2002) *What's Cooking, Jamela?* London: Frances Lincoln.

Edwards, D. (2002) *My Naughty Little Sister*. London: Egmont.

Fine, A. (1990) *Goggle-eyes*. London: Puffin.

Forde, C. (2004) *Skarrs*. London: Egmont.

Fine, A. (2006) *The Book of the Banshee*. London: Random House.

Magrs, P. (2004) *Hands Up*. London: Simon & Schuster.

Gavin, J. (1993) *Granpa Chatterji*. London: Methuen.

Gleitzman, M. (1999) *Bumface*. London: Puffin.

Gleitzman, M. (2006) *Belly Flop and Water Wings*. London: Puffin.

Hoffman, M. (1997) *Grace and Family*. London: Frances Lincoln.

Hughes, S. (1997) *Alfie Gets in First*. London: Random House.

Johnson, P. (2001) *Rescuing Dad*. London: Random House.

Johnson, P. (2003) *How to Train Your Parents*. London: Random House.

McDonald, M. (2001) *Judy Moody*. London: Walker.

McKay, H. (2002) *Saffy's Angel*. London: Hodder.

Nesbit, E. (2005) *The Railway Children*. London: Puffin.

Rai, B. (2004) *Rani and Sukh*. London: Random House.

Rees, G. (2003) *The Mum Hunt*. London: Macmillan.

Simon, F. (2006) *A Giant Slice of Horrid Henry*. London: Orion.

Townsend, J.R. (1999) *Gumble's Yard*. Oxford: Oxford University Press.

Wallace, K. (2002) *Raspberries on the Yangtzee*. London: Simon & Schuster.
Wilson, J. (1996) *Double Act*. London: Random House.
Wilson , J. (2000) *The Illustrated Mum*. London: Random House.

Further reading
Tucker, N. and Gamble, N. (2001) *Family Fictions*. London: Continuum.
Teachers' resources for Indigo's *Star* www.writeaway.org.uk

Other themes and issues in contemporary realistic fiction

A wide range of contemporary social issues have been explored in realistic fiction. The following list is illustrative and not intended to be comprehensive. You may want to extend the range of themes in your reading journal, identifying key titles for each theme:

- Terminal illness: Maurice Gleitzman, *Two Weeks With the Queen*; Ian Strachan, *The Boy in the Bubble*;
- Sexuality: Paul Magrs, *Strange Boy*; James Riordan, *The Cello*;
- Teenage pregnancy: Berlie Doherty, *Dear Nobody*; Catherine Macphail, *Roxy's Baby*; Mary Hooper, *Megan*;
- Drugs: Melvin Burgess, *Junk*;
- Bullying: Anne Fine, *The Tulip Touch*; Nicky Singer, *Feather Boy*; Carl Hiassen, *Hoot*; Keith Gray, *Malarkey*; Michael Coleman, *Weirdo's War*; Graham Gardner, *Inventing Elliott*;
- Friendship: Eoin Colfer, *Benny and Omar*; Elizabeth Laird, *Secret Friends*;
- Death and bereavement: Michael Rosen, *Sad Book*;
- Homelessnes: Robert Swindell, *Stone Cold*; Steven Herrick, *The Simple Gift*;
- Refugees: Morris Gleitzman, *Boy Overboard*; Robert Swindells, *Ruby Tanya*; Beverley Naidoo, *The Other Side of Truth*;
- Racism: Benjamin Zephaniah, *Face*; Eric Brown, *British Front*; Bali Rai, *What's Your Problem?*
- Transplant surgery: Malorie Blackman, *Pig Heart Boy*; Melvin Burgess, *Sara's Face*;
- Child abuse: Jean Ure, *Bad Alice*; Elizabeth Laird, *Jake's Tower*;
- Respect and tolerance: Rumer Godden, *The Diddakoi*; Randa Abdel-Fattah, *Does My Head Look Big in This?*
- Children in care: Malachy Doyle, *Georgie*;
- Disability: Sherry Ashworth, *Paralysed*; Stefan Casta, *Summer with Mary Lou*; Margaret Wild, *Jinx*;
- Football: Michaela Morgan, *Respect*; Mal Peet, *Keeper*;
- Alzheimer's: Mary Arrigan, *Chocolate Moon*; Roise Rushton, *Waving Not Drowning*;
- Mental health: Tabitha Suzuma, *A Note of Madness*;
- Identity: Rachel Anderson, *Red Moon*; Tanuja Desai Hidier, *Born Confused*;
- Religious conflict: Theresa Breslin, *The Divided City*.

ACTIVITY

Review a range of realistic fiction for your journal. The titles listed above provide a good starting point for exploration. Alternatively, you may want to check the lists of recent award winners and start your reading there. What issues interest the children you are working/have worked with? Can you locate a book to match their interests?

The problem novel

Sheila Egoff (Egoff et al., 1980) writes critically about the 'problem novel', which she calls a sub-genre of realistic fiction. This collection of books, she suggests, is reductive in its literary qualities, the motivation for writing being the exploitation of a problem rather than artistic drive: 'While most of these books could be destroyed on literary grounds, or challenged as amateurish forays into the disciplines of psychology and sociology, as a group they are formidable in their popularity and endurance' (1980: 356). Most realistic fiction deals with the problems that children face (physical, psychological, intellectual, emotional) but those that are classified as problem novels can be recognized by the following signs:

- Problem novels are about externals, how things look rather than how things are. They differ from realistic novels in their limited aims. Titles often indicate that the author started with a problem in mind rather than the idea for a plot or character.
- The protagonist is laden with grievances and anxieties which grow out of some form of alienation from the adult world, to which s/he is usually hostile.
- Partial or temporary relief from these anxieties is received in association with an unconventional adult outside the family.
- The narrative is almost always in the first person and its confessional tone is rigorously self-centred.
- The vocabulary is limited and the observations are restricted by the pretence that an 'ordinary' child is the narrator.
- Sentences and paragraphs are short.
- Locutions are colloquial and the language is flat and without nuance.
- There is an obligatory inclusion of expletives.
- Sex is discussed openly.
- The setting is urban.
- The role of the parent in the problem novel is one of failure. Adults are generally shown to be insensitive to anything outside the norm.
- Endings of problem novels can be most revealing: 'A consideration of the endings alone strengthens the impression that it is the problems themselves – or rather the cool anecdotal explication of them – that are the raison d'être of problem novels, for psychologically convincing resolutions seem to be neither required by readers nor demanded by the conventions of the genre' (Egoff et al., 1980: 363).

Values in realist fiction

In realist fiction, Peter Hunt observes, 'It is interesting to see that the religious/didactic element in children's books has been replaced by a movement to be politically correct – socially and racially aware'. During the 1970s, 1980s and 1990s the role of children's literature in transmitting the social values of the dominant culture was vigorously debated among those involved with children and books. Attention has been drawn to the limited and sometimes negative portrayals of sex, race, class, age, sexuality, body type and so on.

When it was first published, Jan Needle's *My Mate Shofique* (1978) was groundbreaking in its exploration of racism but more recently critics have questioned the book's validity on the basis that Jan Needle is writing as an outsider and must therefore necessarily present an outsider's viewpoint. This criticism is voiced by Errol Lloyd writing in *Books for Keeps*:

> In Britain although racism is alive and kicking in subtle forms, mixed neighbourhoods are the norm, and mixed couples and social mixing generally, are very much on the increase, which makes it easier for the white writer, potentially at any rate, to gain insights into patterns of black culture, style etc. as a source of fiction. There are pitfalls however, language for instance can prove a barrier and is shot through with subtle power relations. How familiar will the white writer be with the speech patterns within the black community particularly of black youth? (November 1997: 1)

It is an issue to consider when selecting books. We need to think about issues that are implicitly embedded in the writing process as well as those that are obviously present in the subject.

In recent years picture books have challenged the under-representation and marginalization of children from different ethnic groups. Mary Hoffman and Caroline Binch's buoyant heroine in *Amazing Grace* proves that there is no reason why a black female cannot play Peter Pan in the class play. James Berry and Louise Brierley's *Celebration Song* depicts a black Madonna and child, Verna Wilkins's *Dave and the Tooth Fairy*, a black tooth fairy and in *An Angel Just Like Me*, also by Mary Hoffman, a young boy discovers that angels do not have to be pink and female. All of the books mentioned draw attention to the issue of inequality but a litera-ture of inclusion is emerging more slowly. One example is Malorie Blackman's adventures, where she does not comment on the background of her black charac-ters – they just are.

Attention has recently been drawn to other issues of representation. Positive images of disability are, for instance, still rare. Mark Roberts's *Night Riders* (2001) tells the story of two Down's syndrome teenagers which presents a different view of disability to that commonly held. The boys are individuals whose talents and difficulties reflect the diversity that is found in children with this condition. And Gillian Cross has created an unsentimental and determined wheelchair-bound character in her thriller *Calling a Dead Man* (2001). The International Board on Books for Young People (IBBY) publishes a biennial booklet featuring outstanding books for people with disability which includes the representation of the disabled in literature for the young (see www.ibby.org).

Language

One of the areas guaranteed to cause a reaction is the use of 'bad language' in children's books. This ranges from casual use of expletives to offensive language directed at a particular group (e.g. race, gender and sexual orientation).When Robert Westell's Carnegie Medal-winning *Machine Gunners* was first published by Macmillan in 1975 there was a reaction to its authentic use of language, which was deemed to be offensive. Set during the Second World War it is a story about a gang of boys and one girl (barely tolerated) who collect war souvenirs. Their most dar-ing feat is to smuggle a machine gun out of a German bomber. Puffin published an edition in 1977 and made the decision to retain Westell's original words but by the time the second edition was printed in 1979 they had expurgated the offend-ing language. The 1979 edition is available today.

Here are some of the changes that were made in the later editions:

'Frigg off, Audrey Parton, we're busy.' 'Faff off, Audrey Parton, we're busy.'
'Leave the poor bugger alone.' 'Leave the poor thing alone.' (about
a prisoner of war)
'Frigging fool!' 'Faffing fool!'
'The sodding Germans are coming.' 'The faffing Germans are coming.'
'He bit me, the Nazi sod!' 'He bit me, the Nazi swine!'

The language the boys use is anti-German and has sexual connotations but the ideological content of Westall's book is pacifist not anti-German. The important issue raised by such cases is whether writers can express their views if they are cur-tailed from using the language that reveals prejudice.

ACTIVITY

Consider the extent to which your selection of books for teaching has been influenced by an awareness of the moral, social or political content.

- Has a moral or political issue ever arisen in connection with a child's reading?
- What dilemmas did this create for you?
- How did you resolve them?
- What would you consider to be unacceptable in a book for children aged 0–5 years, 5–7 years, 7–11 years, 11–14 years?
- Why have social, political and moral issues caused enduring debate in the field of children's literature since the 1960s?
- Should teachers and librarians:
  (a) adopt evaluative guidelines for selection?
  (b) remove offending titles from library shelves?
  (c) explain and encourage critical literacy so that children can make their own judgements about literature?

ACTIVITY

Now that you have considered some of the features of literature that has been called 'fantasy' or 'realism'. Select two novels from your reading. One should be predominantly fantasy and the other predominantly realistic. Complete a copy of the grid in Appendix 6.1 for each of the novels. What conclusions can you draw from this activity? If possible share what you have found with a critical partner or group. How does your completed grid compare to theirs?

Appendix 6.1

TITLE:

	FANTASY	REALISTIC
SETTING		
CHARACTERS		
THEMES		
DIALOGUE		
EVENTS		

Chapter 7

Time and Place in Children's Fiction

In this chapter we shall:

- explore the range of writing about the past and consider its relevance to young readers today;
- consider the place of fictions set in the future;
- review the range of fictions set in other parts of the world, including those written from internal and external perspectives;
- consider the case for including literature in translation in children's reading repertoires.

Time and place

The fictions discussed in this chapter are connected by a focus on setting. Whether set in the past, the future or other parts of the world, they offer young readers access to experiences beyond their everyday lives. Such experiences, as we shall see, are not merely escapist but may also provide a means by which children can reflect on their own lives and come to a view of their place in the world.

Bringing the past to life

Writing about the past encompasses a range of fictions. Some semi-autobiographical work such as Nina Bawden's *Carrie's War* might be classified as 'recollection as history'. Other novels, such as Jill Paton Walsh's *A Parcel of Patterns*, deal with a specific historical event. This kind of writing requires some research on the part of the author, although the depth and extent of the research varies from writer to writer. Some writers claim to carry out virtually no background research, while others may take years gathering material in preparation for writing. For some the research is about immersion in the world that they are writing about as Ann Turnbull reflects: 'The need to get the details right is for me as much as it is for the reader. If I know that I've researched everything, I can then start to take it out of the final draft' (from www.writeaway.org.uk). A further type of writing about the past is set in an identifiable period but does not refer to historical events. This might be called period fiction, the novel's equivalent of the costume drama. Books such as Leon Garfield's *Smith* are included in this category. Again there are differences in the extent to which the historical period is accurately drawn. In the detailed descriptions of Garfield's novels, the 18th-century world of Fielding and Smollett is convincingly drawn but other writers may present only the slightest hint at period, being more interested in costume and romance. The past may also be used as a setting for other genres such as the historical fantasy and alternate histories (Joan Aiken *Midnight Is a Place*), historical mystery (Patricia Finney, *Lady Grace Mysteries*) timeslip novel (Helen Cresswell, *Moondial*) or historical adventure (Graham Marks, *Snatched*).

One of the earliest writers of children's historical fiction in English, Geoffrey Trease (1972), drew attention to the distinctions that can be made between different types of writing about the past:

> The author has to be clear from the start what kind of historical fiction he is going to write ... The distinction I have in mind concerns first of all the attitude one adopts to the past. I think most readers of historical fiction ... tend to fall into one of two categories. They are concerned with, fascinated by, either the differences between bygone times and their own, or the similarities. Broadly speaking, the former category read to escape from real life; the latter to illuminate it by comparison and recognition of unchanging human characteristics ... The authors in their turn fall into the same two categories. If they belong to the first they are likely to produce the 'costume' novel. The other type of novel he suggests is the true 'historical novel', seeking not only authenticity of fact – but so far as it is humanly discoverable – a faithful recreation of minds and motives. In the last analysis a good historical novel is a good novel, neither more nor less, whose story happens to be laid outside the time limits of living memory. (Cited in Fox, 1995: 51–2)

You might detect a tone intimating that the 'true historical novel' is superior to other fiction set in the past. Certainly Trease's writing set a standard for historical accuracy which in the 1930s contrasted with earlier romanticized approaches to writing historical fiction (e.g. Robert Louis Stevenson, *Kidnapped*; Baroness Orczy, *The Scarlet Pimpernel*; Walter Scott, *Ivanhoe*). Is it necessarily true that period fiction is less interested in the recreation of 'minds and motives' and is concerned principally with 'escape from life'? You might reflect on this distinction drawing on your experience of children's books set in the past.

ACTIVITY

> Why include fiction set in the past in the repertoire of children's reading? Discuss the special qualities of historical fiction or write notes in your journal.

Commentary

You may have identified some of the following benefits and others that are not included here:

Historical fiction can:

- Arouse interest and curiosity in history.
- Often put historical events in the context of everyday settings – the narrative provides a 'temporal scaffold for historic understanding that is accessible even to quite young children' (Downey and Levstik, 1988: 338).
- Encourage empathy through characterization. The interest is in people and their motivations. In this way it might complement other sources that are used in historical enquiry. Whereas sources for macro-history often privilege male perspectives, historical fiction provides more insight into women's stories. Kay Vandergrift writes, 'Through literature, young people can become familiar with aspects of history absent in most school curricula and with a literary canon that affirms women's lives and represents female heroes independent of the male model' (from www.childrensbooks.about.com).
- Often explore the complexity of a situation. It may be written from a prevailing point of view or from multiple perspectives. Fiction presents models of behaviour and can illuminate ways in which different people solve problems and conflicts.
- In the school context, use historical fiction as a means of integrating the curriculum. A historical novel might be used as stimulus for work in history, literacy/English, citizenship and so on.

Recollection as history

Does the writer remembering the past have any particular responsibilities to the child reader? Jill Paton Walsh (1994) suggests that recollection involves bringing past states of mind into view of the present state of mind and claims that many writers for children have recollected childhood as a lost 'Golden Age'. In her view recollection of childhood is insufficient ground in common with young readers for whom childhood is the present, *'Difficult though it is to achieve it, we must try to see the world, and portray it to children in the light of the present day'* (1994: 219).

One novel based on recollection is Nina Bawden's *Carrie's War*, which is partially based on her childhood experiences of being evacuated to Wales during the Second World War. In her autobiography Bawden writes, 'except in the coded way that most novelists make use of their lives, cannibalizing rough odds and ends of experience to make a tidy whole, *Carrie's War*, is not my story' (1994: 40) but those childhood memories of being supplanted from home, attempts to understand adults in her new environment and explorations in the Welsh countryside have all found their way into the novel:

> During the war – when England was at war with Germany – the Government sent the children out of the cities so they shouldn't be bombed. We weren't told where we were going. Just told to turn up at our schools with a packed lunch and a change of clothes, then we went to the station with our teachers. There were whole train-loads of children sent away like that ... (*Carrie's War* by Nina Bawden)

Similarly, Valerie Bloom's novel, *Surprising Joy* (2004), is about a young girl who has spent her life with her grandmother in Jamaica, steeped in Jamaican culture. Until her mother, who moved to England when Joy was a baby, writes to say that she's ready for her daughter to come and join her. Joy can hardly contain her excitement. Joy goes through an experience that must have been very similar to Valerie's own arrival in England in the late 1970s, though she was older than Joy.

Neither Bloom nor Bawden present childhood as a 'lost Golden Age'. The circumstances that Joy and Carrie find themselves in are similar to those of their respective authors but alienation, coming to terms with changed circumstances and personal growth are universal themes that transcend the authors' particular childhood experiences. The emotional tone of these books will ring true for many children reading these novels today.

Historical fiction

Historical fiction is dependent on temporal setting and thus requires a special commitment and research from the author. How important is historical accuracy? Jill Paton Walsh reminds us that facts alone do not create historical fiction: 'Who cares about facts? We shall not find truth in them. Though we may if we seek for graver and more philosophical meanings be able to forge truth from them' (1987: 202). So can writers of historical fiction write about something that isn't true? Jill Paton Walsh offers a useful distinction between two different definitions of 'not true': (a) not true – meaning *known* to be not true; (b) not true – meaning *not known* to be true. While writers of historical fiction should not write anything known to be not true, she says, they are free to use whatever is 'not known to be true', 'the thrilling quagmire of what might have been'.

Historical fiction concentrates on public events and private consciousness. Some writers are interested in the macro historical events while others, like Jill Paton Walsh, are interested in the impact of history on individual lives. She writes,

> the inner thoughts and feelings of the characters as public events impinge on them has to be invented. Nevertheless, because anybody who has actually lived through a public event ... will remember a mixture of the inner and outer happenings ... a narration that supplies a private element in an account of a historical event will have more credibility to the majority or readers ... In telling children a story about something in the past, I aim therefore at an account which mixes public and private perspectives so as to imitate memory. (Walsh, 1994: 217)

John Stephens (1992) argues that the audience for historical fiction starts at the upper primary level, as a less solipsistic view of the world is required in order to engage imaginatively with characters and events not identifiable in the present.

Readers, he suggests, need to imagine settings and technologies which are exotic in a particular way and need to be able to take interest in such details. In his analysis he demonstrates that historical fiction tends to present some degree of linguistic difficulty in so far as the strategies writers use to make the text seem 'strange' are often linguistic.

Whose history?

Historical fiction tends to reflect the preoccupations of the culture from which it arises. There are different prevailing trends in the books available in the USA, Australia and Britain, for example. In 2005/6 several seafaring books set in the 19th century were published to coincide with the bicentennial of Trafalgar (Susan Cooper, *Victory*; Paul Dowswell, *Powder Monkey*; Michael Molloy, *Peter Raven Under Fire*; and Elizabeth Laird, *Secrets of the Fearless*). It would be unusual for this significant British event to get equal attention anywhere other than Britain.

Conversely, there are lots of interesting stories from world history that may not be readily available to British children. In the USA, for instance, an interest in the African-American experience and pioneers has spawned a body of literature. In Australia the depression is a popular subject and in Ireland publishing books about the Famine (Marita Conlon-McKenna, *Under the Hawthorn Tree*) and Irish political history (Gerard Whelan, *War Children*) find their place. Interestingly, Celia Kennan estimates that about a quarter of children's books published in Ireland are historical, which coincides with the wider cultural interest in history (*The Lion and the Unicorn* 21.3, September 1997).

Even in the UK there are different trends in the history that is retold in England, Wales, and Scotland; Welsh publishing has a large number of titles about blending the mythic, historic and fantasy with King Arthur as the figure representing national identity. Scottish writers including Kathleen Fidler (*The Droving Lad*), Donald Lightwood (*The Long Revenge*), Judith O'Neill (*So Far from Skye*) and Mary Moffat (*The Lothian Run*) have all written about key events in Scottish History. While some historical books may be taken up by mainstream British publishers (e.g. Sonya Hartnett, *Thursday's Child*) others may not travel far from their place of original publication. For teachers prepared to track books down using the internet, there are alternative histories available to broaden the range generally available through mainstream outlets.

Black History Month, held every year in October, has raised the profile of books about prominent black figures. The majority of these books are non-fiction and are concerned with figureheads, people who have made significant achievements. There is still too little fiction available, especially about the lives of ordinary people. One recent exception is Celia Rees, *Pirates*. Rees's heroine Nancy Kington, is 'A Merchant of Bristol's Daughter', and therefore right at the centre of the power, money and privilege generated by the trade in sugar and slaves. She is beautiful, she is wealthy, but as she grows towards womanhood, she finds that she is just as much a commodity as any of the products her family buys and sells. She is sent to Jamaica to fulfil the destiny planned for her. Here she meets Minerva Sharpe, a slave, born on the Kington's Jamaican plantation. On the surface, the two girls couldn't appear more different, but neither can tolerate the position that society has forced upon them, so they rebel together.

Rees finds validation for the authenticity of her depiction of a friendship between a white slave owner and back slave in Aphra Behn's *Oroonoko*.

In the UK the curriculum may also have an impact on the number of books that are written and published about particular historical periods. Romans, Tudors, Victorians and the two World Wars are particularly popular periods for education and non-fiction publishing but fiction set in these periods may also be favoured in schools and libraries book selections. And yet, one of the pleasures of historical fiction is the facility it offers to introduce children to the periods and places that are not formally studied in the curriculum.

Review the range of historical fiction in your class, school local or teachers' centre library. Which periods and countries are represented? Where do the writers come from?

Which periods of history have limited or no representation? Use the internet to search to find examples of historical fiction originating in other countries.

Selected titles:

Beaman, N.G. (2001) *Dragon Mountain*. Milton Keynes: AuthorHouse (Wales).
Breslin, T. (2002) *Kezzie*. London: Egmont (Scotland).
Brink, C.R. (1990) *Caddie Woodlawn*. Atheneum (USA).
Byars, B. (1982) *Trouble River*. London: Scholastic (USA).
Conlon-McKenna, M. *Under the Hawthorn Tree*. Dublin: O'Brien (Ireland).
Curtis, C.P. (2004) *Bud, Not Buddy*. Laurel Leaf (USA).
Cushman, K. (2002) *The Ballad of Lucy Whipple*. London: Macmillan (USA).
Fidler. K. (2003) *The Droving Lad*. Edinburgh: Floris (Scotland).
Harrison, C. (1998) *The Secret of Drumshee Castle*. Merlin Publishing (Ireland).
Hartnett, S. (2002) *Thursday's Child*. London: Walker (Australia).
Hesse, K. (1999) *Out of the Dust*. New York: Scholastic (USA).
Hofmeyr, D. (2003) *The Waterbearer*. London: Hodder (South Africa).
Hunter, M. (2003) *Escape from Loch Leven*. Edinburgh: Floris (Scotland).
Lightwood, D. (2002) *The Long Revenge*. Scottish Children's Press (Scotland).
Llywelyn, M. (1990) *Brian Boru*. Dublin: O'Brien Press (Ireland).
Lutzeier, E. (2002a) *The Coldest Winter*. Oxford: Oxford University Press (Ireland).
Lutzeier, E. (2002b) *Bound for America*. Oxford: Oxford University Press (Ireland/USA).
Morgan, N. (2003) *Fleshmarket*. London: Hodder (Scotland).
O'Neill, J. (1993) *So Far from Skye*. London: Puffin (Scotland).
Park, R. (2001) *Playing Beatie Bow*. London: Barn Owl (Australia).
Reekie, J. (2003) *Tess*. Raincast Books Canada (Canada).
Rhind, M. (2002) *The Dark Shadow*. Edinburgh: Floris (Scotland).
Welch, R. (1994) *The Gauntlet*. Oxford: Oxford University Press (Wales).
Wheatley, N. (1994) *My Place*. Kane/Miller (Australia).
Whelen, G. (1996) *The Guns of Easter*. Dublin: O'Brien Press (Ireland).

Language

The extent to which writers try to create a language that creates the feeling of the past varies. Gillian Lathey writes, 'At its most basic, period vocabulary becomes a stage prop to indicate costume, food, trades, military equipment and the like' (2001: 33) and at its worst vocabulary such as 'zounds' and 'begad' is used to bamboozle the reader into thinking there is research behind the story.

It is interesting to look at the different ways in which writers have attempted to recreate an impression of the past through language. Lathey observes that in *A Parcel of Patterns*,

past language becomes the structure of modern thought patterns in a beautifully constructed conceit. The language of narrator Mall Percival is based on research into the syntax and vocabulary of contemporary documents from the plague village of Eyam in Derbyshire. Mall guides us through the plague years; her thoughtful, earnest nature chimes with the sonorousness of the record she feels compelled to write and leave behind before setting out for a new life in America. Convincing as this narrative strategy is, Mall's written record is no simple country girl's charm; the reader is privy to a modern consciousness couched in period language. (2001: 33–4)

Revolution, is an anti-war statement. The Colliers' view is that fiction that presents history from a single viewpoint is a falsification of truth, which does little to help us understand present or future needs. Other writers would disagree. Hester Burton author of the Carnegie medal winning *Time of Trial* (1963) wrote about the importance of an authentic viewpoint:

> When I come to describe the historical situation which I have chosen, I try to view it through the limited vision of a single character or group of characters. I am not all-wise, or all-knowing as the historian is; but neither, it is well to remember, were the people actually taking part in the historical event I am describing. They had no access to state papers; they could merely use their eyes. Not only is it a wise caution for the writer of historical novels to limit this range of vision but it is also much better art. (Burton, 1973)

ACTIVITY

Write your reflections based on these questions in your journal:

- Should a writer of historical fiction present more than one point of view?
- Is limited vision a falsification of history?
- Is it more important to represent the feelings of a major character or present a broader social perspective?
- Can a writer overcome this dilemma: writing convincingly from the viewpoint of a major character at the same time revealing the character's prejudices to the reader?

Universal human experience

Sometimes it is suggested that we can learn from the mistakes of the past or that the universality of human experience enables us to develop empathy for people living at another time. Stephens (1992: 203) argues against the assumption that there is an essential human nature which is transhistorical:

> This 'humanist' position is challenged by 'cultural relativism' which takes the converse view: the individual subject is constructed where cultural systems and structures intersect. Thus, the cultural assumptions of one period cannot be applied to another. Notions of the universality of human experience need to be handled with great care, since it may amount to no more than a matter of representing the past in our own image. It is easy to see that humans in all periods seek to experience happiness but this is in fact a culturally specific notion. Even in very recent times, middle-class western women tended to conceive happiness rather differently in 1989 to 1959 or 1949.

ACTIVITY

Choose and read one historical novel. You might want to read the same novel as a colleague/group of colleagues. Consider some of these questions and write your reflections in your journal:

- How accurate do you think the description of the historical period is? What makes you think that? What details are used to create a feeling for time and place?
- Are any real historical figures featured in the story? How does the depiction in this novel compare to what you know of the character? You might read a biography and autobiography to compare the similarities/ differences in representation.
- Does the story describe a known historical incident? Does it add anything to what we know about this incident?
- What is the source of the conflict in story? Does it arise out of the historical element? How does it relate to children today?
- Why do you think the author chose to write this story, set in this particular period?
- Is the point of view a partial one?

Period fiction

Period fiction, the equivalent of a television costume drama, is set in an identifiable historical period but is not primarily concerned with a particular event or real figures from history. The 18th-century setting of Fielding and Smollett is depicted in Leon Garfield's period novels, though they also owe something to Dickens and Stevenson for their style and content, which probably accounts for the occasional erroneous attribution of the setting as Victorian London. Garfield's first book, *Jack Holborn*, published in 1964 bears some similarity to Stevenson's *Treasure Island*, being a seafaring adventure with piratical encounters. The story involves a mystery surrounding the hero's long-lost mother. Family secrets and a search for identity also feature in his second book, *Devil-in-the-Fog* (1966). George Treet is happy with his life as part of a family of travelling actors until he discovers that Mr Treet is not his real father, and that he in fact comes from a noble family – a family that has dark secrets. It soon becomes clear that someone is out to kill George. The story is written in the picaresque style, recounting, with characteristic dark humour, the adventures of the roguish hero through the squalid world inhabited by the underclasses of the period. *Smith* (1987) is written in a similar style and the story takes place in familiar Garfield territory. Set in 18th-century London, street urchin Smith witnesses the murder of an old man whose pocket he has just picked. Unable to read the contents of a document that he recovers from the dying man, his possession of it leads him into peril in a plot brimming with intrigue and betrayal. Garfield's work (like Dickens's) with its period flavour, has adapted particularly well for television and film, *Black Jack*, *The December Rose*, and *Devil-in-the-Fog* all benefiting from this treatment.

A recent compelling saga, V.A. Richardson's *The House of Windjammer* (2003) and *The Moneylender's Daughter* (2006) is set against the backdrop of tulip fever in 17th-century Amsterdam where fortunes can be easily won and just as easily lost in crazy speculative markets. Richardson's story charts the progress of one merchant family who lose everything when their ship, the *Sirrus*, is sunk. Their predatory merchant banker, Van Helsen, calls in their debts knowing that it will destroy them. The family is further betrayed by a greedy, ineffectual uncle whose lack of business acumen accelerates the decline. Though the future is bleak for young Adam Windjammer, he finds romantic interest in the guise of Van Helsen's daughter – a recipe for intrigue and drama.

Family chronicle

Richardson's *Windjammer* stories fall into the tradition of the family saga or chronicle and can be compared to the adult equivalents: John Galsworthy's *Forsyte Saga* (1906) or Margaret Mitchell's *Gone With the Wind* (1936). Typically these novels, or sequences of novels, chart the waxing and waning fortunes of a family, or connected families, over a period of time. Early examples include Charlotte Yonge's *The Daisy Chain* (1856) which describes the life of eleven children brought up by their widowed father in the West Midlands, and Louisa May Alcott's *Little Women* (1868) and its sequels, which chart the fortunes of four sisters, Amy, Beth, Jo and Meg, growing up during the American Civil War.

From the 20th century K.M. Peyton's *Flambards* (1967) is a celebrated family chronicle written for children. The series is set before, during and following The Great War. The first book in the sequence is the story of orphaned teenage heiress Christina Parsons on the event of moving to live with her uncle and her cousins on the run-down estate, Flambards. Christina falls in love firstly with Mark, one of her cousins, and then later with the stablehand, Dick, whom she eventually marries. The chronicle format allows for an exploration of changing social circumstances and the impact on individuals. As a result of Christina's commitment, hard work and good management the run-down Flambards is transformed into a working farm that can yield a small harvest. In the controversial later addition to the sequence, *Flambards Divided* (1981), the local gentry refuse to admit Christina and Dick into the social circle and when Mark returns from the war Christina's feelings are very much divided.

Joan O' Neill's Irish saga *Daisy Chain War* (2002) and sequels detail the lives of the Doyle family, covering the timespan from the Irish 'Emergency' to present day. The saga or chronicle is often used as a device, enabling the writer to portray particular historical events and the impact of those events on people's lives. This is certainly the case with O'Neill's books. Book One focuses on the young Lizzie Doyle as she comes to terms with living with her English cousin and the impact of war on an impoverished Ireland. The second, *Bread and Sugar* (2002), set in the late 1940s follows Lizzie's nephew, John Doyle. The third, *Daisy Chain Dream* (2003), returns to a focus on Lizzie as she prepares to marry her childhood sweetheart as the country rebuilds itself after the war. The final book, *Daisy Chain Days* (2004), returns to a first-person narration and brings the family story up to the present. As the population of Ireland changes and becomes more culturally diverse, the central character, Beth, must confront the racial prejudice that her friend Alexandru, a Bosnian refugee faces. As a whole the chronicle presents an interesting comparison of values and attitudes in Ireland in 1941 and 2004.

Alternative histories

Alternative histories engage with the past by posing the questions: What if things had turned out differently? How would the world have been different? What impact would it have had on our lives? Alternative histories focus on a change which would alter history and then explore the ramifications of that change. One example is Michael Cronin's trilogy which takes as its premise the successful Nazi invasion of Britain. The three books, *Against the Day* (1998), *Through the Night* (2003) and *In the Morning* (2005), tell the story of two boys who must learn to live with their new neighbours, the German Gestapo, but are drawn into the secret world of the Resistance. Similarly, Joan Aiken's *The Wolves of Willoughby Chase* (1962) is set in an England where the succession of the monarchy does not follow the line that we know from our history textbook. It takes as its point of divergence the successful Stuart succession in the Jacobite wars. James III is King and the pretender to the throne is called George.

Historical fantasy

Historical fiction shares some common ground with fantasy: both genres are dependent on the creation of convincingly realized settings that are beyond the experience of the reader and may well appeal to readers in similar ways, offering an exotic experience or 'escape' to another world. The connection is taken one step further with the strand of historical fiction – historical fantasy – which does not impose the same constraints regarding accuracy as straight historical fiction. The term covers fictions that might be set in a clearly defined historical period into which an element of fantasy or magic is introduced. One example is Ben Jeapes's *New World Order* (2004). Set during the English Civil War, Oliver Cromwell's New Model Army does battle with the Holekhors as alien airships fly over the skies of 17th-century London. The introduction of aliens into a story set in the 1600s is a startling imaginative leap.

The fantasy element in Kevin Crossley-Holland's *The Seeing Stone* (2001) is less of a disjuncture with the time and place in which it is set. Arthur de Caldicot lives with his uncle and cousins in a manor. He wants more than anything to become a knight but has many lessons to learn before acquiring that privileged status. Arthur is befriended by the mysterious Merlin who gives him a piece of obsidian, the seeing stone, and in its polished surface he has visions of another Arthur who grew up to be a fine King, owner of the sword Excalibur and leader of the Knights of the Round Table. As Crossley-Holland points out,

> The books are historical but they are also legendary in that I'm invoking the resonant motifs within Arthurian legend such as The Round Table, and talking about them not in a historical but in a legendary way: for example, with the idea of Arthur going under the hill, or the three times of throwing the sword into the water. (from www.writeaway.org.uk)

But this is no casual fusion of legend and history. Initially the book was to be a retelling of the Arthurian legend but catching his own reflection in a piece of obsidian Crossley-Holland realized that the 'seeing stone' could be used as a device through which Arthur de Caldicot could glimpse snatches of the legendary Arthur's life and that those visions could resonate with events in his own life, amplifying their meaning.

The year 1200 is a significant date; after that the stories of Arthur, the pan European hero, would have been widespread and it is inconceivable that they would have been unknown to Arthur de Caldicot. Furthermore, the period also has co-incidence with contemporary cultural and religious conflict. In the second and third books in the trilogy the fantasy element is less marked, and in a fourth stand-alone novel, *Gatty's Tale* (2006), the legendary elements are set aside in a purely historical story about Gatty's pilgrimage to Bethlehem.

Some books are set in a purely fantasy world that may bear a strong resemblance to a specific period. Steven Elboz's 'Magic' books are set in a world that is suggestive of Victorian London, complete with recognizable landmarks such as St Paul's Cathedral (not the domed one), the Bank of England and the Tower of London, but it is a world where things are slightly askew – familiar but strange. In *Stravaganza*, Mary Hoffman (2004) uses the same device. Her alternative world, Talia, bears some resemblance to the Italy that we know but it exists in a parallel dimension. The defining moment came at the point when Romulus and Remus fought and the city of Rome was founded. In Talia it is Remus who wins the contest and founds the city, which is named Remora and becomes the capital of the Reman Empire.

Finally, before moving on from historical fantasy, there is one more type to consider: stories which are set in clearly identified historical periods but in imaginary lands. For example, Frances Hodgson Burnett's *The Lost Prince*, set in the 19th century, is the story of Marco and his father who move from place to place. Loyal to the kingdom of Samavia, they are involved in plots and secret councils hoping to restore a Lost Prince who might come to rule his people. Imaginary European states and lost princes are a recurring theme in a strand of fiction that has become known as Ruritanian, taking the name from Anthony Hope's novels set in Ruritania: *The Prisoner of Zenda* (1894), *The Heart of Princess Osra* (1896) and *Rupert of Hentzau* (1898). In these novels, Ruritania is depicted as a German-speaking country located between Saxony and Bohemia, under the rule of an absolute monarchy with inhabitants possessing extreme wealth or suffering from extreme poverty. The political content of Hope's novels was neutralized in film adaptations which reinvented Ruritania using motifs from fairy tales. Other examples of the genre include Robert Louis Stevenson's *Prince Otto* (1885) and Violet Needham's *The Black Riders* (1939) and *The Emerald Crown* (1940). In a spoof by American writer William Goldman, *The Princess Bride* (1973), Prince Humperdinck of Florin plans to marry Buttercup, a country girl ranked number 20 for her beauty so that he can produce and heir and inherit the kingdom from his senile father. His real intentions are to kill her throwing suspicion onto neighbouring kingdom Guilder and thus instigating war.

Historical sources in fictional contexts

As well as blurring boundaries between history and fantasy, the interface between factual historical accounts and the fictionalizing of events is made explicit in some novels. For example, Teresa Tomlinson's *The Flither Pickers* (1987) and *The Herring Girls* (1994), about the lives of the wives and children of the Whitby fishermen, were inspired by contemporary photographs by Frank Meadow Sutcliff. Photographs are included in the book. Sometimes this distinction between historical fact and fiction may be hidden from the reader making it difficult to ascertain the validity of information. The digitext *The Diary of Walter Tull* (2005) is, for example, a fictionalized diary of a real historical character (in electronic form) interspersed with primary-source evidence such as family photographs. The absence of an author's name for the diary makes it appear that the text was actually written by Tull and that letters included are archived material (an author's name does appear in the accompanying teachers' notes).

Review a range of writing about the past including recollection, historical fiction, period fiction and historical fantasy and add details to your book records.

Selected titles:

Avi (2002) *Crispin: The Cross of Lead*. London: Simon and Schuster.
Bawden, N. (1974) *Carrie's War*. London: Puffin.
Branford, H. (1997) *Fire, Bed and Bone*. London: Walker Books.
Breslin, T. (2002) *Kezzie*. London: Egmont.
Crew, G. and Tan, S. (1999) *Memorial*. Melbourne: Lothian Books.
Crossley-Holland, K. (2001) *The Seeing Stone*. London: Orion.
Crossley-Holland, K. (2006) *Gatty's Tale*. London: Orion.
Cushman, K. (1994) *Catherine Called Birdy*. London: HarperCollins.
Doherty, B. (2004) *Granny was a Buffer Girl*. London: Puffin.
Dickinson, P. (1998) *The Kin*. London: Macmillan.
Forbes, E. (1968) *Johnny Tremain*. New York: Yearling Books.
Francis, P. (2007) *Raven Queen*. London: Usborne.
Gardner, S. (2006) *I Coriander*. London: Orion.
Garfield, L. (1968) *Smith*. London: Puffin.
Gavin, J. (2000) *Coram Boy*. London: Egmont.
Geras, A. (2004) *Lizzie's Wish*. London: Usborne.
Golding, J. (2006) *The Diamond of Drury Lane*. London: Egmont.
Grant, K.M. (2006) *Blood Red Horse*. London: Puffin.
Hautzig, E. (1981) *The Endless Steppe*. London: Puffin.
Hearn, J. (2005) *The Merrybegot*. Oxford: Oxford University Press.
Hearn, J. (2006) *Ivy*. Oxford: Oxford University Press.
Hest, A. (1997) *When Jessie Came Across the Sea*. London: Walker Books.
Hoffman, M. (2004) *Stravaganza: City of Masks*. London: Bloomsbury
Hooper, M. (2003) *At the Sign of the Sugared Plum*. London: Bloomsbury.
Hooper, M. (2004) *Petals in the Ashes*. London: Bloomsbury.
Howker, J. (2003) *Isaac Campion*. London: Walker Books.
Hubbard, K. (2007) *Rubies in the Snow*. London: Short Books.
Lawrence, C. (2002) *Thieves of Ostia*. (The Roman Mysteries). London: Orion.
Magorian, M. (1983) *Goodnight, Mister Tom*. London: Puffin.
Marryat (1983) *The Children of the New Forest*. London: Puffin.
McCaughrean, G. (2001) *The Kite Rider*. Oxford: Oxford University Press.
McCaughrean, G. (2003) *A Little Lower than the Angels*. London: Puffin.
Morpurgo, M. (2003) *The Wreck of the Zanzibar*. London: Egmont.
Newbery, L. (2003) *The Shell House*. London: Scholastic.
Newbery, L. (2005) *Polly's March*. London: Usborne.
O'Neill, J. (2002a) *Daisy Chain War*. London: Hodder.
O'Neill, J. (2002b) *Bread and Sugar*. London: Hodder.
O'Neill. J (2003) *Daisy Chain Dream*. London: Hodder.
O'Neill, J. (2004) *Daisy Chain Days*. London: Hodder.
Park, L.S. (2006) *A Single Shard*. Oxford: Oxford University Press.
Patterson, K. (2003) *Preacher's Boy*. Oxford: Oxford University Press.
Patterson, K. (2005) *Lyddie*. London: Puffin.
Peyton, K. M. (2004) *Flambards*. Oxford: Oxford University Press.

▶

Priestley, C.(2006) *Death and the Arrow*. London: Random House.
Prince, A. (2001) *Oranges and Murder*. Oxford: OUP.
Rees, C. (2001) *Witch Child*. London: Bloomsbury.
Rees, C. (2004) *Pirates*. London: Bloomsbury.
Richardson, V.A. *The House of Windjammer*. London: Bloomsbury.
Richardson, V.A. (2006) *The Moneylender's Daughter*. London: Bloomsbury.
Sedgwick, M. (2005) *The Foreshadowing*. London: Orion.
Sutcliff, R. (2000) *Eagle of the Ninth*. Oxford: Oxford University Press.
Tomlinson, T. (2005) *Against the Tide*. London: Random House.
Turnbull, A. (2003) *No Shame, No Fear*. London: Walker.
Turnbull, A. (2004) *Josie Under Fire*. London: Usborne.
Walsh, J.P. (1992) *A Parcel of Patterns*. London: Puffin.
Webb, B. (2006) *Star Dancer*. London: Macmillan.
Westall, R. (1994) *Machine Gunners*. London: Macmillan.

Further reading

Agnew, K. and Fox, G. (2001) *Children at War*. London: Continuum.
Collins, F.M. and Graham, J. (2001) *Historical Fiction for Children*. London: David Fulton.
Fisher, J. (1994) 'Historical fiction', in P. Hunt (ed.), *International Companion Encyclopedia of Children's Literature*. London: Routledge.
Beck, Cathy et al. 'Historical Fiction: Teaching Tool or Literary Experience?', *Language Arts* 77(6): 546–55.

Time-slip

> 'A Sundial!' she exclaimed softly, and then almost immediately and without knowing why, 'Moondial!' And as she spoke the word a cold distinct wind rushed past her and the whole garden stirred and her ears were filled with a thousand urgent voices. She stood swaying. She put her hands over her ears and shut her eyes tight. The whispers faded, the wind died. Minty opened her eyes and was blinded for a moment by the sun, but when she did see, she knew that she was in a now altered morning, not at all the morning she had woken up to. (*Moondial* by Helen Cresswell)

In the time-slip story a contemporary child is transported back into the past, characters from the past reappear in the present, or both. The historical context of the time-slip novel is authentic. Alison Uttley's *A Traveller in Time* (1939) moves between 1910 into the England of Elizabeth, Mary Queen of Scots and the Babington Plot; Penelope Farmer's *Charlotte Sometimes* (1969) slips between the late 1960s and the 1914–18 War. Recent additions include Susan Cooper's *Kingdom of Shadows*, in which a modern boy is enabled to experience the Globe Theatre in the time of Shakespeare and Linda Buckley-Archer's *Gideon the Cutpurse* set in the 18th century when highwaymen owned the roads and public hangings were regarded as entertainment. As well as historically accurate settings characters face genuine historical problems such as child abuse, health and mortality, justice and punishment, labour issues, poverty. In each of these books historical events are filtered through the eyes of a contemporary protagonist. Because that character is usually a contemporary of the implied reader, they can be expected to view events from a similar perspective and with shared values. For the reader this facilitates a connection with the past. The time-slip novel allows the author to explore a period with hindsight and may contrast the values of a historical period with the present as Temple et al. (1998: 343) express it: 'Going back in time allows characters to gain first hand experience that deepens their understanding of how historical events influence the present'.

Unlike the historical novel however, Margery Fisher (1969: 116) notes that fact is subordinate to fantasy:

The House of Arden by E. Nesbit, Alison Uttley's *A Traveller in Time*, Edward Eager's *The Time Garden* – give you far more than just a story of Elizabeth's reign. They give you in various moods, the feelings of boys and girls moving in history but still remembering their own times. The reactions of the children to what they see and hear, the way they are changed by their experience – it is for these things we make the journey. What we learn on the way is incidental.

The qualities of time-slip are magical and mysterious as Linda Hall (1998: 224) explains,

> The sense of mystery is perhaps partly due to the emphasis in such stories on time, a much less easily defined or understood concept than history. Indeed, scientists are still hypothesizing about it, although what time-slip writers seek is not a scientific or even rational explanation of time. Time for them seems to represent the opposite of what we understand by the word history. Whereas history, and especially the history we are taught at school, is perceived to be about change ... time becomes the focus for intuitions about the changeless, timeless matters of human existence and for fear of the loss of such necessary continuities.

As a result time-slip occupies a philosophical-cum-poetic terrain that the materialist nature of history has largely denied itself. It is inevitable, therefore, that time-slip engages with more intangible matters than historical fiction does.

Most frequently time-slip novels begin in the present where the author establishes the credibility of the contemporary world. Although the tone of time-slip differs from the purely historical novel, the only fantastic device that is employed is the portal through which the characters travel back in time. For it to work in a plot that is otherwise written in the realistic mode, the portal must be convincingly capable of inducing a shift in perception or reality. In Philippa Pearce's *Tom's Midnight Garden* (1958), a door to the past is opened (literally) when the clock strikes thirteen.

Time pieces are of course the perfect device for transporting characters between time periods. In Kit Pearson's *A Handful of Time* (1987) a pocket watch is the mechanism by which Patricia is taken back to her mother's childhood past. In *Moondial* it is the symbol of time, a statue of Old Father Time rather than a watch or clock. Objects or talismans that exist in the present but have also existed in the past are also frequently dolls, moneyboxes, jewelry and clothes. Portals can also be uncovered in old buildings. In Melvin Burgess's *An Angel for May* the protagonist, Tam, is sheltering in an old fireplace when he falls through the back and into the time of the Second World War. With the reality time travel now, in theory at least, considered a real possibility there may more serious speculative uses of the devices.

One of the problems for the plot of these novels is the movement of time. How does the writer account for the disappearance of a character for sometimes lengthy periods? It is most usual for time to stand still while the protagonist is in the past, or at least move at a slower pace so that the character will not have been unduly missed. One exception to this pattern is again Melvin Burgess's *Angel for May* where Tam's absence leads to a police investigation.

Existing at the intersection of three different strands of children's literature (historical, fantasy and contemporary realism) time-slip affords characters the opportunity to reflect on universal problems from a more distanced perspective. Though the fantasy element of time-slip is the product of imagination, emotional and psychological truth must be present if the reader is to suspend their disbelief. The catalyst for time travel is often provided by some personal difficulty such as bereavement (*King of Shadows*) separation (*Gideon the Cutpurse*, *Tom's Midnight Garden*) divorce (*An Angel for May*), parental illness (*Follow Me Down*) or even the state of adolescence. Frequently the hero or heroine might be aided by their experience in the past with coming to terms with personal difficulties. For example in Helen Cresswell's *Moondial*, Minty is pulled back in time by the mysterious moondial where she is called upon to help children living in extreme circumstances and through caring for others learns to cope with her own personal difficulties.

ACTIVITY

Review a range of time-slip books and add notes to your records. You may want to consider the following:

- What do the characters learn about the past and present?
- What problems does the main character face in the contemporary world? What do they learn about themselves?
- How does the portal operate between the different time periods and how appropriate is this device?
- How is the problem of the passing of time in the past and present dealt with?

Selected titles:

Almond, D. *Kit's Wilderness*. London: Hodder.
Boston, L. (2000) *The Children of Green Knowe*. London: Faber.
Browne, N.M. (2000) *Warriors of Alavna*. London: Bloomsbury.
Buckley-Archer, L. (2006) *Gideon the Cutpurse*. London: Simon & Schuster.
Burgess, M. (1994) *An Angel for May*. London: Puffin.
Cooper, S. (2000) *King of Shadows*. London; Puffin.
Cresswell, C. (2000) *Moondial*. Oxford: Oxford University Press.
Curley, M. (2005) *The Named*. London: Bloomsbury.
Farmer, P.(2002) *Charlotte Sometimes*. London: Random House.
Hearn, J. (2004) *Follow Me Down*. Oxford: Oxford University Press.
Hedges, C. (2001) *Red Velvet*. Oxford: Oxford University Press.
Jarman, J. (2006) *The Time Travelling Cat and the Egyptian Goddess*. London: Andersen Press.
Kipling, R. (1995) *Puck of Pook's Hill*. London: Penguin.
Mayne, W. (1995) *Earthfasts*. London: Hodder.
Park, R. (2001) *Playing Beatie Bow*. London: Barn Owl Books.
Pearce. P. (2005) *Tom's Midnight Garden*. London: Puffin.
Peyton, K.M. (1972) *A Pattern of Roses*. Oxford: Oxford University Press.
Pratchett, T. (1997) *Johnny and the Bomb*. London: Random House.
Price, S. (2003) *The Sterkarm Handshake*. London: Scholastic.
Sheldon, D.and Blythe, G. (1995) *The Garden*. London: Random House.
Tomlinson, T. (2003a) *Meet Me by the Steelmen*. London: Walker Books.
Tomlinson, T. (2003b) *Errand Lass*. London: Walker Books.
Uttley, A. (1977) *A Traveller in Time*. London: Puffin.

Science fiction: speculation and futuristic settings

A useful working definition of science fiction is proposed by Kornbluth et al., (1959): 'Realistic speculation about possible future events, based solidly on adequate knowledge of the real world, past and present, and on a thorough understanding of the nature and significance of the scientific method'. As this definition suggests, science fiction is future oriented, though it is not always set in the future and does not attempt to predict it, being more concerned with possibilities than certainties. As children's writer Peter Dickinson puts it, 'I believe we have evolved to speculate about possibilities. It's a very useful survival tool for a species expanding into new and different terrains. We still go on doing it because our minds are that shape'. Indeed writers of science fiction are as likely to write about a future that they hope will not come to pass, as a future they think is likely to happen. As Ray Bradbury (1979) put it, *'People ask me to predict the future, when all I want to do is prevent it'*. Science fiction shows the tension that exists between the hopes that society places in science and the fear of technological development. Perhaps this is best symbolized in Mary Shelley's *Frankenstein* (1818), Stevenson's *The Strange Case of Dr Jekyll and Mr Hyde* (1886) and Stan Lee's *The Incredible Hulk* (1962) in which the hubristic scientists are eventually destroyed by their own creations.

The distinction between science fiction and fantasy is not a clear one. Some commentators maintain that fantasy presents a world that never was nor could be and science fiction speculates on future possibilities, given what we know of science. They argue that there are no connections between these genres. However, others insist that this is an over-simplification and that what a lay person understands as scientifically 'realistic' will be different to that of the quantum physicist, for example. In his essay 'Hazards of Prophecy: The Failure of the Imagination' Arthur C. Clarke (1962) wrote that any sufficiently advanced technology is indistinguishable from magic, a law which Terry Pratchett inverted in his *Discworld* novels to read 'Any sufficiently advanced magic is indistinguishable from technology'. Indeed writers of science fiction may also write fantasy (e.g. Ursula Le Guin, Neil Gaiman) and fantasy writers may be awarded science fiction prizes (e.g. Diana Wynne Jones). One common distinction is between 'hard' science fiction dealing with realistic science while 'soft' science fiction is sometimes applied to more fanciful applications. It is a distinction that has existed since the genesis of the genre and is epitomized in the acrimonious exchange of letters between H.G. Wells and Jules Verne. In 1903 Verne wrote, 'It occurs to me that his stories do not repose on a very scientific basis ... I make use of physics [Wells] fabricates'. The retort was equally scathing, 'There's a quality in my "pseudo-scientific" (imbecile adjective) stuff which differentiates it from Jules Verne ... Something one might regard as a new system of ideas – thought'.

Science Fiction encompasses a range of fictions with recurring themes and patterns. A discussion of these follows.

Dystopia

A fictional, socially engineered society usually presided over by a totalitarian regime. While dystopias may bear some resemblance to our world, they are usually set in an imagined future. The defining characteristic of the genre is that human beings are responsible for the dystopic state. In these books we often find that social mobility is restricted, that the state has total control of the economy, black markets emerge, that there is general conformity and discouragement of dissension, though there may be informal or organized resistance. The strapline of Oisin McGann's *Small Minded Giants* (2006) sums it up perfectly: 'If you mess with the Machine, the Clockworkers will come for you'. The human race has been forced to live underground in an engineered dome following a catastrophic climate change and when Sol's father goes missing, Sol discovers what lies beneath the veneer of his so called civilized society. *Shade's Children* by Australian writer Garth Nix (2006), takes place in a future where evil overlords have ruled since the catastrophic 'change' which caused all people over the age of 14 to disappear. The 14th birthday is known as Sad Birthday. Children are taken to the Meat Factory and their organs harvested to create the cyborg creatures that are servants to the overlords. Chilling stuff indeed.

Cyberpunk

A portmanteau label combining cybernetics and punk, cyberpunk focuses on advanced technologies combined with the breakdown in social order. Generally cyberpunk is concerned with conflict between hackers and the mega-corporations that have ultimate control and power. Usually they are set on a near future earth rather than inter-galactic territory. The Feed, in M.T. Anderson's (2003) novel of the same title, is a constant flow of information and advertising plugged straight into the brain via a microchip insertion. There is no need to think as the Internet and Shopping Channels will make suggestions as to what you need or want to know. It's a sick and dying world where skin lesions have become fashion accessories. When Titus meets Violet, a girl with a cheap defective feed, he is offered the chance to think for himself, but is it worth the effort? Written in an American slang first-person idiolect, this is an outstanding book for teenagers.

Post-apocalypse

Post-apocalyptic fiction is set after a catastrophic change, perhaps climatic, or the aftermath of a nuclear holocaust. In Robert Swindells's *Brother in the Land* the teenage first-person narrator, Danny, recounts his experiences of surviving the devastation of a nuclear bomb. Set in Shipley in the North of England, this is a story about surviving by using your wits and the determination to fight to protect family and possessions. In this society new groups of people are formed. 'Badgers' are the survivors holed up in the basements, hoarding food and often the target for raids and attacks from other groups. 'Spacers' are people who have lost everything, wandering through the land in a dazed, detached existence. 'Purples' are the feared cannibals, named after the song 'Purple People Eaters'. 'Goths' are outsiders who raid the area looking for food and their attacks are vicious. It is a bleak vision of a future where the worst aspects of human nature come to the fore.

Robert O' Brien's *Z for Zachariah* has a female narrator, 16-year-old Ann. At first she believes that she is the sole survivor of a nuclear attack until a stranger clad in a radiation suit finds her house. When he becomes sick Ann nurses him back to health but as he grows stronger he becomes more menacing and controlling and one night attacks Ann in her room. Ann executes a plan to steal the radiation suit and escape the valley to look for survivors elsewhere. This is a claustrophobic novel focusing on themes of power, control and freedom.

In contrast Louise Lawrence's *Children of the Dust* is ultimately a more optimistic novel. Following a full-scale nuclear attack, Sarah and her family are confined in a bunker. Above ground survivors survive the nuclear winter and adapt to conditions becoming the dominant species. This futuristic family saga follows the fortunes of three generations concluding with Simon's story and his emergence from the bunker accepting that humans are a dying species. Lawrence's book offers some hope of survival after catastrophic events.

Julie Bertagna's *Exodus* (2002) and *Zenith* (2007) are set in an imagined future where climate change has submerged entire countries under water. A group of teenagers fighting for survival set sail in search of Greenland. Bertagna writes, 'I feel I'm caught within a fragile membrane that separates what is from what may be, as the future I have imagined seems to rip through the real world of now' (from www.juliebertagna.com).

Robots

Robots, artificial aliens, have been popular in children's literature since the 1950s. The treatment of the subject varies from the gently humorous, through the anarchic, to the deeply disturbing. For older teenagers, Asimov's *I Robot* (1950) is a collection of nine short stories that explore the interaction between humans, robots and morality. In Kevin Brooks's hard-hitting but sensitive novel, *Being* (2007), Robert is in hospital for a routine examination. Anaesthetized but conscious he is aware of the surgeons talking about him, as the endoscopy reveals plastic casings and fibre optic filaments. Robert is forced to flee for his life, desperate for the answers that will tell him who, or what, he is.

For readers from around 10 years old, Helen Fox's *Eager* (2004) is the story of an experimental robot, EGR3. Released into a world that is accustomed to robots that simply do as they are programmed, Eager is designed to learn, think and make choices and his creator sends him to live with a family called the Bells, in order that he may learn how the world works. Fox, like Asimov and Brooks, is interested in the moral dimension of advanced robotics. Does a machine capable of thinking, learning and feeling have rights? Can it be good or evil? The morality of robots is explored more schematically in the *Transformers* comics. Controlled by the Robotmaster, the heroic protagonists, Autobots, battle with the evil antagonists, Decepticons.

Frontiers of exploration

Much early science fiction was concerned with exploration, including space travel and journeys to the deepest oceans. Jules Verne, one of the early pioneers of the

I see now that for this task of writing I have undertaken I lack wit and skill, and set things down awry. For Catherine Momphesson, her dress, is already written here, and how she came to Eyam is yet to be set down. But then it is no matter if it be disordered, like enough as long as it is told.

So then, at the time of the parcel, of parsons we had two. Parson Stanley had been with us many years, longer than I can remember otherwise. But older folk well remembered a time before him, when we had a wicked parson, who had sorely vexed the people, and at last departed, leaving no one here to christen or to marry, or to pray over the dead. Then a number of the men of Eyam agreed together and fetched Thomas Stanley to be our parson, and petitioned Mr Saville in whose gift the living lies, that he might consent to have Stanley, and he agreed. All this was many years before my birth, but here I set down the history of it as I had it from John Stanley, Parson Stanley's son with whom I have played catch-and-tag, all round the churchyard wall, and whom grew to man's estate as one among all the boys of Eyam. (*A Parcel of Patterns* by Jill Paton Walsh)

Ann Turnbull also considered how she would need to adapt language for her story about relationships and religious tension set during the early reign of Charles I. Her solution was to use language that would not alienate a modern readership but at the same time to avoid words and phrases that would be too readily located in the 21st century and would therefore sound anachronistic in her story: 'I didn't struggle too much. I knew that Susanna had to use the pronouns 'thee' and 'thou' because that was central to the story':

Mary regarded me gravely. My employer is not given to shows of emotion, but I saw that she was glad for me. 'I shall miss thee,' she said. 'But thou hast earned thy happiness – and hast served out the time of the agreement.' (*Forged in the Fire* by Ann Turnbull)

ACTIVITY

> Select and read two historical novels.
>   Write notes comparing the different ways in which the writers recreate a sense of the past through use of language.
>
> Suggested authors:
>
> Henrietta Branford
> Sally Gardner
> Leon Garfield
> Jamila Gavin
> Adele Geras
> Linda Newbery
> Rosemary Sutcliff
> Geoffrey Trease.
> Ann Turnbull
> Jill Paton Walsh

Point of view and artistic integrity

Reading historical fiction provides an opportunity to reflect on a narrative point of view. John Stephens (1992: 202), writes, 'One of the areas of writing for young readers which can be most radically ideological is the area of historical fiction. This is either because writers are trying to forge truth from facts or else because the idea of telling it how it was tends implicitly to mask more complex issues such as the retrospective construction of causality and the impossibility of creating narrative without a point of view'.

In writing *Johnny Tremain*, Esther Forbes (1944) chose mainly to follow historians who believed that the American Revolution was a just cause, whereas James and Christopher Collier's *My Brother Sam Is Dead* (1974), also about the American genre, wrote *20,000 Leagues Under the Sea* (1870) before submarines were perfected, and *From the Earth to the Moon* (1865) before space travel was possible. Now that both of these forms of travel are commonplace, exploration of the universe must take other forms. As early as (1895) H.G. Wells had considered the possibility of time travel in *The Time Machine*. More recently *Dr Who*, resurrected in 2004 as a TV series with accompanying tie-in novels, travels through space and time in his police box spacecraft, the Tardis. His travels may not be entirely fanciful with scientific researchers seriously investigating the possibilities of string theory and circular space time. Jamila Gavin's *The Wormholers* (2003) was developed from the combination of the after-effects of anesthetic and a fascination with notions of time, space and travel, black holes and wormholes.

Aliens

Alien stories are part of the exploration theme with characters encountering aliens in other parts of the galaxy. When this happens the writer has to make the world credible in the same way that the writer of fantasy has to realize an alternative setting: 'If the story takes place on an alien world, the reader must be able to believe humans can walk there. Everything, from gravity and atmosphere, geology and life forms, must fit and be part of that world if it is to ring true ...' (H.M. Hoover). Alternatively, aliens make the journey across space and visit earth. H.G. Wells's *The War of the Worlds* was written after the close observation of Mars in 1894 which led to speculation that there could be life on the red planet.

Alien presence is frequently treated as malevolent. K.A. Appplegate's *Animorph Series* for young adults, first published in 1996, is about five teenagers and an Andalite alien who attempt to prevent the takeover of the earth by parasitic aliens called Yeerks. The teenagers, granted the powers of alien technology, are able to morph into animals if they touch them. In Nicholas Fisk's *Grinny*, the alien takes the form of an elderly, seemingly benign, relative who plays mind tricks on the adults in the family. She is eventually trapped by the children who remain unaffected by her powers. Aliens disguised as humans is a recurring theme in children's fiction and television. The popular *My Parents Are Aliens* (CITV) features two ingenuous aliens disguised as human foster parents in order to learn about the human race. Jeanne Willis's series of Dr Xargle picture books are young aliens learning about the idiosyncratic behaviour of the human race, and misunderstanding it.

Investigating genre reading
This activity can be adapted for other genres (e.g. horror, chick lit, thriller).

Find an adult whose reading preferences include science fiction (or an alternative genre). Talk to them about how their identity was constructed through reading this genre. The following prompts might be helpful. Make notes in your journal. Reflect on what you have learnt and the implications for working with young readers.

- How long have you been reading science fiction?
- When you were younger did you read science fiction written for children?
- When you were younger did you have any favourite science fiction authors? If so, who?
- What were the particular qualities of science fiction that you enjoyed as a child?
- What qualities do you look for in science fiction as an adult reader?
- Do you read anything other than science fiction? If so, what?
- To what extend do you think reading science fiction has influenced your view of the world (e.g. politics, religious beliefs, moral or social values)?

Read two or three science fiction titles. Include at least one classic book and one modern science fiction novel. Make notes in your reading journal. If possible, discuss your thoughts with a group or partner.

▶

Investigate the range of science fiction titles that are currently available in the book-shops. Are there any recurring themes (e.g. climate change, genetic engineering, cloning)?

Investigate the range of technologies that children have or the things on their current wish lists. What do they consider to be the most exciting uses of technology? What do they anticipate the 'next generation' technologies will be able to do? What possibilities for problems/conflicts/stories might emerge from these futuristic technologies?

Selected science fiction titles:
Proto-science fiction and scientific romances

Doyle, A.C. Sir (1994) *The Lost World*. London: Puffin.
Shelley, M. (2004) *Frankenstein*. London: Puffin.
Verne, J. (2004) *20,000 Leagues Under the Sea*. London: Puffin.
Verne, J. (2005) *Around the World in Eighty Days*. London: Puffin.
Wells, H.G. (1968) *The War of the Worlds*. London: Heinemann.
Wells, H.G. (2004) *The Time Machine*. London: Pheonix.

Modern science fiction for younger readers

Anderson, M.T. (2003) *Feed*. London: Walker Books.
Blackman, M. (2004) *Dangerous Reality*. London: Random House.
Burgess, M. (2006) *Sara's Face*. London: Andersen Press.
Colfer, E. (2005) *The Supernaturalist*. London: Puffin.
Dickinson, P. (2001) *Eva*. London: Macmillan.
Dickinson, P. (2003) *The Weathermonger*. London: Macmillan.
Farmer, N. (2003) *House of Scorpion*. London: Simon & Schuster.
Fox, H. (2003) *Eager*. London: Hodder.
Gavin, J. (1996) *The Wormholers*. London: Mammoth.
Halam, A. (2002) *Taylor Five*. London: Orion.
Jeapes, B. (2003) *The Xenocide Mission*. London: Random House.
Jeapes, B. (2004) *The New World Order*. London: Random House.
Lassiter, R. (1999) *Hex*. London: Macmillan.
Lawrence, L.(2002) *Children of the Dust*. London: Random House.
McGann, O.(2006) *Small-minded Giants*. London: Random House.
Nix, G. (2006) *Shade's Children*. London: Harper Collins.
O'Brien, R. (2004) *Z for Zachariah*. London: Puffin.
Philbrick, R. (2002) *REM World*. New York: Scholastic.
Rose, M. (2005) *Hurricane Force*. London: Simon & Schuster.
Rose, M. (2006) *The Death Gene*. London: Simon & Schuster.
Rose, M. (2006) *Luke Harding: Role Call*. London: Kingfisher.
Sedgwick, M. (2000) *Floodland*. London: Orion.
Singleton, J. (2006) *Angel Blood*. London: Puffin.

Another place: a world view

As well as being a key to unlocking the past or the future, children's literature also offers readers possibilities of vicariously experiencing unfamiliar places. Books can be windows looking out to the world, showing how children grow up in different places, rich cultural heritages, the universality of human experience as well as highlighting sometimes difficult circumstances that children have to endure perhaps due to war, totalitarianism, poverty or extraordinary events.

Ideally children should have access to literature originating in other countries. Historically, publishing books from abroad, especially books translated into English, has not been a strength in British publishing. There are indications that this is beginning to change. The Marsh Award for Children's Literature in Translation has in recent years raised the profile of children's literature from other countries and the books submitted for this prize are more numerous than they were at the outset. Recent winners include Sarah Adams for her very fine translation of Daniel Pennac's *Eye of the Wolf* (2002) which tells the story of a young African refugee and his deep empathetic relationship with a caged wolf, blinded in one eye by human hunters. A guide to translated children's literature, *Outside In* (2005), is an excellent resource for those wanting to select books or find out more about this aspect of children's books. Books written in English may also originate from other parts of the world. Linzi Glass, Lauren St John, Beverley Birch and Beverley Naidoo, for example, have all written stories based on their experiences of living in Africa.

There are also some very good books written by writers who, although they do not live in the places they are writing about, have visited or conducted careful research. Elizabeth Laird's *Oranges in No Man's Land* (2006) draws on her experience of living in Lebanon in the 1970s and *A Little Piece of Ground* was written after a visit to Ramallah. One question to consider is whether an outsider can legitimately tell the story of a group to which they do not belong. Balanced against this we have to consider by what other means those stories would be made available to children. Furthermore, it can be argued that in some cases an outsider's point of view is important both for objectivity and because this viewpoint can mediate to make the unfamiliar understandable.

Children who are fortunate to experience picture books from other countries have the opportunity to develop a broader aesthetic sensibility. For instance, European picture books are generally more painterly in style, while British books have a strong graphic design. Picture books are, as Jane Doonan reminds us, histories of art and style. As such they draw on the artistic and cultural traditions from which they arise. They vary in tone, style and treatment of subject matter. A good starting point for discovering European picture books is the website for the European Picture Book Collection (www.ncrcl.ac.uk/epbc/EN/index.asp). The internet is also a good source for finding books that are not distributed through large chains.

ACTIVITY

Reading the World

Select one or more books set in another part of the world.

- After reading make some notes about what you have learnt from reading the book.
- Put the book in context: find out more about the country where the story is set using a range of resources including the internet.
- What was the author's relationship to the country they were writing about? Did the book include any special uses of language?
- If the book you have selected is a picture book, consider how the words and images combine to create meaning.
- If you were reading this book with a group or class of children, what would be interesting to explore and talk about with them?
- To find out more about children's literature from other countries visit the IBBY's (International Board on Books for Young People) website at www.ibby.org.

Selected titles:

Beake, L. (2006) *Home Now*. London: Frances Lincoln.
Binch, C. (1997) *Gregory Cool*. London: Frances Lincoln.
Birch, B. (2006) *Rift*. London: Egmont.
Bloom, V. (2004) *Surprising Joy*. London: Macmillan.
Cattell, B. and Agard, J. (2006) *Butter-finger*. London: Frances Lincoln.
Cornwall, Nicki (2006) *Christopher's Story*. London: Frances Lincoln.
Daly, N. *Jamela's Dress*. London: Frances Lincoln.
Desai, A. (2001) *The Village by the Sea*. London: Puffin.
Ellis, D. (2004) *The Breadwinner*. Oxford: Oxford University Press.
Forbes, C. (2003) *Flying with Icarus*. London: Walker Books.

▶

Freud, E. (1993) *Hideous Kinky*. London: Penguin.
Gavin, J. (2001) *The Wheel of Surya*. London: Egmont.
Gavin, J. (2001) *The Eye of the Horse*. London: Egmont.
Grifalconi, A. (2002) *The Village That Vanished*. Bath: Ragged Bears.
Glass, L. (2006) *The Year the Gypsies Came*. London: Puffin.
Guene, F. (2006) *Just Like Tomorrow*. London: Walker Books.
Heide, F.P. (1992) *Sami and the Time of Troubles*. Boston, MA: Houghton Mifflin.
Heide, F.P. (1997) *The Day of Ahmed's Secret*. London: Puffin.
Hicyilmaz, G. (1998) *The Frozen Waterfall*. London: Faber.
Laird, E. (2001) *Kiss the Dust*. London: Egmont.
Laird, E. (2004) *The Garbage King*. London: Macmillan.
Laird E. (2004) *A Little Piece of Ground*. London: Macmillan.
Laird, E. (2006) *Oranges in No Man's Land*. London: Macmillan.
McCaughrean, G. (2006) *The White Darkness*. Oxford: Oxford University Press.
Mitchell, P. (2005) *Petar's Story*. London: Frances Lincoln.
Naidoo, B. (1999) *Journey to Jo'Burg*. London: HarperCollins.
Naidoo, B. (2007) *Burn My Heart*. London: Puffin.
Naidoo, B., Naidoo, M. and Littlewood, K. (2004) *Baba's Gift*. London: Frances Lincoln.
Pennac, D. (2002) *The Eye of the Wolf*. London: Walker Books.
St John, L. (2006) *The White Giraffe*. London: Orion.
Tadjo, V. (2006) *Stories from Africa*. London: A & C Black.
Tulloch, J. and Tulloch, S. (2007) *I am a Cloud, I Can Blow Anywhere*. London: Egmont.
Winter, J. (2005) *The Librarian of Basra*. London: Harcourt.

Chapter 8

Picture Power

This chapter examines the special qualities of the picture book and their place in children's reading repertoire. You will:

- reflect on the special qualities or the picture book and consider what it offers the reader;
- review your knowledge of the range of picture books written for children and your knowledge of illustrators;
- consider what needs to be taken into account when selecting picture books for the classroom.

We have already referred to picture books in the preceeding chapters, so here we will just sketch some of the specific qualities of picture books.

Margaret Meek (1991) writes 'Picture Books are not simply privileged reading for or with children. They make reading for all a distinctive kind of imaginative looking'. In this chapter we will be looking at ways in which picture books provide a unique reading experience for readers of all ages, not only the very young. Perhaps when you were writing your personal reading history (Chapter 1) you mentioned some picture books that were important to you when you were younger. Those books may have continued to be important to you as an adult, you may have read them to your own children or kept your childhood copies as treasured possessions. If you have access to these books re-read them and write notes in your reading journal. What do you remember of the book from childhood? How do you respond to the book as an adult? Do you think the book will appeal to children today?

ACTIVITY

Gather together a collection of picture books from your own collection or from the library. Take time to explore, read and share them with colleagues or children. What do these books have in common? Try writing a definition of a picture book.

Commentary

In surveying the range of picture books, you probably found that lots of different types of books fit this category. There are alphabet books, concept books poetry, non-fiction, thrillers and science fiction, early readers and wordless picture books, to name just a few. So what do these books have in common? Barbara Bader (1976:) writes, 'A picture book is text, illustrations, total design, an item of manufacture and a commercial product; a social, cultural, historical document; and foremost, an experience for a child. As an art form it hinges on the interdependence of pictures and words, on the simultaneous display of two facing pages, and on the drama of the turning page'. That's a fairly comprehensive definition and we'll return to it later in this chapter.

The anatomy of the picture book

First of all we'll turn our attention to the design of the picture book. Some illustrators play a large part in the design of their books. For Lauren Child, for instance, the design is integral to the way she conceptualizes her books. In other cases a designer may play a much larger role in the selection of font and layout as well as the overall production of the book. The arrangement of illustrations and text on the page is called the anatomy of the picture book.

Book shape

The choice of shape for a book is important. Generally books are rectangular or square. A rectangular book may have the spine positioned so the book opens horizontally or vertically. Tony Ross and Jeanne Willis use a horizontal format to good effect for their book *Tadpole's Promise*: the spine is positioned across the long top edge so that when the book is opened the illustrations on facing pages are positioned one above the other. The top illustration shows the airy world of the caterpillar/butterfly, while the bottom picture shows the watery world of the tadpole/frog.

Endpapers

The endpapers, especially in hardback editions, are carefully selected to suit the mood and tone of the book and may be integral to the storytelling. For example, *Farmer Duck* by Martin Wadell and Helen Oxenbury has endpapers that depict different seasons: winter at the beginning of the book and spring at the end of the book. It can be interesting to talk to children about reasons that these two illustrations have been chosen to bookend the story. Anthony Browne's *The Tunnel* has images of art nouveau floral paper and imitation brick wall at both the beginning and end of the book, but at the back of the book we notice that a ball and book of fairy tales now occupy the same space. Even where the endpapers are blank, choices about colour have to made. The glossy black endpapers for Istvan Banyai's *Zoom* are an apposite choice we realize as the book moves towards its conclusion in outer space.

Borders

Borders are used around text and illustration. They can be heavy or light, complete or broken, varying sizes or non-existent, allowing the illustration to bleed to the edges of the page. In *Where the Wild Things Are*, Maurice Sendak starts the story in small frames contained within tight borders, but as Max enters his imaginative space, the size of the frame increases and the borders dissolve. Some artists such as Marcia Williams and Jan Brett use elaborate page borders which contain details that amplify the meaning of the main text or illustration.

Single- and double-page illustrations

Where illustrations are placed on one side of the page, the facing page will often be used for text. A double-page spread may be used for showing landscape as in Susan Hill and Angela Barrett's *Beware Beware*, or sometimes a wordless double-page spread may be introduced to allow the pictures to take over the storytelling as they do in the wild rumpus in Maurice Sendak's *Where the Wild Things Are*.

Frames

Sometimes illustrations will be divided into frames. Jez Alborough's *Where's My Teddy?* and *Duck in the Truck* are told using a series of comic book-style frames of varying sizes and are particularly good for showing a sequence of movement from looking at a scene from different angles, rather like a film camera. David Wiesner's *Tuesday* opens with a series of panels showing a turtle on a log. Each frame moves closer by increments giving the effect of moving closer to the turtle which increases in size and detail. In this case the frames work in a similar way to an establishing shot at the beginning of a film.

Gutter

The gutter lies in the fold of the book and presents a challenge especially for double-page spreads. The illustrator and designer need to take account of the gutter to make sure an important element of the illustration does not literally disappear in the gutter. Sometimes an illustrator will make imaginative use of the gutter turning it to their advantage.

Typeface and text layout

The typeface selected should be sympathetic to the type of picture book. Some font faces would look patronizing in a picture book aimed at older readers. There are also optimum sizes for text: too small or too large and it will be difficult to read. The positioning of the text and its relationship to the illustration can affect the mood, tone and readability of the story. The amount of white space around the text also needs to be given consideration. Lauren Child is known for her imaginative use of typeface and text layout which breaks with conventional directionality. Dual-language books create particular challenges for text layout, especially when combining languages that follow different directional rules.

The turning page

It's also worth noting here the importance of the turning page. Good picture book makers create suspense and surprise. As we turn the page we may laugh aloud or gasp in horror or breathe a sigh or relief. Jeanne Willis and Tony Ross's *Tadpole's Promise* is a perfectly paced story with a punchline that hinges entirely on the turn of the final pages.

The language of pictures

Picture books are composed from text and illustration. Pictures have their own language and vocabulary to describe them. By talking to children about the ways pictures are created we can introduce ways of talking that enable them to describe and analyse what they see. Jane Doonan (1993) provides a working vocabulary for talking about pictures that children can begin to acquire from a young age. For Doonan drawing children's attention to the intent in picture making and teaching that every mark matters is important to the development of visual literacy. She calls this close looking. Doonan identifies the following ingredients in illustrations:

- a scheme of colour;
- a scheme of light and dark;
- a system of scale and intervals;
- an arrangement of shapes;
- on order of linear and largescale patterns;
- a network of linear rhythms.

Colour and its constituents, hue, tone and saturation may be used to create a particular mood or to suggest symbolic associations, In Anthony Browne's *Gorilla* for instance, there are two contrasting scenes in which the child character, Hannah, is pictured eating at a table. The first with her distracted father, who pays her little attention, is painted mainly in cold blue tones, while a later scene in which Hannah is seene enjoying a feast with her new-found friend the gorilla is dominated by a bright saturated red.

Light and dark lines can be made with different implements, with pen, or brush, or pencil or marker. They can be decorative or be used to show movement or stasis. The versatility of line can be seen by comparing the free-flowing, broken, dynamic line of Quentin Blake's illustrations with the heavy black unbroken outline of a Dick Bruna or the fluid inky line of Charles Keeping's *The Highwayman*. In addition to the line the artist makes, a picture will have a linear emphasis: horizontal, vertical, diagonal or wavy, for instance. These emphases will have a different impact and rhythm.

The interplay of text and illustration

Maurice Sendak wrote, 'You must never illustrate exactly what is written. You must find a space in the text so that pictures can do the work. Then you must let the words take over where words do it best'. The interplay of text and illustration works in diverse ways. At their most simple text and illustration appear to tell the same story: 'My cat Flossie' printed below a picture of a tortoiseshell cat. However, while text and image are in agreement, they provide different kinds of information. The text tells us who the cat belongs to; this is not evident in the illustration; the illustration shows us the type of cat, this is not explained in the text. Pictures are most effective at showing what characters are like, the setting in which they move, body language can show how characters are feeling. Text, on the other hand is good for naming, generalizing and telling us what characters are thinking or saying.

In other pictures text and image may tell entirely different stories. In Chapter 3 we saw how the dissonance between the story told in pictures and the story told in words in the picture book classic *Rosie's Walk* results in dramatic irony. Similarly, most children read Anthony Browne's *Zoo* as a text that is critical of zoos and yet there is no mention of this in the text which is narrated objectively. The inference is made on the basis of paratexual clues such as the framing of the pictures as well as the animals' body language and lack of eye contact made with the reader. As Kimmerling Meibauer (1999) expresses it, 'Ironic meaning comes into being as a consequence of a relationship, a dynamic performative bringing together the said and the unsaid, each of which takes on meaning only in relation to the other'.

Several attempts have been made to categorize the ways in which pictures and text work together. For instance, Jane Golden (1990), offers this categorization:

- text and picture are symmetrical;
- text depends on pictures for clarification;
- illustration enhances and elaborates text;
- text carries primary narrative, illustration is selective;
- illustration carries primary narrative, text is selective.

While these classifications may be help us to reflect on the ways in which picture books work, they should not be taken as comprehensive or absolute. The picture book is a dynamic and flexible form and a site for innovation and indivudal books may not fit easily into predefined categories.

ACTIVITY

- Select one of the picture books from the recommended list, or a book of your own choice.
- Read through the book once. Jot down your initial responses in your reading journal.
- Now re-read taking particular account of the pictures. Pay attention to colour, shapes, lines, patterns and the arrangement. Make a few notes about the illustrations.

- Re-read paying particular attention to the text, to rhythm, rhyme, pace and so on. Make a few notes about the quality of the text in your reading journal.
- Read again, this time taking account of the way in which the pictures and text inter-animate each other. Jot your observations in your journal.
- Finally consider the design of the book and how this affects the reading experience.
- Reflect on your own responses to the book and then consider what the book has to offer a younger reader.

If possible, compare your responses with a partner who has read the same book.

Selected picture books:

Baker, J. (1991) *Window*. London: Random House.
Baker, J. (2004) *Belonging*. London: Walker Books.
Banyai, I. (1995) *Zoom*. London: Viking.
Banyai, I. (2005) *The Other Side*. California: Chronicle.
Briggs, R. (1990) *Fungus the Bogeyman*. London: Puffin.
Browne, A. (1997) *Changes*. London: Walker Books.
Browne, A. (1997) *The Tunnel*. London: Walker Books.
Browne, A. (1998) *Voices in the Park*. London: Picture Corgi.
Browne, A. (2001) *Willy's Pictures*. London: Walker Books.
Crew, G. and Tan, S. (illus.) (2003) *The Viewer*. Melbourne, Australia: Lothian.
Crew, G. and Tan, S. (illus.) (2003) *Memorial*. Melbourne, Australia: Lothian.
Crew G. and Woolman, S. (illus.) (1997) *The Watertower*. Brooklyn Park, Australia: Era Publishing.
Fanelli, S. (2001) *Dear Diary*. London: Walker Books.
Innocenti, R. (1985) *Rose Blanche*. London: Jonathan Cape.
Popov, N. (1996) *Why?* London: North South Books.
Preston, T. and Bartram, S (illus.) (2001) *Pumpkin Moon*. Dorking: Templar.
Scieszka, J. and Johnson, S. (1994) *The Frog Prince Continued*. London: Puffin.
Scieszka, J. and Smith, L. (illus.) (1991) *True Story of the Three Little Pigs*. London: Puffin.
Scieszka, J. and Smith, L. (illus.) (1993) *Stinky Cheese Man*. London: Puffin.
Scieszka, J. and Smith, L.(illus.) (1999) *Squids Will Be Squids*. London: Puffin.
Sendak, M. (1981) *Outside Over There*. London: Puffin.
Sis, P. (2003) *The Tree of Life*. London: Walker Books.
Tan, S. (2001) *The Lost Thing*. Melbourne, Australia: Lothian.
Tan, S. (2003) *The Red Tree*. Melbourne, Australia: Lothian.
Thompson, C. (1998) *How to Live Forever*. London: Random House.
Thompson, C. (2002) *Falling Angels*. London: Random House.
Thompson, C. (2006) *Castles*. London: Random House.
Van Allsburg C. (1984) *The Mysteries of Harris Burdick*. Boston, MA: Houghton Mifflin.
Van Allsburg, C. (1993) *The Widow's Broom*. London: Andersen Press.
Wiesner, D. (1995) *Tuesday*. New York: Clarion Books.
Wiesner, D. (1994) *Freefall*. Mulberry.
Wiesner, D. (1999) *Night of the Gargoyles*. New York: Clarion Books.
Wiesner, D. (2006) *Flotsom*. New York: Clarion Books.
Wisniewski, D. (1994) *Golem*. Boston, MA: Houghton Mifflin.

Further reading

Baddeley, P. and Eddershaw, C. (1994) *Not So Simple Picture Books*. Stoke-on-Trent: Trentham Books.
Cotton, P. (2000) *Picture Books Sans Frontiere*. Stoke-on-Trent: Trentham Books.
Doonan, J. (1993) *Looking at Pictures in Picture Books*. Stroud: Thimble Press.
Evans, J. (1998) *What's in the Picture?* London: Paul Chapman Publishing.
Lewis, D. (2001) *Reading Contemporary Picture Books*. London: Routledge.
Nodelman, P. (1990) *Words About Pictures*. Athens, GA: University of Georgia.
Styles, M. and Arizpe, E. (2002) *Children Reading Pictures*. London: Routledge.

Chapter 9

The Pleasure of Poetry

This chapter explores some ideas about poetry written for and read by children. We shall:

- reflect on the special qualities of poetry and consider what poetry offers the reader;
- review your knowledge of the range of poetry written for children and your knowledge of children's poets;
- consider what needs to be taken into account when selecting poetry for the classroom;
- learn about approaches that you can use to develop and refine children's response to poetry;
- find out about resources that can support your teaching of poetry.

Does the thought of poetry conjure up memories of delight or fill you with dread? In the years that I have worked with teachers and student teachers I have found that many report that the reading and writing of poetry was a highly pleasurable experience and those fortunate teachers will often quote at length from favourite poems experienced in childhood. Those who had less happy experiences most frequently talk about the reading of poetry being a painful comprehension exercise in which they were expected to guess at the obscure meaning of poem, usually answering questions on the poet's intention and to which the teacher already had privileged access and information.

All children are entitled to positive experiences with poetry and it is important that if we carry residual prejudices we address them and avoid passing on negative feelings to new generations of readers. In Linda Hall's (1989) survey of children reading poetry she found that 47 per cent of pupils indicated they read no poetry out of school, as many as 36 per cent professed to be utterly hostile to it. The National Literacy Trust survey into children's reading choices and preferences found that a similarly dispiriting picture with only 41.5% of girls reading poetry outside school and 22.4% of boys. And yet teachers who positively promote poetry in their classrooms will attest to children's engagement with and enjoyment of poetry.

To begin it will be helpful to spend some time reflecting on your early experiences, to rediscover the joys of those early experiences or, if more appropriate, to begin to analyse why your memories are less bright.

Memories of poetry

ACTIVITY

- What poetry can you remember from childhood? Nursery rhymes, jingles, songs, classic poems, humorous poetry or playground rhymes?
- Write down the actual lines from a poem or poems that you can remember.
- If possible share these memories and your lines of poetry with a colleague.
- Reflect on your early experiences and consider implications for your own teaching.
- Consider the lines of poetry you have remembered. What makes these lines/phrases or words memorable?

Commentary

I was fortunate to have a poetry-rich childhood. Nursery rhymes were the earliest memories and my favourite was the little nut tree, which always seemed to me to have something of the 'minor key' that appealed to me more than energetic rhymes such as 'Humpty Dumpty', 'Jack and Jill' or 'Georgie Porgie':

> I had a little nut tree
> Nothing would it bear
> But a silver nutmeg
> And a golden pear
> The King of Spain's daughter
> Came to visit me
> And all for the sake
> Of my little nut tree.

Poems were frequently read to me at bedtime and poetry books were a popular choice for birthday and Christmas presents. In particular my father enjoyed sharing the poems that he had enjoyed when he was younger. He introduced me to Walter de La Mare, John Masefield and Wordsworth. Much of the poetry he read was not written exclusively for children and the words were often unfamiliar and deliciously exotic. John Masefield's *Cargoes* was a much requested favourite and I loved rolling the the sounds of the opening line 'Quinquireme of Ninevah from distant Ophir' around my tongue, although I had no idea then what a Quinquereme was or where Ninevah or Ophir were. What mattered was that those few words allowed them to be richly realized in my imagination. Language was undoubtedly a vital part of the poetic experience. In your remembered poems what was the relative importance of the ideas or the words used to express those ideas?

I loved the flowing rhythm and intuitively felt the contrast in the rhythms Masefield used describing the

> 'Dirty British coaster with a salt-caked smoke stack/Butting through the Channel in the mad March days'.

Rhythm is one of the characteristics of poetry that makes it highly memorable. In the 1970s I enjoyed the punchy fast delivery of a well-known cola advert:

> *Lipsmackinthirstquenchinacetastinmotivatingoodbuzzincooltalkinhighwalkin-fastlivinevergivencoolfizzin ...*

Of course this language isn't intentionally poetic but there are potential poems to be found in everyday language, an advertising slogan, a newspaper headline, a few lines of a well-written travel report or the description of a recipe. You might look for instances of this unintentional poetry and encourage the children in your classes to develop this awareness by sharing examples with them.

Perhaps represented in the poems you remember from childhood are those with equally strong rhythms or rhyme, which are characteristic features of this highly memorable language. Students and teachers that I have worked with often cite strong rhythm as one of the features they enjoyed: Thomas Hood's 'I Remember, I Remember', Robert Louis Stevenson's 'View From a Railway Carriage', W.H. Auden's 'Night Mail' and John Masefield's 'Sea Fever' frequently feature in these lists of remembered poems. You may also have observed children reciting rhymes and poems they have memorised, clearly enjoying their mastery and control over words that they can recall word for word.

I also enjoyed stories told in verse form. The section called 'Unforgettable Stories' in Louis Untermeyer's *Golden Treasury of Poetry* was well thumbed. The drama and romance of Moy Castle, Barbara Fretchie, Lochinvar, and Casablanca sustained many rereadings. Romance and heroic deeds fed my imaginative life and I read myself into these stories. And top of the list was Alfred Noyes's 'The Highwayman' with its air of tension and atmospheric setting:

> The wind was a torrent of darkness among the gusty trees,
> The moon was a ghostly galleon tossed upon cloudy seas,
> The road was a ribbon of moonlight over the purple moor,

And the highwayman came riding –
   Riding – riding –
The highwayman came riding, up to the old inn-door.

Perhaps you included some narrative poems in your list of remembered poems. These might have been classic poems or more recent poems such as Roald Dahl's 'Revolting Rhymes', Kit Wright's 'The Special Person' or Michael Rosen's, 'The Hollywood'.

While Spike Milligan's nonsense poems irritated me and I was fairly indifferent to Lewis Carroll's verse, I had a taste for the more melancholy nonsense of Lear, 'The Jumblies' with its lilting refrain:

Far and few, far and few,
Are the lands where the Jumblies live;
Their heads are green, and their hands are blue,
And they went to sea in a Sieve.

Likewise Hilaire Belloc's anarchic parodies of cautionary tales with their implausible morals thrilled me. I had complete mastery of Matilda (who told dreadful lies and was burned to death) and enjoyed reciting it to patient family members and friends. This memorizing of favourite poems was learning 'by heart' in the truest sense rather than the verbatim reciting of poems that we were sometimes required to do at school, regardless of whether we liked or understood the poem.

What is poetry?

ACTIVITY

Which of the following statements fits with your definition of poetry? Do any of these statements make you reassess your definition of poetry? Which do you like? Discuss your thoughts with a colleague.

- 'The best words in the best order' (Samuel Taylor Coleridge);
- Nursery rhymes;
- 'Bits of stuff' (Michael Rosen);
- 'A mode of apprehension, not an area of comprehension' (Elizabeth Cook);
- Felt thought;
- Memorable speech;
- Verse in greetings cards;
- 'Simply the most beautiful, impressive and widely effective mode of saying things' (Mathew Arnold);
- Difficult to understand;
- 'Semantic squeeze' (Jérome Bruner);
- 'Language used with the greatest inclusiveness and power' (*The Bullock Report*);
- 'What oft was thought, but ne'er so well express'd' (Alexander Pope);
- Lyrics of your favourite song;
- 'Manifestation of the human spirit and a relief from, or expression of, emotion' (James Reeves);
- Flowery old-fashioned language;
- Enjoyed by women and girls;
- 'Poetry is what gets lost in translation' (Robert Frost);
- 'Poetry is being, not doing' (e.e. cummings);
- 'Poetry lifts the veil from the hidden beauty of the world, and makes familiar objects be as if they were not familiar' (Percy Bysshe Shelley);
- 'Painting is silent poetry, and poetry is a speaking picture' (Simonides);
- 'Poetry is feeling – not knowing or believing or thinking' (e.e. cummings);
- 'The poem means more, not less, than ordinary speech can communicate (T.S. Eliot);
- 'If I read a book and it makes my whole body so cold no fire can ever warm me, I know that is poetry' (Emily Dickinson);
- 'Poetry is the spontaneous overflow of powerful feelings' (William Wordsworth).

Commentary

You may have found it easier to say what poetry is not than to produce a succinct definition. Indeed, what we call poetry encompasses many different kinds of writing from the verse novel to the short syllabic form, Haiku; from tragic narrative ballads to humorous limericks.

It can be illuminating to read poets' aphorisms about the cardinal characteristics of poetry. As a collection, they reveal how inadequate simple definitions are in their attempts to capture the essence of poetry. For instance, it would be possible to apply the rules for writing a sonnet and produce a piece of writing that perfectly satisfied the criteria for the sonnet form, but nevertheless fell short of being what might be called a poem. Some of the earlier quotations focus on the compression of meaning – Bruner's 'semantic squeeze' – while others privilege the special ways in which poetry uses language or emotion.

Though simple definitions may be elusive, it *is* possible to talk about the qualities of poetry. These qualities include compression, allusiveness and patterning. Compression of language creates concentrated, multilayered meanings, the ambiguities that allow for more than one interpretation; the imagery and metaphors that reveal meanings beyond the literal or superficial. Figurative devices may be used like similes that compare two things using words 'as' 'like' or 'than' for example, 'as sly as a fox'. Metaphor is a more sophisticated comparison in which the subject takes on the attributes of the thing to which it is being compared: 'The moon was a ghostly galleon/tossed upon cloudy seas'.

Personification is the attribution of human or animal qualities to inanimate objects. For example in James Reeves's poem, 'The Sea', the sea, in all its seasonal moods, is described as if it were a dog:

> The sea is a hungry dog. Giant and grey
> He rolls on the beach all day.
> With his clashing teeth and shaggy jaws
> Hour up on hour he gnaws
> The rumbling, tumbling stones,

The compression of language in poetry means that many poems offer themselves up for different interpretations. So, for example, Sylvia Plath's poem, 'Mushrooms', can be read literally as a poetic description of mushrooms growing overnight, as mushrooms do, but equally it bears a feminist reading in which the mushrooms are a metaphor for 'mild-mannered' women who will 'inherit the earth'. Others have interpreted the poem as being about pregnancy, with the physical qualities of the mushroom bearing a resemblance to the unborn child and, following this interpretation, it is the younger generation that will in years to come 'inherit the earth'. The allusiveness is the extent to which poetry refers covertly or indirectly to Robert Browning's poems about Renaissance artists and his 'Pied Piper of Hamelin' alludes to other literary and artistic texts. Not all poets value this allusiveness: William Carlos Williams, the American poet, expressed a dislike of T.S. Eliot's poetry because it was so heavily allusive.

Patterns relate to the form of words rather than their meaning. A poem's patterns may play with the auditory qualities of the poem: patterns of rhythm, rhyme, alliteration, assonance and the repetitions of words. Rhymes can occur at the end of lines (end rhyme) or in the middle of lines (internal rhyme). They can be full rhymes as in *sane/lane* or half rhyme as in *dame/lane*. Many forms of poetry have regular rhyme schemes which can be described using letters to show the distribution of the rhyme. The rhyme scheme of a Limerick has the following pattern:

There was a Young Lady whose chin,	a
Resembled the point of a pin;	a
So she had it made sharp,	b
And purchased a harp,	b
And played several tunes with her chin.	a

(Edward Lear)

While the rhyme scheme of Thomas Hardy's 'The Darkling Thrush' has an alternate rhyme scheme which can be described as:

I leant upon a coppice gate	a
When frost was spectre-grey	b
And Winter's dregs made desolate	c
The weakening eye of day	b
The tangled bine-stems scored the sky	d
Like strings of broken lyres,	e
And all mankind that haunted nigh	f
Had sought their household fires.	e

Other patterns of sound include alliteration, the repetition of consonant sounds in neighbouring syllables. In the following line taken from Wilfred Owen's 'Anthem for Doomed Youth', the repetition of the consonants/s//t/ and/f/ imitate the machine gun fire that is being described in the poem: 'The stuttering of the rifles' rapid rattle'. Vowel sounds may also be repeated to create particular effects and this is called assonance.

A poet may also use visual patterning, line breaks, the arrangements of lines on the page and the use of capitalization. e. e cummings, for instance, made good use of a word's visual form in his poetry. And Lewis Carroll's famous 'The Mouse's Tale' is shaped like a mouse tail thus amplifying the play on words.

Poetry, like narrative, is written with a voice which implies someone speaking the poem. This speaker is not usually the same as the poet but an assumed persona. Take for example the following poems by Christina Rossetti and Robert Louis Stevenson: what can be said about the voices in which they are written?

Love Me – I Love You
Love me – I love you,
Love me, my baby;
Sing it high, sing it low,
Sing it as may be.
Mother's arms under you,
Her eyes above you;
Sing it high, sing it low,
Love me – I love you.

(Christina Rossetti)

Bed in Summer
In winter I get up at night
And dress by yellow candle-light.
In summer quite the other way,
I have to go to bed by day.

I have to go to bed and see
The birds still hopping on the tree,
Or hear the grown-up people's feet
Still going past me in the street.

And does it not seem hard to you,
When all the sky is clear and blue,
And I should like so much to play,
To have to go to bed by day?

(Robert Louis Stevenson)

In Rossetti's poem the speaker takes the persona of a young mother addressing her baby, though Rossetti had no children of her own. And in Stevenson's poem the voice of a young child is affected. Read a selection of poems and write notes on the voices used in each of them.

Types of poetry

There are three main groups of poetry: dramatic, lyric and narrative. Narrative poetry is considered to be the oldest form of poetry with its roots in the oral, bardic tradition. Indeed in some cultures the tradition of recitation of traditional verse still thrives. Features of traditional ballads such as regular metre, repetition and alliteration may well have been aids to memory assisting the bards in the passing-on of stories from one generation to the next. Narrative poetry encompasses the epic poems of *The Illiad* and *The Odyssey* as well as shorter traditional ballads such as the Robin Hood cycle and story poems such as Robert Browning's 'The Pied Piper of Hamelin' and Ogden Nash's 'The Tale of Custard the Dragon'. Dramatic poetry uses character and discourse to tell a story or depict a situation. This includes dramatic verse in plays, such as Shakespeare's works which may be written in rhymed or blank verse as well as dramatic monologues such as those written by Robert Browning or Alfred Tennyson. In children's poetry 'Please, Mrs Butler', an altercation between the teacher, Mrs Butler, and her pupils, follows this tradition. Lyric poetry is the most frequently occurring in modern poetry and is concerned primarily with the expression of thought and feeling in a way that appears to be personal. It includes poems ranging from complex meditation to playful wit and includes the poetic forms of ode and elegy. Ted Hughes's nature poems for children are examples of lyric poems.

Within the broad categories of narrative, dramatic and lyric is a range of form. The following categories include some popular forms that are often recited, read or taught in school:

Nursery rhymes

Rhymes for the very young gathered under the generic label nursery rhymes, and often found in collections called Mother Goose rhymes, include action rhymes, counting rhymes and riddles. Recognized as an important part of children's early language experience, the number of rhymes that children are able to recite at the age of 5 has been identified as a predictor of their future reading success (Bryant and Bradley, 1985). This is attributed to the use of alliteration, rhyme and half-rhyme, which help children to discriminate sound and develop phonological awareness. The lap bumping, hand-clapping, finger movements, arm tickling that accompanies many of the rhymes makes rhyme-time into a pleasurable shared experience. Many of the rhymes started as political squibs not specifically intended for children but have been appropriated by the nursery and, accompanied by gentle illustrations, have acquired an idyllic pastoral flavour. The Opies' *Nursery Rhymes* provides a fascinating insight into the origins of the rhymes for anyone interested in the subject.

Limerick

The limerick is a five-line irreverent poem with a regular metre and AABBA rhyme scheme. Made famous by Edward Lear, whose collection of nonsense verse included:

> There was an old man with a beard
> Who said it is just as I feared
> Two owls and a hen
> Four larks and a wren
> Have all built their nest in my beard.

Sonnet

The sonnet is a fixed-verse form of 14 lines that accords with one of a number of schemes, most commonly the Petrachan or Shakespearean sonnet. Originating in the 13th century it continues to be a popular verse form today. The Shakespearean sonnet consists of three quatrains (four-line stanzas) each with its own rhyme scheme and ending with a rhymed couplet. Shelley's 'Ozymandias' and Wordsworth's 'Upon Westminster Bridge' are often included in anthologies for young readers.

Haiku

Haiku is a Japanese-inspired form of poetry. Though there are variations, English Haiku are most usually syllabic forms possessing 17 syllables distributed over three lines in groups of five, seven and five syllables. Traditionally haiku uses natural imagery to express some truth about the natural world. If following a strict form, the third line provides a contrast or comparison to the first two lines.

Renga

Renga is a collaborative form based on the haiku and comprising a stanza of 5–7–5 syllables followed by a two line stanza of 7–7 syllables, a further three-line stanza then two-line stanzas and so on.

Cinquains

Influenced by Japanese forms of poetry, the American poet Adelaide Crapsey developed the Cinquain. Cinquains are five-line poems which adhere to the following structure:

    Line 1 is one word (the title);
    Line 2 is two words that describe the title;
    Line 3 is three words that tell the action;
    Line 4 is four words that express the feeling;
    Line 5 is one word that recalls the title.

Elegy

A poem or praise and lament written following the death of a particular person and often sorrowful in tone. Tennyson's long poem, 'In Memoriam', written for a university friend who died young of a brain hemorrhage is one of the best-known examples.

Ode

A poem which is often elevated in tone and addressed to a praised person or object. Sometimes the poem may be divided into sections which represent transitions in thought. Line lengths are usually varied and there is no fixed rhyme scheme. Well known examples include John Keats's 'Ode to a Nightingale' and 'Ode on a Grecian Urn'.

Free verse

Free verse is a form of poetry composed of either rhymed or unrhymed lines that have no set fixed metrical pattern. Emerging at the beginning of the 20th century, free verse allowed poets to break from the formula and rigidity of traditional poetry.

Concrete poetry

In concrete poetry the typographical arrangement of words is important for conveying the meaning. A well known example is Lewis Carroll's 'The Mouse's Tale'.

Ballad

A ballad is a story poem, most usually a traditional story written in ballad form and recited or sung. Traditional ballads are usually written in quatrains (four-line stanzas) with a strong memorable metre. Though this varies, a frequent pattern is to have four stresses in the first and third lines (iambic tetrameter) and three stresses in the second and third lines (iambic trimester). The rhyme schemes is typically abab or abcb. See this introduction from the traditional ballad 'Robin Hood and Allen A'Dale':

> Come listen to me, you gallants so free,
> All you that loves mirth for to hear,
>   And I will you tell of a bold outlaw,
> That lived in Nottinghamshire.
>
> As Robin Hood in the forrest stood,
> All under the green-wood tree,
>   There was he ware of a brave young man,
> As fine as fine might be.

Nonsense verse

Nonsense poetry uses words which appear to be written in English but in fact do not carry any identifiable meaning such as Lewis Carrol's 'Jabberwocky':

> Twas brillig, and the slithy toves
> Did gyre and gimble in the wabe:
> All mimsy were the borogoves,
> And the mome raths outgrabe.

In this poem, although some of the words are made up, the syntax is correct. So the poem makes grammatical sense but not semantic sense. Some poems do not use nonsense words but are still nonsense poems such as this one:

> As I was going up the stair
> I met a man who wasn't there
> He wasn't there again today
> Oh how I wish he'd go away

> (Hugh Mearns)

ACTIVITY

Create an anthology

Collect a range of poems on a particular topic or theme. Include some older, classic poems as well as recent ones. Try to find poems written in a variety of forms including syllabic poetry, free verse and visual poems. Decide which poems you will include in your anthology. Think about how you want to arrange the poems. Which poem should open the anthology and which should close it? Think carefully about which poems are placed next to each other. How does the juxtaposition of one poem next to another enhance the collection? You may want to include illustrations such as children's drawings, photographs, found images, your own artwork. When you have produced your anthology, read and share the poems with children and discuss their responses to the poems.

Suggested themes:

- Family
- People
- The natural world
- Cats
- Magic
- Stories
- Earth, Wind, Water, Fire
- What do you hear?
- Poetry about Poetry
- Children through the ages
- So you think it's funny?

How well do you know your poets?

How familiar are you with the range of poetry available for children? Do you have knowledge of some classic and contemporary collections? Light-hearted and more serious poetry? Which of the following children's poets' names do you recognize? Have you read their poetry?

John Agard
Allan Ahlberg
Michael Rosen
Valerie Bloom
Jackie Kay
Tony Mitton
Gerald Benson
Charles Causley
Walter de la Mare
Ian McMillan
Brian Moses
Brian Patten
Wendy Cope
Roger McGough
Adrian Mitchell
Ted Hughes
John Masefield
Grace Nichols
Kit Wright
Benjamin Zephaniah
Robert Louis Stevenson
Christina Rossetti
Eleanor Farjeon
Elizabeth Jennings
Judith Nicholls

Commentary

This list of well-known children's poets includes some classic writers such as Christina Rossetti, Walter de la Mare and John Masefield, as well as more recent poets such as Tony Mitton, Michael Rosen and Jackie Kay. Use the list as a starting point for updating your knowledge. Seek out poems and collections by each of these poets and write entries for your reading journal. Useful reference sources include Morag Styles's excellent history which charts the development of children's poetry from the pastoral to the urban, as the title expresses it, *From the Garden to the Street*; Deborah Halford and Ed Zaghini's *Universal Verse,* a comprehensive guide to recent poetry books; *The Oxford Book of Children's Verse* and *The New Oxford Book of Children's Verse*, which include iconic poems for children from the Middle Ages to the present day.

The CLPE Poetry Award, inaugurated in 2003, celebrates the best in poetry publishing for children. Obtain copies of the winning books in bookshops or libraries. The winners to date are:

2003 John Agard and Grace Nichols *Under the Moon and Over the Sea*
2004 Roger McGough *All the Best, Selected Poems*
2005 Roger McGough (ed.) *Sensational Poems Inspired by the Five Senses*
2006 Fiona Waters (ed.) *Why Does My Mum Always Iron a Crease in My Jeans?*

The experience of poetry

So, what do children gain from reading poetry or from having poetry read to them? Write a few notes in response to this question or discuss with a colleague. Consider

▶

the following points. What would you add to this list?
Poetry can:

- motivate children to read by generating delight in language;
- through its special qualities of patterned language help to develop the 'auditory imagination';
- develop understanding beyond the literal due to the use of symbolism and imagery;
- through its compression, provide an enriching and challenging reading experience for able pupils who have not yet developed reading stamina;
- through its themes and subjects contribute to children's emotional life providing opportunities to safely experience the full range of emotions;
- extend children's experience and insight of the world;
- contribute to the development of imagination;
- support the development of beginning readers through encounters with rhyme;
- develop the imagination and help children to create pictures in the mind;
- enrich vocabulary.

Poetry for the classroom

ACTIVITY

Consider, or discuss with a colleague, the range of poetry that you think should be available in the school or class library. You might conduct a quick audit to ascertain what is currently available. Is the library well stocked with poetry? Is there a good range of different types of poetry? Are there any gaps in provision? How is poetry promoted in the class/school? Do children select poetry to read independently?

As a benchmark you might start by examining current curriculum documents and establishing what they have to say about the range of poetry. For example the renewed *Framework for Literacy in England* recommends a programme of units with the following titles:

- Using the Senses;
- Pattern and Rhyme;
- Poems on a Theme;
- Patterns on the Page;
- Really Looking;
- Silly Stuff;
- Poems to Perform;
- Shape Poetry and Calligrams;
- Language Play;
- Creating Images;
- Exploring Form;
- Poetic Style;
- Classic and Narrative Poems;
- Choral and Performance;
- The Power of Imagery;
- Finding a Voice.

What view of poetry underpins this selection of topics? Are there other considerations to make when choosing poetry for children?

Commentary

Scanning the aforementioned list of units, it is evident that an eclectic view of poetry underpins the renewed framework. Attention is given to exploration of a variety of genres and forms, to increasing knowledge of poetic form, to ways of reading and approaches to writing. We might start by stocking our classrooms with the poetry books that will resource the teaching of these units. Certainly there will be ample material available from publishers to help us do that. However, no curriculum or syllabus is objective and it is worth reflecting on other ways in which we might think about poetry for the classroom. We should certainly be offering a range of material broader than that required specifically for curricular purposes and we should endeavour to ensure that children's experience of a particular type of poetry is not limited to the space allocated in curriculum plans. For example, classic and narrative poetry should be ever present in the classroom, not confined to the Year 5 class. Children should be able to select collections of classic poetry and to hear it read aloud.

Here are some suggestions for alternative or complementary ways of thinking about poetry resources. What would you add to this list?

- A range of poetry anthologies: when selecting anthologies, pay attention to the anthologist. Do they have the expertise to produce a good anthology? Does the range of poems include the well known and some surprises or is the anthology simply rehashing selections that have been made many times before? How are the poems arranged in the anthology? Has it been put together in a sensitive, thoughtful and interesting way?
- Thematic collection: thematic collections facilitate the comparison of poems on a similar theme and can support curriculum topics. However, they may also limit interpretation. Placing Ted Hughes's 'Jaguar' in a collection of animal poems, for instance, reduces the poem simply to an animal poem whereas in fact it can be a poem about many things like freedom, for example.
- Single-poet collections: a collection of poems written and assembled by a single poet is one of the best ways of coming to know the poet, their range of style, mood and tone. Sadly, the single-poet collection seems to be under threat in the market place with purchasing power seemingly pushing for more anthologies and collections that more explicitly reference the curriculum. This is problematic in that it makes the publishing of children's poetry less fertile territory for new and aspiring poets and could well lead to an impoverished selection in the future. There are then both educational and commercial imperatives for supporting the single-poet collection.
- Picture book poetry: books with strong rhyme and rhythm such as those written by Tony Mitton, Julia Donaldson or Kay Umanksy, visual interpretations of single poems such as Charles Keeping's illustrated versions of 'The Highwayman' and 'The Lady of Shalott'.
- Poetry written by children: collections of published poems by children such as *Paint Me a Poem* by Grace Nichols, which includes children's poems alongside her own.
- Poetry written for adults: poetry that was not intended specifically for children should also be included. Children may apprehend deep levels of truth and beauty in poems even when they do not fully comprehend them.
- Audio poetry: children need regular opportunities to hear poetry read aloud. Undoubtedly the best classroom experience is the intimate sharing of poetry when the teacher or children read poems aloud for each other. However, there are benefits to having professional audiobooks as well. These can be used independently by the children. Some teachers may also feel more confident listening to poems written with obvious accents or dialects read by professional readers.
- Digital poetry: poetry and multimedia have much in common, both being multi-sensory forms of communication. Digital poetry which uses words, images, colour and sound is becoming increasingly popular and should be available to children in school.

Reading poetry with children

Before reading or introducing new poems consider how you will engage the children's interest or help them to gain maximum benefit from the poetry session. Simple introductions may really help children to understand or appreciate a difficult poem. Introductions should not over-explicate but might say something along the lines of, 'This poem appears to be about a jaguar in a zoo, but perhaps it's about much more than that. Listen carefully and at the end you can tell me what you think'. More demanding poems may require longer introductions and it might help to discuss complex vocabulary beforehand but paraphrasing the poem should be avoided at all costs. Another way in is to help children connect the poem to their personal experience. So, prior to reading e.e. cummings's 'maggie and milly and molly and may' you might invite the children to recall a time they visited the seaside and talk about what they did there. You might draw attention to particular language features or devices or to the visual patterns of the poem.

Reading aloud

There are many ways in which you can help children to develop and refine a response to poetry. Most poetry is written to be read aloud, so frequent opportunities to hear poetry read expressively is paramount. Listening to the same poem read by different voices will bring fresh nuances of meaning to the poem which can be discussed and reflected upon. Children will also need opportunities to read aloud either individually or in groups regardless of whether the teaching focus is performance or choral poetry.

Use some simple warm-up exercises prior to reading to help children make the best use of their voices. Exercises can include controlled breathing, tongue twisters to aid articulation, exercises that draw attention to pace (e.g. counting 1–10 starting slow and getting faster), exercises that draw attention to volume (e.g. counting from 1–10 starting quietly and increasing the volume).

Over time teach children how to read aloud with variety and interest. They can be taught to think about:

- Pace: reading fast or slowly increasing or decreasing pace;
- Pause: spaces are never empty. As with music, use pauses for effect;
- Pitch: vary the pitch using higher or lower than normal pitch;
- Power: varying the energy in the voice. You can read loudly, softly, shout, whisper, firm but gentle;
- Emphasis: making one or more words in a line more important than others. Try reading a sentence like Would you like a cup of tea? several times emphasizing a different word each time;
- Inflection: musical pattern conveying emotion, feeling, meaning (falling/rising, rising/falling).

To begin with, choose poems that can be read aloud by the whole class and demonstrate how to annotate a poem to aid expressive reading. When children are more experienced they can work independently in groups to arrange and organize their reading. Musical instruments might also be used.

Talking in groups

Talking about poems can enhance children's appreciation. Some children find it more difficult to offer their views and participate in discussion so use teaching approaches that make the experience enjoyable and are non-threatening. For instance, after reading a poem, you might invite the children to respond in writing or drawing, then use these initial jottings to stimulate discussion. In small groups, ask each child to share what they have drawn or written. These should be accepted without comment in order to give validity to each response. After the initial sharing revisit the poem. Reread and discuss the poem line by line.

A variation is to invite one child to read the poem, while other children in the group follow reading silently. Then invite a second child to read the poem aloud. At this point each member of the group offers a response which can be a thought, connection, feeling, question. Responses are recorded on a flip chart, whiteboard or large sheet of paper. When everyone has contributed open up the discussion using the initial responses as a starting point.

Small-group activities

Occasionally disrupting the text of a poem can help to focus discussion. Cloze procedure (see Chapter 2) can be used to focus attention on rhyme, alliteration, imagery or other poetic devices.

Sequencing activities might also help children to identify and talk about patterning as well as the meaning of a poem. Take a copy and cut out the poem (Appendix 9.1). Reassemble the poem in the order in which you think the original is produced. As you are doing this task take particular note of the clues you are using to help your complete the task. What knowledge and understanding do you use? Ideally this activity should be undertaken with a partner so that you can talk about the task. This will demonstrate the role of collaborative learning in this and similar small-group activities.

Withholding the title of a poem and then asking children to write and justify the most suitable title can be used to help children identify main themes or the essence of a poem. If children haven't done this before, demonstrate with the class first, modelling your thought processes. Alternatively, read a poem but withhold the final three lines. In pairs or small groups the children complete the poem again first modelling how to do this with the class.

Drama responses

Drama can be used to help the children 'inhabit' the poem. The range of drama activities might include improvising scenes from a narrative poem, exploring structure using freeze frame images, creating a sound collage to accompany a dramatic reading, staging a dramatic performance of a poem, hotseating characters in order to explore thoughts and feelings.

Dance and music

Poetry is multisensory and is sympathetic to the performance arts. Musical instruments can be used to create soundtracks to accompany lyric poetry. And the rhythms of poetry lend themselves to exploration through movement. Contrasting qualities, heavy and light, fast and slow, sharp and flowing can be accentuated through words and gesture.

Visual and multi-media responses

Poetry has much in common with multi-media: both make use of a range of sensory material, patterns of sound, typography, imagery and so on. Invite children to produce a multi-media presentation of a poem using digital cameras, digital video, images found on the internet, sound files, musical composition, drama and children's artwork. The presentation can be assembled using Powerpoint or a simple video-editing package such as Microsoft Moviemaker. If children have little experience of working with digital media it may be best to start with still images rather than video.

Resources for poetry

There are many resources available to support the teaching of poetry. The following are good starting points:

- *The Poetry Society:* The Poetry Society organizes National Poetry Day and has a range of services for teachers including poets in school, Foyle Young Poets of the Year Award, Poems on the Underground, poetry posters and other resources.
- *Poetry Book Society –Children's Poetry Bookshelf:* The PBS runs a children's poetry book club. Teacher members receive a parcel of the best two or three new poetry books for 7–11 year olds every term. They are also sent posters, teaching tips and discussion ideas based on the selected books.
- *Poetry Library:* The Poetry Library houses the most comprehensive collection of British poetry from 1912. It has an extensive children's collection and excellent education service providing support for schools.

Selected poetry titles

Agard, John (2002) *Einstein, the Girl Who Hated Maths*. London: Hodder.
Ahlberg, Allan (1984) *Please, Mrs Butler*. London: Puffin.

Belloc, Hillaire (1995) *Cautionary Verses*. London: Random House.
Bloom, Valerie (ed.) (2003) *One River, Many Creeks: Poems from All Around the World*. London: Macmillan.
Bloom, Valerie (2004) *Whoop an' Shout*. London: Macmillan.
Causley, Charles (1997) *Collected Poems for Children*. London: Macmillan.
Chatterjee, Debjani (2005) *Masala*. London: Macmillan.
De la Mare, Walter (2001) *Peacock Pie*. London: Faber.
Eliot, T.S. (2001 *Old Possum's Book of Practical Cats*. London: Faber.
Harrison, M. and Stuart-Clark, C. (eds) (2000) *The Oxford Book of Story Poems*. Oxford: Oxford University Press.
Hughes, Ted (2005) *Collected Poems for Children*. London: Faber.
McGough, Roger (1998) *Bad Bad Cats*. London: Puffin.
Nichols, Grace (2005) *Paint Me a Poem*. London: A & C Black.
Patten, Brian (2001) *Juggling with Gerbils*. London: Puffin.
Patten, Brian (ed.) (1999) *The Puffin Book of Utterly Brilliant Poetry*. London: Puffin.
Stevenson, R.L. *A Child's Garden of Verses*.
Webb, Kaye (ed.) (1979) *I Like This Poem*. London: Puffin.
Wright, Kit (1989) *Cat Among the Pigeons*. London: Puffin.
Zephaniah, Benjamin (2001) *Wicked World*. London: Puffin.

Further reading

Lambirth, A. (2002) *Poetry Matters*. Royston: UKLA.
Wilson, A. and Hughes, S. (1998) *The Poetry Book for Primary Schools*. London: Poetry Book Society.

Appendix 9.1

Between the woods and frozen lake The darkest evening of the year
The only other sound's the sweep Of easy wind and downy flake
He gives his harness bells a shake
And miles to go before I sleep
Whose woods these are I think I know His house is in the village, though
To stop without a farmhouse near
The woods are lovely, dark and deep And miles to go before I sleep
My little horse must think it queer But I have promises to keep
To ask if there is some mistake
He will not see me stopping here To watch his woods fill up with snow

Chapter 10

Reading in Schools and Classrooms

In this chapter we shall:

- explore the scope of a classroom book collection;
- consider approaches to auditing book stock and setting targets for future
- acquisitions;
- reflect on how we might evaluate books for children;
- consider the importance of reading spaces;
- examine the benefits of working in partnership with other key professionals.

If children are to develop their knowledge and skills in reading and studying literature, they need to have access to a wide range of texts. To ensure that the range within the collection is comprehensive and will meet the needs of all the children, it is helpful if schools have a book acquisition policy. This will ensure that:

- the current book stock is audited and catalogued;
- targets are set for future purchasing;
- full use is made of loan books through local authorities (LA) provision for schools;
- children's needs are met in terms of levels of difficulty and range of texts available.

The Ofsted report, *Reading for Pleasure and Purpose: An Evaluation of the Teaching of Reading in Primary Schools* (2004) stated that 'although schools were successfully raising reading attainment and were teaching pupils the skills they needed to read with accuracy and understanding, few were successfully engaging the interest of those who, though competent readers, did not read for pleasure. Schools seldom built on pupils' own reading interests and the range of reading material they read outside school'. One obvious implication of the report is that an acquisitions policy should take account of children's out-of-school interests as well as reading choices. Furthermore, teachers might consider ways in which pupils can be involved in the selection of books for school and class libraries.

Having a policy in place ensures that when funds become available, as they sometimes do at short notice through various national and local policy management decisions, there can be a prompt and efficient decision regarding priorities. When the National Literacy Strategy was introduced in England, for example, schools were provided with grants for book purchase. The grants came sometimes at short notice, with very short time constraints for spending. Schools with priorities already established were able to target books into areas of need: mainly, at that time, in purchasing 'big books', enlarged texts for whole-class sharing, or sets of multiple copies of books for group sharing. Whether the money spent so fast was spent on books in the genres, styles and levels of difficulty most urgently needed in the school will have depended on the clarity of understanding of the current book stock matched against the needs of the children.

Spending on books in schools

> Effective teaching also requires ... sufficient resources to support learning. About one in 15 primary schools, and nearly a quarter of secondary schools, are judged to have insufficient learning resources. (Annual Report of Her Majesty's Chief Inspector of Schools 1999–2000)

Over 27 per cent of the books published in the world are in English (BA Report 1997). In the UK alone, the number of new titles for children published annually has risen dramatically in recent years (Table 10.1), perhaps reflecting changing priorities in spending with the introduction in 1998 of the National Literacy Strategy.

Table 10.1 *Number of new children's titles published annually (1995–2000)*

Year	Number of titles
1995	7,631
1996	8,012
1997	8,049
1998	8,399
1999	9,043
2000	10,397

Source: www.whitaker.co.uk

The figures in Table 10.1 are interesting as they also reflect increased spending on children's books within the market as a whole from 13.3 per cent in 1998 to 14.7 per cent in 2000 (www.thebookseller.com.). Indications are that publishing for children in English is thriving, with major contributions from Australia, USA and Ireland in particular, enriching the scope of books available and a small but significant increase in translated titles.

Changing policy and curriculum emphases will undoubtedly affect funds available for developing the school fiction collection. For example, between 1994 and 1999, school spending on textbooks went up, but the spending on school library books went down in the same period from £51.8 million to £42.6 million. The Publishers Association (2003) reported a decline in 2002–03 in spending on books for primary schools of 4.9 per cent in England and 3.1 per cent in Wales. The cumulative effect of the decline in England is that spending was 25% below its peak in 1998/9. 47% of primary schools spent less than £2,000. In the independent sector 25% of schools spent more than £10,000. Striking regional differences were highlighted in the report which showed that Northern Ireland continued to spend more than the other countries with an increase of 11.9%. Scotland also increased book spending by 7.7%. The figures for secondary schools showed increases in spending in England and Wales of 18.8 and 38.8% respectively, stable spending in Scotland and a decline of 16.3% in Northern Ireland.

In monetary terms the spending per school was equal across the four countries. Independent schools again outstripped state schools. Over 50% of schools reported that their spending on books in 2002/3 was inadequate. 52.3% of primary schools believed that good book stocks were highly effective in raising standards and 41.4% of secondary schools.

Research conducted in 2006 indicates that the decline is continuing and that book use and educational standards are under threat. Steve Hurd, OU researcher, has argued that 'there is an appallingly low number of books in our primary schools. Many schools would say "oh, we've got loads of books" but when you dig a bit deeper you find there aren't very many at all. There are few new books because schools are using their money elsewhere' (*Independent*, 6 June 2006). This research also stated that pound for pound, money spent on books had a greater impact on educational achievement than money spent on ICT.

Regardless of educational initiatives, school libraries and class collections will require an annual sum to be budgeted for maintenance and development. Book Trust (2002) recommended that spending on books per head for a primary pupil should be £53 for adequate provision and £87 for secondary students. The report suggests that while there may need to be substantially greater spending to make up for inadequate provision, schools that have recently restocked might spend less than the recommended average. The report highlighted difficulties that schools found in estimating cost based on real need rather than historic spending.

When schools were asked whether they were in favour of the earmarking of funds for books and other resources 68% of primary schools said 'yes' and 55.5% of secondary schools. However, 65 per cent of schools felt that the amount allocated within their schools for book purchasing was inadequate or grossly inadequate (Publishers Association, 2003). Because of depleted book stocks Steve Hurd (2006) argued that £100 per child would need to be injected for adequate book provision.

- Find out the allocation per head of spending on books in your school.
- How much of that is spent on fiction and poetry? How much on non-fiction?
- How does it compare to the national averages and recommended figures?
- Is there a budget and policy for book purchasing in school?
- Who decides what the priorities are for book purchasing?

Commentary

If there is not a fixed budget, you will need to find out what the processes are for identifying book needs and organizing purchases. Schools sometimes spend on major projects but omit to allocate funds on a regular basis for maintaining and developing stock.

A framework for creating a book collection

- What do you think a good classroom collection should include?
- Make a list of the categories of literary texts you feel a good classroom collection should contain.

Ensure that your list includes compliance with any curriculum documents which inform your teaching. Note that the ranges outlined only address minimum requirements and do not reflect the scope of many good classroom collections. For example, the *National Curriculum for England at Key Stage 1* (KS1) requires children to have access to texts 'with familiar settings'. However, as we have seen in earlier sections, children can cope with texts which make demands beyond the familiar, and these texts have an important role to play in extending the possibilities of text with children and developing literacy skills.

Commentary

Schools will wish to develop their own categories of books, but groups of students and teachers studying children's literature produced the following list to guide formation of a collection.

A good collection of books in the classroom should include the following range, depending on the age of the children:

- fairy tales;
- adventure;
- traditional tales;
- classics;
- myths and legends;
- true stories;
- fables;
- humorous stories;

- science fiction;
- historical;
- horror;
- school stories;
- animal stories;
- books dealing with 'issues';
- fantasy;
- contemporary realism;
- mysteries;
- graphic novels (comic strips);
- nursery rhymes;
- books reflecting popular culture;
- rhyming stories;
- television and film tie-ins;
- poetry – single-poet collections;
- poetry – anthologies;
- poetry – thematic collections;
- poetry from diverse cultures;
- picture books;
- picture books without words;
- picture books for older readers;
- graphic novels;
- anthologies;
- books in series;
- plays;
- books written by the children themselves;
- stories from a range of cultures;
- autobiography;
- biography;
- non-fiction – information books;
- creative non-fiction.

In addition, within this the collection should include:

- books by a range of significant established authors and newly published work;
- multiple copies of some texts;
- big books for sharing as a class;
- collections of books by particular authors, illustrators or on themes;
- books of different sizes and lengths;
- hardback and paperback versions;
- dual textbooks and other books written in different languages and scripts;
- books written with different formats, for example in letters;
- a range of levels of textual difficulty and style;
- books in different formats, for example pop-up books, novelty books;
- CD-ROM talking books;
- audiobooks of favourite texts;
- video/DVD versions of books;
- multi-media texts (e.g. books on CD-ROM)
- a permanent collection supplemented by loan books from internal and external sources.

How does this compare to your list? You may have included some categories which are not identified here, or you may wish to adjust your list to ensure that you have sufficient breadth to meet all the children's needs. This list only addresses categorization by genre and format: there are other considerations, such as ensuring that there are texts which challenge children's comprehension beyond the literal level, texts written in a different narrative and linguistic styles and using different literary devices. The data bank you set up in Chapter 1 will help you ensure that this range is covered. The books provided should also be at varying levels of reading difficulty.

Assessing levels of difficulty in fiction

Attributing reading age levels to texts is not as simple as is implied by the common practice of labelling children's books by age in bookshops and libraries. Readability indices have been devised to assess levels of textual difficulty and there are now computer programmes that will do the computation on a selected passage. However, there are shortcomings to this approach. Most readability indices work on an analysis of the number of polysyllabic words in a sample of text, and the length of the sentences used. These figures are then used to compute a number relating to reading age. This is a rather simplistic approach though, and your reading of Chapters 6 and 9 will have highlighted the many other factors affecting comprehension of a text.

ACTIVITY

Readability

- Use the readability index in Appendix 10.1 to analyse the readability level of a children's novel.
- Then read and review the book, considering the narrator, style, subject content and use of language, use of literary devices such as flashbacks, major themes and so on.
- Is there anything you have noticed that would make you challenge the outcome of the readability index?
- Can literature be reduced to this numerical level of analysis?

Commentary

As you will quickly realize, unless you have selected a very simple text, the numerical analysis is an inadequate indicator of textual difficulty. Readability formulae rarely take account of context. Furthermore the simplistic correlation of sentence length fails to address the difference children would find in reading a long compound sentence compared to a long complex sentence with subordinate clauses. The T-unit length would indicate the complexity but would not address the issue of word length. However, even word length is an unreliable indicator of textual difficulty, as we saw in Chapter 9. The phrase 'be that as it may' contains monosyllabic words and could be in a short sentence but may be more difficult for a young child to comprehend than, for example, the closing of *Noisy Nora*: '"but I'm back again," said Nora, with a monumental crash'. Most young children are highly motivated to read this book with its wonderfully patterned language and take the polysyllabic finale well in their stride having heard it read to them once or twice. A word of caution here: while it is useful to categorize books into broad levels of difficulty to monitor provision, labelling books with levels can be problematic.

Although children may benefit from some guidance about approximate levels of difficulty, coding book levels by colour or symbol can be very restricting. Children may limit their reading to a narrow band of titles within a grade and not exhibit the behaviours of the effective reader, which is to vary the level of textual difficulty according to need. There are three main levels at which children read (Southgate, 1981):

- independent level: the level at which children can read a text on their own, with errors of less than 1 per cent;
- instructional level: the level at which children can read with support, with errors of about 5 per cent, that is, 1 in 20 words;
- frustration level: the level at which the text is too difficult for children to draw meaning from the text with errors of 10 per cent or more, 1 in 10 words.

Children who are still learning to read will learn most when reading at instructional level. However, effective readers do not always read at their optimum levels: they often read easier books for relaxation, pleasure and consolidation, and may attempt very demanding texts if motivated. This mirrors adult behaviours. We may re-read favourites or unwind with a formulaic series book or a popular best-seller. Children who know they are 'red-level' readers may be reluctant to try a harder 'blue' book or to re-read a favourite text if it is categorized as several grades below their current level. Having levels prominently displayed also means that children may not develop the ability to assess for themselves whether a book is of a suitable level. They need to learn to evaluate the cover and scan the contents, pausing to sample parts of the text to assess readability for themselves. A strategy to help those who lack confidence in book selection at their own level of difficulty is to introduce the five-finger test.

ACTIVITY

The five-finger test

- Find a page with at least a paragraph of text on it and start to read.
- If you get to a word that you cannot read put your little finger on it.
- Read on, and if you come to another word you cannot read, put the next finger on it.
- If you run out of fingers before you finish the page, the book may be a little hard for you to read.
- Try the test with some children in school, particularly those with a poor image of their own reading levels who find choosing hard.
- This does actually have a scientific basis: if the child reads a sample of 100 words and makes more than five errors, he or she is moving towards frustration level.
- The five-finger test is a good way to encourage children to assess for themselves whether they will be able to cope with a particular text.

There are a number of ways in which checking levels of difficulty in book stock can be approached to make it manageable. Published lists of graded books can help and many publishers produce their own lists for guidance. The Centre for Language in Primary Education (CLPE) has produced broad-banded descriptive reading scales that can be used for assessing children's levels of reading. They can also work for categorizing the books. The Individualized Reading Levels from the National Centre for Language and Literacy have been used by many schools, but the number of levels can be tedious to work with and have the effect of creating one massive graded reading scheme from a book collection. Graded booklists to match the National Curriculum for England are available on the Qualifications and Curriculum Authority (QCA) website.

Auditing the current book stock

The next stage in the process of developing a good collection is to audit the current collection to record strengths in provision and identify gaps. The complete current stock of books in classrooms, the library and other resource collections (e.g. sets of multiple copies or author packs) should be audited. This involves listing and sorting by:

- genre/theme;
- author/illustrator/title;
- level of difficulty;
- number of copies;
- site;
- condition.

The children can be involved in this process. A similar trawl should be done for the range of authors to be included in the collection. It is a constant complaint of writers visiting schools that the children have not read their books, which limits the value of any visit. If children are to be encouraged to become familiar with the works of a particular author, then this is essential. However, care should be taken to ensure that the collection is appropriate to the age ranges of children involved. Many authors writing for children also write for adolescents and adults, and it can be disappointing for children to meet an impenetrable text or meet inappropriate themes in a text by a favourite author (e.g. Jacqueline Wilson, Judy Blume or Philip Pullman).

The condition of the texts is a further issue, as unattractive, worn texts may not attract children used to the graphics and quality of electronic texts and the high quality of modern paperbacks. Some older paperbacks that are on yellowed paper may not be selected by the casual browser but may be of use as part of multiple collections or when the children have already been captivated by a text through having it read aloud to them. Old copies of books with different covers and blurbs can be useful for comparisons and discussion of marketing policies, as well as critical analysis of artistic interpretation of a text.

Some schools have a core collection in each classroom with 'travelling book boxes' which are switched around each term. This works well where there are two or three form entry and parallel classes. In addition, classroom collections can be supplemented from the school central library collection or LA loan books. From this audit, targets can be set for book provision either from loans for temporary provision, or for future purchasing. The target list should be prioritized so that book purchasing can be planned into the school development plan, and full benefit derived from unexpected opportunities when funds are available from various sources for purchasing at short notice.

The purchasing policy will thus include:

- filling in gaps in the range of genres/themes/authors;
- ensuring there are sufficient books at each level of difficulty;
- replacing worn copies of popular books;
- contingency funds to purchase a long-awaited sequel, new title by a favourite author, book being made into film, television series and so on. Such purchases allow for a response to feed children's motivation and enthusiasm to read books.

Taking account of children's needs and interests

The children's levels of literacy should be audited and cross-referenced to the collection available in each classroom. This can be through matching to broad band descriptors such as the CLPE reading scale or the National Curriculum levelling, or though formal testing. In matching the book collection to children's reading levels, it will be necessary to ensure that you project ahead, allowing for the improvement that should take place across the year. Try to ensure that there are sufficient books at each level of difficulty to meet the needs of all the children. It may be necessary to adjust classroom collections, particularly when children are regrouped and moved around the school. When providing easier books for older, non-fluent readers it is a good idea to prioritize new book buying for this age group so that children are motivated by new books and do not have always to read books familiar from earlier classes.

Involving children in book selection is important and some schools have found innovative ways of doing this. Children can be involved in book picks at the library or book supplier with teachers making sure there is enough balance in the range of material selected as well as sufficiently challenging books to extend the children's reading.

The question of quality in children's books

We started off with the question of quality in the Introduction and if you have read the chapters in between, and at least some of the children's books referred to within those chapters, you should feel fairly knowledgeable about children's books by now. So it may be a good time to review this issue.

Because it has been precisely the self-imposed task of children's literature critics to judge which books are good for children and why, all children's literature criticism and reviews abound with both implicit and overt statements concerning the definitions of 'children's literature', 'children' and 'literature' (Lesnik-Oberstein, 1999: 18).

Throughout this book we have explored the nature of literature and have touched on the nature of childhood. The work of Aries (1961) and Cunningham's (1995, 2006) later reassessment of changing concepts of the child have provided challenges to the stance we may take as 'experts' working with children in our 'knowing' and understanding of the child. These are concepts and definitions, therefore, that those of us working with children tend to revisit throughout our careers as societal, cultural and political change impacts on them. Our 'knowing' and understanding of children and their books will therefore be a dynamic state.

The issue of what counts as a good children's book has been influenced by the question of who decides. Hollindale (1988) is critical of those who would argue that it is the child who is the arbiter of a good book for children. Some of those involved with children would argue that popularity with children is the main factor, and yet we do not accept in other aspects of life that children should set the boundaries. As they are inexperienced and we are still supporting their learning, we would intervene if we saw children behaving cruelly to an animal, for example. We would challenge the rationale that the child might use to justify such behaviour and encourage alternative behaviour. So the child as critic may require guidance to explore the concept of the good book. We might, as a starting point in our own exploration, take a text regarded as a 'classic' as being one where we have a consensus that it embodies, in some way, quality.

ACTIVITY

Read the opening chapters of a children's book considered a 'classic'. *The Secret Garden*, *The Wind in the Willows* and *Treasure Island* are all available in imprints labelled 'classics', and any titles in these imprints would be safe choices.

Now imagine you have been commissioned to produce a simplified version of the book for inexperienced young readers. Rewrite the opening few paragraphs, simplifying the text.

When you have done this, compare the two versions. Is the simplified version still a 'classic'? What has changed? Is it still good literature?

Commentary

Comparing different versions of a text can be useful for exploring notions of quality.

The two versions of *Alice in Wonderland* and *Black Beauty* printed next pose some immediate questions:

The first place that I can well remember was a large pleasant meadow with a pond of clear water in it. Some shady trees leaned over it, and rushes and water-lilies grew at the deep end. Over the hedge on one side we looked into a ploughed field, and on the other we looked over a gate at our master's house, which stood by the roadside; at the top of the meadow was a plantation of fir trees, and at the bottom a running stream overhung by a steep bank. When I was young I lived upon my mother's milk, as I could not eat grass. In the day time I ran by her side, and at night I lay down close by her. When it was hot, we used to stand by the pond in the shade of the trees, and when it was cold, we had a nice warm shed near the plantation. As soon as I was old enough to eat grass, my mother used to go out to work in the day time, and came back in the evening. There were six young colts in the meadow besides me; they were older than I was; some were nearly as large as grown-up horses. I used to run with them, and had great fun; we used to gallop all together round and round the field, as hard as we could go. Sometimes we had rather rough play, for they would frequently bite and kick as well as gallop. (*Black Beauty* by Anna Sewell)

The very first place that I can remember was a large pleasant meadow. To start with, I lived on my mother's milk. As soon as I could eat grass, however, she had to go out to work, and came home in the evening. There were six young colts in the meadow besides me. We had great fun galloping around although they would sometimes bite and kick. (Ladybird version of *Black Beauty* 'retold by' Betty Evans)

Alice was beginning to get very tired of sitting by her sister on the bank, and of having nothing to do: once or twice she had peeped into the book her sister was reading, but it had no pictures or conversations in it, 'and what is the use of a book,' thought Alice, 'without pictures or conversations?'

So she was considering, in her own mind (as well as she could, for the hot day made her feel very sleepy and stupid), whether the pleasure of making a daisy-chain would be worth the trouble of getting up and picking the daisies, when suddenly a White Rabbit with pink eyes ran close by her. There was nothing so *very* remarkable in that; nor did Alice think it so *very* much out of the way to hear the Rabbit say to itself, 'Oh dear! Oh dear! I shall be too late!' (when she thought about it afterwards, it occurred to her that she ought to have wondered at this, but at the time it all seemed quite natural); but when the Rabbit actually *took a watch out of its waistcoat-pocket*, and looked at it, and then hurried on, Alice started to her feet, for it flashed across her mind that she had never before seen a rabbit with either a waistcoat-pocket, or a watch to take out of it, and burning with curiosity, she ran across the field after it, and was just in time to see it pop down a large rabbit-hole under the hedge.

In another moment down went Alice after it, never once considering how in the world she was to get out again. (*Alice's Adventures in Wonderland* by Lewis Carroll)

Alice was tired of sitting by her sister on the grassy bank and having nothing to do. Her sister was reading a book with no pictures or conversations in it.

It looked very dull.

It was a hot day, and Alice was sleepy. She was wondering whether to get up and make a daisy chain, when suddenly a white rabbit with pink eyes ran close by her. (Ladybird version of *Alice in Wonderland* 'retold by' Joan Collins)

The simplification retains the storyline of the original, but loses some of the narrative and linguistic devices that guide the reader through the text. The simplified versions tend to emphasize and encourage a literal reading, losing the complexities of language, the high-value connectives and interrelations, with a corresponding loss of inferential reading. The reader will know the main characters and plot but will not have entered the same relationship with the writer, the narrator and text that the original offers.

The question of what counts as quality, then, may or may not be something which children can read, choose to read or love reading. In your school, as part of your book provision policy, you should explore your understanding of what counts as quality in children's books. That does not mean to say that we would only want children to read the most 'worthy' of books. Peter Dickinson in a seminal article, 'A Defence of Rubbish', argued that children should be allowed and encouraged to read from a wide range of texts including those that form part of children's sub-culture and may be disapproved of by adults (Dickinson, in Fox et al., 1976).

Kim Reynolds (2000) has demonstrated that sub-cultures such as horror series, while causing anxiety to adults fearful for the morals and minds of children, are often very moral texts. The status quo may be challenged by strong and dangerous forces, but after temptation, danger and personal transformation, the moral order is restored in the end.

What makes a classic?

What makes a children's classic? Defining 'literature' and even a 'child' is not as simple as it might at first appear and there is no easy formula that sets 'children's literature' apart from other literature as a distinctive genre, so it is not surprising notions of the 'classic children's book' are problematic.

Take a few minutes to jot down your personal list of top ten classic children's books. Now spend a few moments reflecting on your choices:

● What informed your selection?
● Have you included any books that have been written in the last 10 years/30 years/50 years?
● Are any of the authors on your list still alive?
● Have you included any picture books?
● Did your list contain any poetry collections?
● Are the books those you enjoyed as a child or those that have been enjoyed by your own children? Or the children you teach?
● Have any of the books been made into films, televised or adapted for radio?
● Was 'quality' one of the indicators that informed your choice? If so what do you consider to be the hallmarks of 'quality' writing?

Commentary

Writing of quality?

According to Ezra Pound the true classic has 'a certain eternal and irrepressible freshness', a criterion which has also been applied to children's classics. Geoff Fenwick (1990) claimed that classics are a body of fiction that is enduring, at the heart of literature and represent *the best* in children's writing. Endurance and quality are thus regarded as the main indicators of classic literature, although it could be argued that endurance has more to do with popularity than quality of the writing. In this sense *Black Beauty* and *The Lion, the Witch and the Wardrobe* and *Charlie and the Chocolate Factory* might be called ' classics'.

It is also interesting to observe that books that have acquired the 'classic' accolade are not necessarily those that are most admired at the time of writing. A quick review of prize-winning books from, for instance, the Carnegie list, shows that many of these books are no longer remembered although other books published in the same year may still be in print and their titles more familiar to a modern readership. Peter Hunt (1994a) suggests that the children's classic is different from the adult classic in that it is always 'alive', passed down from one generation to the next. When they cease to be read they fade from the publishers' lists whereas adult 'classics' may survive to be read only by academics.

In a short but illuminating article in *Books for Keeps*, 'What makes a Children's Classic?', Victor Watson (n.d.) describes how a group of 10-year-old children responded to the question, 'What is a classic?' One child suggested, 'books written by dead people'. Watson suggests that this indicates that children know that a classic book's popularity survives the age in which it is written. But he agrees with Hunt that this is not simply a case of survival: 'such a book does not simply endure like a fossil in a glass case but is constantly re-made and improvised upon so that its qualities and its appeal are transformed and revealed to new generations of readers'. He goes on: 'A characteristic of the classic children's story is its capacity to offer from within itself new meaning and fresh emphases while retaining its original integrity'. In this sense the notion of classic is tied in to rewritings and remakings through adaptation, illustration, dramatization and so on.

Do the classics have common features?

Watson (n.d.) asks whether we can identify any features that children's classics have in common. He suggests that they are 'love stories', by which he means the relationships between adults and children are characterized by the certainty that the relationship between them will change. The intimacy with a child is never an equal one because of the acute difference in understanding about life, death and the ephemeral nature of childhood. Children's classics arise out of the intimate spaces between adults and children. In fact, many of the books we have come to regard as classic were once written with a particular child in mind, *Alice in Wonderland*, *The Wind in the Willows* and *Winnie-the-Pooh* for example. Watson suggests that C.S. Lewis's books cannot be called classic because 'the conception of children is distant and narrow'.

Classics for modern children?

Are the classics still relevant to children today? Liz Waterland writing in *Signal* describes how she planned a programme of reading with her 5–7-year-old city children. Every day her class had two story sessions, one based on reading modern picture books and one reading classic fiction. The books read included *Winnie-the-Pooh*, *Alice in Wonderland*, *The Wind in the Willows*, *The Lion, the Witch and the Wardrobe*, *A Christmas Carol*, *Black Beauty* and *The Secret Garden*. The children were read the original texts, which were on the whole unabridged, though some exceptions were made (e.g. Pipers at the Gates of Dawn in *Wind in the Willows* was cut). Waterland reports that the children's responses to these classics were very positive. In describing the value of the experience she writes,

> The first and greatest value is certainly the new worlds that were opened for them and the willingness with which they entered those worlds. Second comes the value of offering children books in their original form and language and the demands this makes on them. There is no doubt that their language was enriched and their understanding of the unfamiliar deepened. Third, I value the links the children have begun to forge with their literary roots. Books like *Alice* are part of a heritage that fewer children nowadays have access to. It is important that children should make connections when they hear people say, 'He's a real Scrooge' or 'God bless us every one'. Lastly and perhaps most satisfying of all, there is the value that children themselves found in the books, and that led them to want to go on exploring the worlds they had entered. Many children found copies of the book I was reading and read along with me or at home.

The question of suitability: childhood and values

Closely related to the issue of quality is the question of suitability. This has been a hot topic throughout the history of children's books. Universal literacy was an early aim of the Puritans, not to provide pleasure for the masses, but to facilitate their Christianity and religious observance. The dilemma has always been for some, that once literate, the child reader has freedom to read what is available to be read as opposed to what some adults think should be read.

Literature for children has its roots in both didactic and pedagogic texts designed for learning to read and for learning to live according to a moral code, and in adult literature, where some texts written for adults have appealed to and been appropriated by children. *Gulliver's Travels* was one of the first books to appear in versions for children and is still available in simplified versions. These versions focus on one or two episodes from the adult narrative, usually not only simplified, but also censored. When Gulliver is in Lilliput, the huge moral dilemma of whether Gulliver should have extinguished the fire in the royal palace in the way he did is rarely presented in children's versions, yet it provides a wonderful example of Tucker's 'cognitive dissonance'.

It is the impact of the stories on an 'unformed mind' that has caused disquiet for adults from the beginnings of children's literature. Once fairy tales were thought to be dangerous to children's minds, with their themes of jealousy, covetousness, hatred and rags-to-riches wish fulfilment: 'for surelye vayne woordes doo worke no smal thinge in vayne, ignoraunt and younge mindes' (Ascham, 1545). Even in the later part of the 20th century fairy tales were criticized for their gender stereotypes, for example. However, the messages in some of the 'updated' versions of these tales can be just as controversial. Babette Cole's *Princess Smartypants* for example, eschews the traditional ending for a tale of the princess marrying the prince who has chosen her. The princess decides to live without a prince: a radical feminist solution, perhaps: Roald Dahl's princess who decides to choose her own non-royal partner is a less radical alternative. But we have realized that through books such as Alison Lurie's *Clever Gretchen and Other Forgotten Folk Tales* that the older versions of the stories, not collected by Perrault or Grimm, often contain much more independent females (see Kate Crackernuts, p. 78.)

You will need to decide where your own boundaries lie in deciding what to include or not within the collection. The 'Harry Potter phenomenon' (Zipes, 2001) has bred a rash of articles by anxious adults concerned about the negative impact on their children of the world of witches and magic. So the earlier Ascham quote, dating from over 400 years ago, may still reflect the concerns of adults in our very different society. We might need to consider whether it is better to share controversial texts with children, and trust that they will be no more corrupted by them than by real life itself or the images and narratives they encounter in other media, than to censor them. However, the choices made at home and at school may be different, and the school fiction collection may have to take into account the sensitivities of the community it serves.

Reading spaces and the reading environment

Reflect for a moment on your personal reading habits and preferences. Do you have a favourite place for reading? A comfy chair? The bath? In bed? Do you prefer reading during the day? At night? In the summer holidays?

While it isn't possible to replicate the conditions of reading at home, schools need to be mindful of the spaces that they set aside for reading. Is there a class or school library? Are these spaces conducive to browsing and selecting books? Are books easily located and is there a system for shelving returned books? Does the school have a library management system such as Junior Librarian, which enables pupils to take control of the management of resources and conduct their own library investigations with ease and efficiency? Does someone have responsibility for the library and is it a welcoming place? Does the furniture allow children to read in comfort? Do pupils have access to the library after school and at lunchtimes? In 2004 the DfES produced a self-evaluation document to help schools assess the effectiveness of the library in school. The document focuses on six key questions:

1. How high are standards?
2. How well are pupils' personal qualities, attitudes, and values developed?
3. How effective are library-focused learning and teaching?
4. How well does the library meet the pupils' needs?
5. How well are pupils guided and supported?
6. How well is the library managed and supported?

Are there spaces in school for quiet sustained and absorbed reading, as well as sharing books with friends? Perhaps a classroom is set aside for quiet reading during lunch breaks.

As well as setting aside places for reading, schools need to consider how the environment promotes a reading culture. Aidan Chambers's *The Reading Environment* (1991) provides excellent advice and features ideas for book displays.

School librarians and school library services

Few primary schools have dedicated school librarians, though there will usually be someone with responsibility for overseeing the library. Most usually this is an enthusiastic teacher who might be supported by parent or pupil helpers. The Ofsted Report *Good School Libraries* (2004b) highlights the importance of well-trained specialist librarians, yet the School Librarian of the Year Award 2007 had only one primary school librarian on the shortlist, and that was a librarian from a school in Hong Kong. Secondary schools are better served with qualified librarians or full-time teacher librarians, though their status varies from school to school. The Ofsted report states that where librarians are regarded as having middle-management status they are best placed to work effectively with teaching staff.

Schools Library Services (SLS) are local authority services dedicated to support-ing schools through book provision, training and specialized consultancy. In most authorities the SLS is part of the library or cultural services, but in some authori-ties the SLS is managed by the education authority. There is no unified pattern of provision so it is important to investigate and find out what is on offer in your local area. Book Trust (2003) found that schools valued the SLS role in ensuring adequate book provision. The following are typical of the comments made by teachers when asked for their opinions about their SLS:

> Most texts are borrowed from the local library education section or come from the school library service to cut down on costs.
>
> Texts are purchased to fit topics, taken from the school library or borrowed from the Library Education Service to save school costs.
>
> In addition: subscribe to Schools Library Service – approx 1000 non-fiction books per year specifically to support subjects + 500 fiction books per year to add to general library stocks. Without this subscription we would be lost.

However, these services are by no means universal. The SLS have increasingly faced delegation of funding to schools with many services dependent on schools' option to buy back into the service. Where schools have failed to due this, services have been cut and even disbanded, with the percentage of school pupils served by Schools Library Services continuing to fall in England. The result is that Schools Library Service provision across the country is patchy and services vary in their capacity to support schools in the ways they would. Those that have survived are finding innovative ways of marketing themselves and offering new and diverse loan and advisory services to schools including INSET, mobile provision and auditing services.

The School Library Association (SLA) is a charitable organization dedicated to the advocacy of both School Librarians and School Library Services. It offers train-ing and supportive networks to those working in the sector. The organization pub-lishes the *School Librarian* and runs annual conferences for professionals working in the sector.

ACTIVITY

Familiarize your self with the Schools Library Service provision in your area. If your local authority does not have a SLS, where is the nearest one? Do they offer support for schools out of their area? Are services available for student teachers? What types of service are offered (e.g. library loan, topic collections, non-book resources)? Does the library offer training to help teachers keep up to date with their book knowledge? If possible arrange a visit to your local schools library service to see what's on offer. Keep a record of contact details in your reading journal.

Time to read

In recent years, much discussion has focused on reading teaching and instruction. In England, for example, the National Literacy Strategy has provided training and curriculum materials to help teachers develop strategies for shared and guided reading, but less attention has been devoted to independent reading practices. In fact for children to become fully independent they need opportunities to:

- listen to skilled and experience readers reading aloud;
- read to their teachers and other experienced readers;
- read by themselves.

Sustained and absorbed reading requires time and it is worth reflecting on how much time is devoted to children's independent reading as well as the quality of engagement during this reading time. For children to develop into committed life-long readers they need opportunities to experience and practise sustained reading in childhood and adolescence but this practice is not as prevalent as it was prior to the introduction of the National Literacy Strategy, with teachers citing insufficient time for including USSR (Universal Sustained Reading) in regular classroom routines.

ACTIVITY

> Carry out an investigation into one class's reading over the period of a week.
>
> - How much time is devoted to the teaching of reading?
> - Is reading taught during literacy lessons?
> - Is reading taught (rather than practised) in other curriculum subjects?
> - What do children do in independent reading sessions?
> - Does reading aloud to children occur regularly?

In this chapter we have:

- considered what might be necessary to include in a classroom collection of fiction;
- introduced ways of auditing the book stock and the needs of the children;
- reflected on the factors that might inform the creation of a book policy;
- considered the importance of the reading environment;
- identified professionals who can support teachers through their specialized expertise and availability of resources for school and classroom.

Further reading to support this chapter is contained in Chapter 11.

Controversial statements

Copy and cut out the controversial statements in Appendix 10.2. In a group, sort them into the statements you agree with, those you disagree with, and those you are either unsure about or on which you cannot reach agreement. These central cards are the tricky ones and worth spending some time exploring. You might want to follow up some of the suggestions for further reading to help you in resolving the issues raised on these problem cards.

Appendix 10.1

Readability formula

This is one of the simplest formulae to use. You could also try using the Fry Readability Graph. Computerized readability formulae are now available which makes the whole process much easier, but when you have completed this activity you may question their validity as measures of contextual difficulty.

FOG Index (Frequency of gobbledegook)

Select three sample passages of 100 words from different parts of the book.

Divide each sample by the number of sentences it contains to find the average sentence length. For each sample count the number of 'hard words', indicated here by words of three or more syllables. Total these two numbers and divide by 0.4 to obtain the Fog Index. The average score for the three samples should indicate the overall level of the text. The index relates to American grades and you should add 5 to obtain a 'reading age'.

Appendix 10.2

Controversial statement cards

There is more poor quality fiction produced for children today than when I was a child	Comics serve an important purpose for children
Teachers should use comics in school with children	If children want to read *Rainbow Fairies* and Darren Shan's *The Demonata* books, they should be on the shelves in classrooms and school libraries
Teachers have a duty to use only the best literature for children	It is dreadful that in the 21st century we are barraged with trashy books for children
The *Harry Potter* books will never stand the test of time and will be looked back on as the *Enid Blyton* novels of the late 20th and early 21st centuries	Popular fiction can co-exist with quality fiction and meet different needs for children
There is no comparison between *Alice in Wonderland* and *The Series of Unfortunate Events* series	The ultimate test of children's fiction is whether it endures for future generations
The ultimate test of quality in children's fiction is whether children want to read it	Enid Blyton's books are biased and trite and can damage children's perceptions of the world
It does not really matter what children read as long as they are reading something	Series books serve an important function in children's development as readers
If children rely too much on series books they will have a very narrow reading experience	It is important that children read quality fiction to aid their development
Teachers should tune in to children's popular culture to help bridge the gap between home and school	Children need to have their own literary sub-cultures as part of taking 'ownership' of reading for themselves
Books such *as The Secret Garden*, with wonderful language and sensitive themes serve an important purpose in children's development	If adults do not introduce children to good books, they will find their own reading matter through friends
If children are forced to read books they do not want to read they will switch off from reading	Boys do not enjoy fiction as much as non-fiction
The influx of American fiction has reduced the quality of literature for children	Film and television tie-in books are generally poor quality

Chapter 11

Keeping in Touch with Children's Books

> This chapter is organized in five sections to help you locate up-to-date children's book information:
>
> - organizations;
> - book prizes and awards;
> - magazines and journals;
> - useful websites.

Organizations

Booktrust

45 East Hill
London
SW18 2QZ
Tel: 020 8516 2977

Booktrust is an independent charity working for those concerned with young children and their books. It initiates and manages a range of projects including Bookstart. The website has a wealth of teachers' resources.

Website: www.booktrusted.com

Seven Stories

St Peter's Wharf
St Peter's Marina
Newcastle upon Tyne
NE6 1TZ
Tel: 0191 276 4289

Website: www.sevenstories.org.uk

Seven Stories is where our rich heritage of British children's books is collected, explored and celebrated. Books are our inspiration for all kinds of exhibitions, activities and events, for seeing and hearing, making and doing, writing and drawing, music and drama.

Centre for Literacy in Primary Education (CLPE)

Webber Street
London
SE1 8QW
Tel: 020 7401 3382/3

Website: www.clpe.co.uk

The CLPE is a resource centre, which provides INSET courses in all aspects of language, literacy and children's literature. An extensive library has an excellent collection of children's books and a teachers' reference section.

Children's Books Ireland

Children's Books Ireland,
17 North Great Georges Street,
Dublin 1
Ireland

Website: www.childrensbooksireland.com

Children's Books Ireland is the national children's book organization of Ireland. The aim of CBI is to promote quality children's books and reading throughout the country. The organization was formed in 1996.

Federation of Children's Book Groups (FCBG)

The National Secretary
2 Bridge Wood View
Horsforth
Leeds
West Yorkshire
LS18 5PE

Website: www.fcbg.org.uk

FCBG is a voluntary organization for teachers, librarians, booksellers, parents and children. It aims to bring children's books, the love of reading and children together. It organizes National Share a Story month, the Red House Children's Book Award and a prestigious annual conference.

International Board on Books for Young People (IBBY)

PO Box 20875
GB – London
SE22 9WO

Website: www.ibby.org

IBBY is an international network committed to bringing children and books together. It aims to:

- promote international understanding through children's books;
- give children everywhere the opportunity to have access to books with high
- literary and artistic standards;
- encourage the publication and distribution of quality children's books especially in developing countries.

Listening Books

12 Lant Street
London
SE1 1QH
Tel: 0207 7407 9417

Website: www.listening-books.org.uk

Listening Books is a registered charity, which provides a postal library service of audio books on cassette for people who have difficulty holding a book, turning the page or reading in the normal way.

National Association for the Teaching of English (NATE)

50 Broadfield Road
Sheffield
S8 OXJ
Tel: 0114 255 5419

Website: www.nate.org.uk

NATE is the UK English teachers' subject association and has members from all age phases. NATE aims to support effective teaching, to keep teachers informed about current developments and provide teachers of English with a national voice. NATE publishes professional books, classroom resources, journals and magazines. It organizes a full programme of regional and national conferences.

National Literacy Association

1st Floor
Leonard House
321 Bradford Street
Digbeth
Birmingham
B5 6ET

Website: www.nla.org.uk

The objective of the National Literacy Association is to ensure that when they leave school 99 per cent of children will be equipped with the literacy skills necessary for modern living. The Association works in partnership with other organizations to support literacy in schools, at home and in the community.

National Literacy Trust

Swire House
59 Buckingham Gate
London
SW1E 6AJ
Tel: 0207 828 2435

Website: www.literacytrust.org.uk

The National Literacy Trust aims to make an independent, strategic contribution to the development of literacy standards in the UK. It organizes the *Reading Is Fundamental* campaign and helps parents become involved in their children's reading. It organizes an annual conference as well as courses and training events.

Poetry Book Society

Poetry Book Society
Fourth Floor
2 Tavistock Place
London
WC1H 9RA

Website: www.childrenspoetrybookshelf.co.uk/default.asp

Runs the Children's Poetry Bookshelf and an annual poetry compettion for children aged 7–11 years.

The most comprehensive and accessible collection of poetry from 1912 in Britain. It houses an extensive children's collection and has an excellent education service. Details are available on the website.

Poetry Library

Poetry library
Level 5
Royal Festival Hall
London
SE1 8XX

Website: www.poetrylibrary.org.uk

The Roald Dahl Museum and Story Centre

81–3 High Street
Great Missenden
Buckinghamshire
HP16 0AL

Website: www.roalddahlmuseum.org

The Roald Dahl Museum and Story Centre was established in 2001 with the aim of setting up a centre to tell Roald Dahl's life story, to care for his archive and to promote a love of creative writing in everyone.

School Library Association (SLA)

Unit 2, Lotmead Business Village
Lotmead Farm
Wanborough
Swindon
SN4 0UY
Tel: 01793 791 787

Website: www.sla.org.uk

The SLA promotes the development of school libraries as an integral part of the curriculum. It produces guidelines on running the school library, a quarterly journal, training courses and has an information and advisory service. It campaigns to ensure that school libraries and school library services have appropriate provision.

Scottish Book Trust

Scottish Book Centre
137 Dundee Street
Edinburgh
EH11 1BG

Website: www.scottishbooktrust.com

This organization is committed to the promotion of reading and writing in Scotland. It organizes book events including National Poetry Day and publishes booklists and the magazine *Shelf Life*.

The Story Museum

Website: www.storymuseum.org.uk

The Story Museum is a charitable company set up in 2003 to create a museum for children about children's books

United Kingdom Literacy Association (UKLA)

4th Floor
Attenborough Building
University of Leicester
Leicester
LE1 7RH

Website: www.ukla.org

UKLA exists to support, inform and give voice to those concerned with the teaching of literacy and language at all levels. It publishes the scholarly *Journal of Research in Reading* and, for teachers, *Literacy*, as well as a newsletter, *Literacy News*.

Welsh Books Council

Castell Brychan
Aberystwyth
Ceredigion
SY23 2JB
Tel: 01970 624 151

Website: www.cllc.org.uk

The Welsh Books Council advises on children's books in Wales. It undertakes a wide range of activities with children and provides a support and information service to schools and libraries.

Write Away

Write Away UK Ltd
9 Notley Green
Great Notley
Braintree
Essex
CM77 7US

Website: www.writeaway.org.uk
E-mail info@writeaway.org.uk

Write Away is an organisation specializing in children's literature, creative writing and cross-arts projects in education. It runs courses and conferences for teachers, students and children. Bespoke consultancy services are available. The Write Away website provides reviews, interviews and free downloadable book-related resources.

Magazines and Journals

Books for Keeps

A well-established bi-monthly magazine which includes articles, author profiles, children's book news and reviews. Subscription details from:

6 Brightfield Road
Lee
London
SE12 8QF

Carousel

Three issues a year featuring book reviews, children's book articles, interviews and reviews. Subscription details from:

Carousel
7 Carrs Lane
Birmingham
B4 7TG

INIS

The magazine of Children's Books Ireland. Includes, informative articles and reviews. Subscription information from:

Children's Books Ireland
First Floor,
17 Lower Camden Street
Dublin 2
Ireland

Shelf Life

A termly magazine produced by the Scottish Book Trust. Includes news, reviews and author information. Subscription information from:

Scottish Book Trust
137 Dundee Street
Edinburgh
EH11 1BG

Website: www.scottishbooktrust.com

Bookbird

Children's Literature in Education
An international journal publishing original articles of interest to librarians, teachers, students, writers and all those interested in children's books. Subscription information from:

Human Sciences Press, Inc.
233 Spring Street
New York
NY 10013–1578
USA

The School Librarian

Journal of the School Library Association containing articles on children's literature and school library organizations, and reviews of recent books, CD-ROMs and websites across the age ranges. Subscription details from:

SLA
Unit 2, Lotmead Business Village
Lotmead Farm
Wanborough
Swindon
Wiltshire
SN4 0UY

Book prizes

Book prizes are useful signposts to guide your reading. Reading shortlisted books for the major prizes is one way of keeping up-to-date and some prizes encourage involvement from schools and children.

The Hans Andersen Awards

The highest international recognition given to authors and illustrators whose work has made a lasting contribution to children's literature. The award is presented biennially at the IBBY Congress. For previous winners see www.ibby.org.

The Blue Peter Book Awards

The Blue Peter Awards were launched in 2000. They are organized by the BBC children's programme, *Blue Peter*. The Judges' Awards are judged by a celebrity panel and the Voters' Awards are voted for by children through public libraries. See www.bbc.co.uk/cbbc/bluepeter/bookclub/awards/.

Branford Boase Award

Awarded to an outstanding first-time novel for children with recognition to the Editor for encouraging new Talent. See www.branfordboaseaward.org.uk/home.html.

Caldecott Medal

Named after the English illustrator Randolph Caldecott (1846–86), this award is presented for the most distinguished American picture book for children. See www.ala.org/ala/alsc/awardsscholarships/literaryawds/caldecottmedal/caldecott medal.htm

Canadian Library Association Awards

Awarded for outstanding Canadian children's book.
See www.cla.ca/awards/bookaw.htm

The Carnegie Medal

Awarded by the Youth Libraries Group of CILIP for an outstanding British book for children. See www.carnegiegreenaway.org.uk/carnegie/carn.html.

The Red House Children's Book Award

The winner of the Children's Book Award is chosen by nominations from children throughout the UK. See www.redhousechildrensbookaward.co.uk.

Children's Book Council of Australia Award

This award for Australian children's books is given for five categories which are judged primarily on criteria of literary quality. See www.cbc.org.au/awards.htm.

Coretta Scott King Award

Awarded each year to an author and illustrator of African descent whose distinguished books promote an understanding and appreciation of the American Dream. See:
www.ala.org/ala/emiert/corettascottkingbookawards/winnersa/cskawardwinners.htm.

Kate Greenaway Medal

The Kate Greenaway Medal is awarded to an artist who has produced the most distinguished work in the illustration of children's books. The medal is awarded on the basis of nominations from the Youth Libraries Group of CILIP. See www.carnegiegreenaway.org.uk/carnegie/carn.html.

The Guardian Fiction Award

Awarded to an outstanding work of fiction for children (not picture books) written by a British or Commonwealth author. The winner is chosen by a panel of authors and the Review Editor for the *Guardian*'s children's books section.

The Marsh Award

Awarded to the best translation of a children's book, by a British translator, from a foreign language into English, and published in the UK by a British publisher.

The Nestlé Award

The awards are given to fiction and poetry in three age categories. Shortlisting is done by a panel of judges and children select bronze, silver and gold winners. See www.booktrusted.co.uk/nestle/.

The Newbery Medal

Named after John Newbery (1713–67), a London bookseller and first British publisher of children's books, *The Newbery Medal* is an American award given annually for the most distinguished contribution to American literature for children published during the previous year. See www.ala.org/ala/alsc/awardsscholarships/literaryawds/newberymedal/newberymedal.htm.

The CLPE Poetry Award

The award honours excellence in children's poetry. See http://www.clpe.co.uk/poetry/poetry.html.

The Costa Book Award

An award for excellence in literature written by authors who have been resident in the UK or Eire for three years. It has a children's category and the children's award winner is eligible for the overall prize. Formerly the Whitbread Award. See http://www.costabookawards.com/.

Useful websites

Achuka: http://www.achuka.co.uk
Booktrust www.booktrusted.com
Reading Matters: www.readingmatters.co.uk
Reading Zone http://www.readingzone.com/
The Word Pool: www.wordpool.co.uk
Writeaway: www.writeaway.org.uk

Select Bibliography

Abbs, P. and Richardson, J. (1990) *The Forms of Narrative*. Cambridge: Cambridge University Press.

Agnew, K. and Fox, G. (2001) *Children at War*. London: Continuum.

Andrews, R. (1994) *International Dimensions in the National Curriculum*. Stoke-on-Trent: Trentham.

Applebee, A. (1978) *The Child's Concept of Story*. Chicago: University of Chicago Press.

Appleyard, J.A. (1990) *Becoming a Reader: The Experience of Fiction from Childhood to Adulthood*. Cambridge: Cambridge University Press.

Aries, P. (1996) *Centuries of Childhood*. London: Pimlico/Random House.

Baddeley, P. and Eddershaw, C. (1994) *Not So Simple Picture Books*. Stoke-on-Trent: Trentham.

Barrs, M. and Cork, V. (2001) *The Reader in the Writer*. London: CLPE.

Barthes, R. (1972) *Mythologies*. London: Vintage.

Barthes, R. (1995) *S/Z*. London: Jonathan Cape.

Bearne, E. (1996) 'Mind the gap: critical literacy as a dangerous underground movement', in M. Styles, E. Bearne and V. Watson (eds) *Voices Off*. London: Cassell.

Bettelheim, B. (1988) *The Uses of Enchantment*. London: Penguin.

Book Trust (2002) *Recommended Spending on Books in Schools*. London: Booktrust.

Booker, C. (2004) *The Seven Basic Plots*. London: Continuum.

Bromley, H. (1996) 'Madam Read the Scary Book, Madam: Mohal and her picture books – the emergent bilingual reader', in V. Watson and M. Styles (eds) *Talking Pictures*. London: Hodder & Stoughton.

Bryson, N. and Kappeler, S. (1983) *Teaching the Text*. London: Routledge and Kegan Paul.

Buckingham, D. (1993) *Children Talking Television: The Making of Television Literacy*. London: Falmer.

Bycock, J. (trans.) (2000) *The Saga of the Volsungs: The Norse Epic of Sigurd the Dragon Slayer*. London: Penguin.

Carpenter, H. (1994) *Secret Gardens*. London: Unwin Hyman.

Carter, J. (1999) *Talking Books*. London: Routledge.

Carter, J. (2001) *Creating Writers*. London: Routledge.

Chambers, A. (1991) *The Reading Environment*. Stroud: Thimble Press.

Chambers, A. (1993) *Tell Me: Children, Reading and Talk*. Stroud: Thimble Press.

Chapman, J. (1987) *Reading: From 5–11 Years*. Buckingham: Open University Press.

Clark, C. and Foster, A. (2005) *Children's and Young People's Reading Habits and Preferences* London: National Literacy Trust.

Clark, M. (1976) *Young Fluent Readers: What Can They Teach Us?* London: Heinemann.

Collins, F.M. and Graham, J. (2001) *Historical Fiction for Children*. London: David Fulton.

Crago, H. (1999) 'Can stories heal?' in P. Hunt (ed.) *Understanding Children's Literature*. London: Routledge.

Cunningham, H. (1995) *Children and Childhood in Western Society Since 1500*. Harlow: Longman.

Daly, I. and Willey, B. (2001) *Irish Myths and Legends*. Oxford: Oxford University Press.

Dalley, S. (trans.) (1988) *Myths from Mesopotamia*. Oxford: Oxford University Press.

Dickinson, P. (1976) 'In Defence of Rubbish' in G. Fox et al. (eds) *Writers, Critics and Children*. London: Heinemann.

Dickinson, P. (1986) 'Fantasy: the need for realism' in *Children's Literature in Education*, 17(1): 39–57.

Doonan, J. (1993) *Looking at Pictures in Picture Books*. Stroud: Thimble Press.

Downey, M.T. and Levstik, L.S. (1988) 'Teaching and learning history: the research base', *Social Education* (September): 336–42.

Eddershaw, C. and Baddeley, P. (1994) *Not So Simple Picture Books*. Stoke-on-Trent: Trentham.

Egoff, S., Stubbs, G. and Ashley, L. (1980) *Only Connect* (2nd edn). Ontario: Oxford University Press.

Egoff, S., Stubbs, G., Ashley, R. and Sutton, W. (1996) *Only Connect: Readings on Children's Literature*. Ontario: Oxford University Press.

Evans, J. (ed.) (1998) *What's in the Picture? Responding to Illustrations in Picture Books*. London: Paul Chapman.

Fairclough, N. (1989) *Language and Power*. London: Longman.

Fenwick, G. (1990) *Teaching Children's Literature in the Primary School*. London: David Fulton.

Fish, S. (1980) *Is There a Text in This Class? The Authority of Interpretative Communities*. Cambridge: Harvard University Press

Fisher, J. (1994) 'Historical fiction', in P. Hunt (ed.) *International Companion Encyclopedia of Children's Literature*. London: Routledge.

Fisher, M. (1969) *Intent upon Reading*. London: Brockhampton Press.

Foster, J. and Simons, J. (1995) *What Katy Read: Feminist Re-readings of 'Classic' Stories for Girls*. London: Macmillan.

Fox, C. (1993) *At the Very Edge of the Forest: The Influence of Literature on Storytelling for Children*. London: Cassell.

Genette, G. and Lewis J.E. (trans.) (1993) *Narrative Discourse*. New York: Cornell University Press.

Grainger, T. (1997) *Traditional Story Telling in the Primary Classroom*. Leamington Spa: Scholastic.

Hall, C. and Coles, M. (1999) *Children's Reading Choices*. London: Routledge.

Hall, L. (1989) *Poetry for Life*. London: Cassell

Hall, L. (1998) 'The pattern of dead and living: Lucy Boston and the necessity of continuity', *Children's Literature in Education*, 29(4): 223–36.

Halliday, M. (1978) *Language as Social Semiotic*. London: Arnold.

Halliday, M.A.K. and Hasan, R. (1976) *Cohesion in English*. Harlow: Longman.

Harding, D. (1977) 'Psychological processes in the reading of fiction', in M. Meek, A. Warlow and G. Barton (eds) *The Cool Web: The Pattern of Children's Reading*. London: The Bodley Head.

Hardy, B. (1997) 'Narrative as a primary act of mind', in M. Meek, A. Warlow and G. Barton (eds) *The Cool Web: The Pattern of Children's Reading*. London: The Bodley Head.

Heath, S.B. (1983) *Ways With Words: Language, Life and Work in Communities and Classrooms*. Cambridge: Cambridge University Press.

Hodges, G.C. (1996) 'Encountering the different', in M. Styles, E. Bearne and V. Watson (eds) *Voices Off*. London: Cassell.

Hollindale, P. (1988) *Ideology and the Children's Book*. Stroud: Thimble Press.

Hollindale, P. (1997) *Signs of Childness in Children's Books*. Stroud: Thimble Press.

Hume, K. (1984) *Fantasy and Mimesis*. London: Routledge

Hunt, P. (1991) *Criticism, Theory and Children's Literature*. Oxford: Blackwell.

Hunt, P. (ed.) (1992) *Children's Literature: The Development of Criticism*. London: Routledge.

Hunt, P. (1994a) *An Introduction to Children's Literature*. Oxford: Oxford University Press.

Hunt, P. (ed.) (1994b) *International Companion Encyclopedia of Children's Literature*. London: Routledge.

Hunt, P. (ed.) (1999) *Understanding Children's Literature*. London: Routledge.

Hunt, P. and Lenz, M. (2001) *Alternative Worlds in Fantasy Fiction*. London: Continuum.

Iser, W. (1978) *The Act of Reading*. London: Routledge and Kegan Paul.

Jackson, R. (1981) *Fantasy: the Literature of Subversion*. London: Routledge.

James, A. and Prout, A. (eds) (1997) *Constructing and Reconstructing Childhood*. London: Falmer Press.

Jenks, C. (1996) *Childhood*. London: Routledge.

King, C. (2001) '"I like group reading because we can share ideas": the role of talk within the literature circle', *Reading*, April.

Kornbluth,C., Bester, A. and Block, R. (1959) 'Science fiction: its nature, faults and virtues', in *The Science Fiction Novel: Imagination and Social Criticism*. Chicago: Advent.

Kress, G. and Knapp, P. (1994) 'Genre in a social theory of language', in *English in Education*. Sheffield: NATE.

Lathey, G. (2001) 'A havey-cavey business: language in historical fiction with particular reference to the novels of Joan Aiken and Leon Garfield', in F. Collins and J. Graham *Historical Fiction for Children*. London: David Fulton.

Le Guin, U.K. (1992) *The Language of the Night: Essays on Fantasy and Science Fiction* (2nd edn). New York: HarperCollins.

Lee, A. (illus.) and Guest, C. (trans.) (2000) *The Mabinogion*. London: Voyager/Collins.

Lesnik-Oberstein, K. (1999) 'Essentials: what is Children's Literature? What is Childhood?' in P. Hunt (ed.) *Understanding Children's Literature*. London: Routledge.

Lewis, D. (1990) 'The constructedness of texts: picture books and the metafictive', *Signal* 62, May.

Lewis, D. (2001) *Reading Contemporary Picture books: Picturing Text*. London: Routledge Falmer.

Lodge, D. (1993) *The Art of Fiction*. London: Penguin.

Longacre, R. (1976) *An Anatomy of Speech Notions*. Lisse: Peter de Riddes.

Lunzer, E. and Gardner, K. (eds) (1979) *The Effective Use of Reading*. London: Heinemann.

Lyotard, J. (1984) *The Post-modern Condition: A Report on Knowledge*. Manchester: Manchester University Press.

Mallett, M. (1992) *Making Facts Matter*. London: Paul Chapman.

Mallett, M. (1999) *Young Researchers*. London: Routledge Falmer.

Manlove, C. (1975) *Modern Fantasy: Five Studies*. Cambridge: Cambridge University Press.

Manlove, C. (1999) *The Fantasy Literature of England*. London: Palgrave Macmillan.

Manlove (2003) *From Alice to Harry Potter: Children's Fantasy in England*. Christchurch: Cybereditions.

Marsh, J. and Millard, E. (2000) *Literacy and Paper Culture: Using Children's Culture in the Classroom*. London: Paul Chapman.

Meek, M. (1988) *How Texts Teach What Readers Learn*. Stroud: Thimble Press.

Meek, M. (1996) *Information and Book Learning*. Stroud: Thimble Press.

Meek, M., Warlow, A. and Barton, G. (1977) *The Cool Web: The Pattern of Children's Reading*. London: Bodley Head.

Melnik, A. and Merritt, J.M. (1972) *Reading: Today and Tomorrow*. London: University of London Press for OU Press.

Moebius, W. (1990) 'Introduction to picturebook codes', in P. Hunt (ed.) *Children's Literature: The Development of Criticism*. London: Routledge.

Morrison, B. (1997) *As If*. London: Grant.

Nodelman, P. (1988) *Words About Pictures: The Narrative Art of Children's Picture Books*. Atlanta, GA: University of Georgia Press.

Nodelman, P. (2002) *The Pleasures of Children's Literature* (3rd edn). White Plains, NY: Longman.

Ofsted (2004a) *Reading for Pleasure and Purpose: An Evaluation of the Teaching of Reading in Primary Schools*. Manchester: Ofsted.

Ofsted (2004b) *Good School Libraries*. Manchester: Ofsted.

Opie, I. and Opie, P. (1980) *The Classic Fairy Tales*. London: Paladin Books/Granada Publishing.

Paul, L. (1987) 'Enigma variations: what feminist theory knows about children's literature', in P. Hunt (ed.) *Children's Literature: The Development of Criticism*. London: Routledge.

Philip, N. (1981) *A Fine Anger: A Critical Introduction to the Work of Alan Garner*. London: Collins.

Philip, N. (1989) *The Cinderella Story*. London: Penguin.

Propp, V. and Scott, L. (trans.) (1968) *The Morphology of the Folktale*. Austin, TX: University of Texas Press.

Reid, J. and Donaldson, H. (1977) *Reading: Problems and Practices*. London: Ward Lock.

Reynolds, K., Brennan, G. and McCarron, K. (2001) *Frightening Fictions*. London: Continuum.

Robinson, M. (1997) *Children Reading Print and Television*. London: Falmer.

Smith, S. (1996) 'The lion, the witch and the drug addict', in S. Egoff, G. Stubbs and L. Ashley (eds) *Only Connect* (2nd edn). Ontario: Oxford University Press.

Southgate, V., Arnold, H. and Johnson, S. (1981) *Extending Beginning Reading*. London: Heinemann.

Stephens, J. (1992) *Language and Ideology in Children's Fiction*. Harlow: Longman.

Styles, M., Bearne, E. and Watson, V. (1994) *The Prose and the Passion*. London: Cassell.

Styles, M., Bearne, E. and Watson, V. (1996) *Voices Off*. London: Cassell.

Tatar, M. (ed.) (1998) *The Classic Fairy Tales*. New York: W.W. Norton.

Thomson, S. (1992) *Folktale*. Berkeley, CA: University of California Press.

Todorov, T. (1973) *The Fantastic: A Structural Approach to a Literary Genre*. New York: Cornell University Press.

Toolan, M.J. (1998) *Language in Literature*. London: Arnold.

Townsend, J.R. (1990) *Written for Children*. London: The Bodley Head.

Trease, G. (1972/1995) 'The historical novelist at work', in G. Fox (ed.) *Celebrating Children's Literature in Education*. London: Hodder & Stoughton.

Tucker, N. (1981) *The Child and the Book: A Psychological and Literary Exploration*. Cambridge: Cambridge University Press.

Tucker, N. and Gamble, N. (2001) *Family Fictions*. London: Continuum.

Wall, B. (1991) *The Narrator's Voice: The Dilemma of Children's Fiction*. London: Macmillan.

Walsh, J.P. (1987) *Language and Ideology in Children's Fiction*. New York: Longman.

Walsh, J.P. (1994) 'Memory and writing for children especially', in M. Styles, E. Bearne and V. Watson (eds) *The Prose and the Passion*. London: Cassell.

Walsh, J.P. (1996) 'The masks of the narrator', in M. Styles, E. Bearne and V. Watson (eds) *Voices Off*. London: Cassell.

Waterland, L. (1989) 'Reading classics with young children' in *Signal* 60, September.

Watson, R. (2003) *Schoolbook Sending in the UK 2002/2003* London: Educational Publishers Council.

Watson, V. (n.d.) 'What makes a children's classic', in *Books for Keeps*.

Watson, V. and Styles, M. (1996) *Talking Pictures: Pictorial Texts and Young Readers*. London: Hodder & Stoughton.

Zipes, J. (1989) *Beauties, Beasts and Enchantments: Classic French Fairy Tales*. New York: Penguin.

Zipes, J. (1995) *Fairy Tales and the Art of Subversion*. London: Routledge.

Zipes, J. (2001a) *Sticks and Stones: the Troublesome Success of Children's Literature from Slovenly Peter to Harry Potter*. London: Routledge.

Zipes. J. (2001b) *The Great Fairy Tale Tradition*. New York: W.W. Norton.

Index